Barnstormers, Wing-Walking and Flying Circuses

Barnstormers, Wing-Walking and Flying Circuses

Peter C. Brown

First published in Great Britain in 2022 by
Pen & Sword Air World
An imprint of
Pen & Sword Books Ltd
Yorkshire – Philadelphia

Copyright © Peter C. Brown 2022

ISBN 978 1 52679 418 5

The right of Peter C. Brown to be identified as Author of this work has been asserted by him in accordance with the Copyright, Designs and Patents Act 1988.

A CIP catalogue record for this book is
available from the British Library.

All rights reserved. No part of this book may be reproduced or transmitted in any form or by any means, electronic or mechanical including photocopying, recording or by any information storage and retrieval system, without permission from the Publisher in writing.

Printed and bound in the UK by CPI Group (UK) Ltd,
Croydon, CR0 4YY.

Pen & Sword Books Limited incorporates the imprints of Atlas, Archaeology, Aviation, Discovery, Family History, Fiction, History, Maritime, Military, Military Classics, Politics, Select, Transport, True Crime, Air World, Frontline Publishing, Leo Cooper, Remember When, Seaforth Publishing, The Praetorian Press, Wharncliffe Local History, Wharncliffe Transport, Wharncliffe True Crime and White Owl.

For a complete list of Pen & Sword titles please contact

PEN & SWORD BOOKS LIMITED
47 Church Street, Barnsley, South Yorkshire, S70 2AS, England
E-mail: enquiries@pen-and-sword.co.uk
Website: www.pen-and-sword.co.uk

Or

PEN AND SWORD BOOKS
1950 Lawrence Rd, Havertown, PA 19083, USA
E mail: Uspen-and-sword@casematepublishers.com
Website: www.penandswordbooks.com

Contents

Note from the Author		vii
Chapter 1	The Early Years	1
Chapter 2	The Races	15
Chapter 3	The 13 Black Cats	33
Chapter 4	Post-First World War and Barnstorming	45
Chapter 5	The Flying Circuses	49
Chapter 6	Across the Pond	61
Chapter 7	The Pilots	87
Chapter 8	Women in Aviation	119
Chapter 9	Movies and Television	145
Chapter 10	Wing-Walkers	159
Notes		165
Glossary		175
Bibliography		179
Index		181

Note from the Author

I have used the word airplane to describe the machines that the early aviators used because it was first coined in 1906, about three years after the Wright brothers took to the air on the first successful flight with the 'flying machine'. Little more than bolted and welded pieces of metal, wood and fabric, it was more than twenty years after the Wright brothers took flight that Charles Lindbergh became the first person to fly solo across the Atlantic non-stop, helping to cement airplane travel across the Atlantic and around the world. The word 'aero', although favoured in scientific jargon, was deemed 'too fancy', and 'planes' became more common things to talk about. In *Scientific American* in 1906, there had already been a claim that 'air-plane' was a much better word than aeroplane. Ten years later, 'airplane' was adopted by the National Advisory Committee for Aeronautics as their term.

Chapter 1

The Early Years

Airplanes were just coming into military use at the outset of the Great War, and while their impact on the course of the war was mainly tactical rather than strategic, most important being direct cooperation with ground forces – especially ranging and correcting artillery fire – the first steps in the strategic roles of aircraft in future wars was also foreshadowed. At the 1911 meeting of the Institute of International Law in Madrid, legislation was proposed to limit the use of airplanes to reconnaissance missions and banning them from being used as platforms for weapons.[1] This legislation was rooted in a fear that airplanes would be used to attack undefended cities, violating Article 69 of the Den Hague Reglement (the set of international laws governing warfare).[2]

However, the initial campaigns of 1914 proved that cavalry could no longer provide the reconnaissance expected by their generals, in the face of the greatly increased firepower of twentieth-century armies, and it was quickly realized that aircraft could at least locate the enemy, even if early air reconnaissance was hampered by the newness of the techniques involved.[3]

Aviation was one of the most romanticized elements of the First World War. 'Air aces' in particular achieved celebrity status both during and after the war and their photographs regularly appeared in newspapers. The French first coined the term 'ace' to describe the high-scoring fighter pilot Adolphe Pégoud and the expression stuck, and then applied to any fighter pilot credited with shooting down five or more enemy aircraft. Lone aerial combat provided an outlet for acts of personal bravery, and the aces were seen as chivalrous heroes engaged in honest and impressive one-to-one fighting. However, the lives of air aces were often cut short through combat or because of mechanical failure. This only fuelled their status as heroic martyrs when they were killed in action between 1916 and 1918 or died in flying accidents during or after the war.[4]

2   Barnstormers, Wing-Walking and Flying Circuses

Many countries signed up to the proposal at the meeting in Madrid for banning the use of airplanes in war, except for the major countries that had aircraft just before the First World War, which in effect catalysed the development of the aircraft industry.[5] Thus the plane became a full war machine with decisive influence on the modern battlefield.[6]

At the start of the war, there was some debate over the usefulness of aircraft in warfare. Many senior officers, in particular, remained sceptical. However, aircraft were to prove their worth by mid-war and early scepticism and low expectations quickly turned to unrealistic demands beyond the capabilities of the primitive aircraft available.[7]

Even so, air reconnaissance played a critical role in the 'war of movement' of 1914, especially in helping the Allies halt the German invasion of France. On 22 August 1914, British Captain Lionel Evelyn Oswald Charlton and Lieutenant Vivian Hugh Nicholas Wadham reported that German General Alexander von Kluck's army was preparing to surround the British Expeditionary Force (BEF), contradicting all other intelligence. The British High Command took note of the report and started to withdraw from Mons, thus saving the lives of 100,000 soldiers. Later, during the First Battle of the Marne, observation aircraft discovered weak points and exposed flanks in the German lines, allowing the Allies to take advantage of them.[8]

In Germany, the great successes of the early Zeppelin airships had largely overshadowed the importance of heavier-than-air aircraft. Out of a paper strength of about 230 aircraft belonging to the army in August 1914 only 180 or so were of any use.[9] The French military aviation exercises of 1911, 1912 and 1913 had pioneered cooperation with the cavalry (reconnaissance) and artillery (spotting), but the momentum was if anything slacking.[10]

Great Britain had 'started late' and initially relied largely on the French aircraft industry, especially for aircraft engines. The initial British contribution to the total Allied air war effort in August 1914 (of about 184 aircraft) was three squadrons with about thirty serviceable machines. By the end of the war, Great Britain had formed the world's first air force independent of either army or naval control, the Royal Air Force.[11] The American army and navy air services were far behind; even in 1917, when the United States entered the war, they were to be almost completely dependent on the French and British aircraft industries for combat aircraft.[12] The Germans' great air 'coup' of 1914 was at the Battle of Tannenberg in East Prussia, where an unexpected Russian attack was reported by pilots Lieutenants Ernst Canter and Karl Mertens, resulting in the Russians being forced to withdraw.[13]

Aerial reconnaissance using heavier-than-air machines was an entirely new science that had to be improvised step by step. Early operations were low-level flights with the pilot often dismounting from the plane to report verbally to the nearest officers. Photographic support was urgently developed, initially requiring a full-time photographer on board to handle the heavy, awkward equipment, and the interpretation of the resulting aerial images became an important new speciality, essential for accurate mapping. It would be 1917 before two-way air-to-ground radio would be in use for reconnaissance pilots, and until then, it was not uncommon for aircraft to land next to command posts so the pilot could personally pass on urgent information. The French employed air-dropped messaging, coloured flares and prearranged aircraft manoeuvres to convey information.

The Wright Flyer

In 1896, the newspapers were filled with accounts of flying machines, but Wilbur and Orville Wright noticed that all these primitive aircraft lacked suitable controls, and how the pilots might balance an aircraft once in the air. They began experimenting using kites, and then a series of gliders to test and made improvements to a system they developed using warped wings, which caused a roll to the left or the right.

They conducted their first controlled flight tests at Kitty Hawk, North Carolina, where the strong winds on the shores of the Atlantic helped to launch the gliders, and the soft sand helped to cushion the fall when they crashed back down again. Their first two tests in gliders in 1901 failed to perform despite reaching heights of around 300 feet on each test flight; not enough lift or not enough control available, so during the winter they constructed a wind tunnel at their bicycle shop in Dayton, Ohio. They employed a belt drive from a small gas engine that they used to power the tools used in their shop to turn the fan of their tunnel. This was a simple, single-speed, open-return design with a fan pushing a flow of air through a long wooden box and then exiting into the room.

4   Barnstormers, Wing-Walking and Flying Circuses

Their experiments allowed the brothers to investigate a wide range of design variables to help them determine the best wing shape for an airplane, and enabled them to build a glider with sufficient lift, allowing them to concentrate on the problem of control. By the end of 1901, they had accrued the most detailed data in the world for the design of aircraft wings, and by the end of the 1902 flying season, their third glider became the first fully controllable aircraft, with roll, pitch, and yaw controls.[14]

The most prominent competitor to the Wright brothers in the race for powered flight was the secretary of the Smithsonian Institute, Samuel Pierpont Langley. At the age of 50, Langley had already achieved prominence through his work as an astronomer, but he wanted to make a discovery that was on a par with Alexander Graham Bell and Thomas Edison. So, he turned to the problem of flight, spending the 1880s and 1890s perfecting an unmanned flying machine he called an aerodrome. The craft looked like a giant dragonfly. It was fifteen feet long, with two sets of wings, and launched by catapult off a houseboat on a river. In 1896, Langley made several successful trials with the machine and began imagining how a human might fit into the picture. Of the few serious scientists working on manned flight, Langley was the most eminent. Author James E. Tobin said that Wilbur and Orville Wright were inspired by Langley's early work.[15] Anyone who wanted to fly had to solve three problems: lift, balance and power. The Wright brothers concentrated on balance, using the image of a bird in flight as their model. Langley was focused on power and the image of an arrow shot through the air: put enough force behind the machine and it would fly.

In 1903, Langley and his mechanics felt ready to test the aerodrome. On 7 October, pilot and chief mechanic Charles Manly climbed aboard the craft, mounted to the top of a houseboat on the Potomac. Reporters swarmed to the site. A catapult launched the aerodrome, and it crashed straight into the river. Now short on funds, Langley made one more attempt. The trial on the following day also ended with failure when the aerodrome shot straight up, and then plummeted backward into the water.

The Wright brothers' mechanic Charlie Taylor had helped with the brothers' design to build a gasoline engine light enough and powerful enough to propel an airplane but were delayed by problems with their propeller shafts – they also designed the first true airplane propellers –

and bad weather, but in the Kill Devil Hills of North Carolina, on 17 December 1903, Wilbur and Orville Wright made the first sustained, manned controlled flights in the 'Wright Flyer', which was constructed using spruce wood for the framework[16] and 'Pride of the West muslin', procured from the Rike-Kumler Company, a local department store located in downtown Dayton, for the surface coverings.[17] While this first practical airplane could only fly in a straight line for less than a minute, by the end of 1905, they were flying figure-eights over Huffman Prairie, staying aloft for more than half an hour (or until their fuel ran out).

Following the 1905 flying season, the Wrights kept a low public profile and did not fly in public again for two years while they contacted the United States War Department, as well as governments and individuals in England, France, Germany and Russia, offering to sell a flying machine. They were turned down time and time again – some government bureaucrats thought they were crackpots; others thought that if two bicycle mechanics could build a successful airplane, they could do it themselves. But their perseverance paid off, and in late 1907, the U.S. Army Signal Corps asked for one aircraft. Just a few months later, in early 1908, a French syndicate of businessmen agreed to purchase another. Both had asked for an airplane that was capable of carrying a passenger, and the Wright brothers hastily adapted their 1905 Flyer with two seats and a more powerful engine. The testing was carried out in secret at Kitty Hawk, North Carolina.

Then the brothers parted company, and between 1908 and 1909, Wilbur went to France to demonstrate their aircraft in Europe, while Orville flew at Fort Meyer, Virginia. Their schedule went well until Orville lost one of the pusher propellers on the Military Flyer and crashed, breaking his leg and killing his passenger, Thomas Selfridge, who was a first lieutenant in the U.S. Army and the first person to die in an airplane crash. While Orville recuperated, Wilbur remained in France, flying, and breaking record after record. Once back home in Dayton, Orville and Wilbur returned to Fort Meyer with a new Military Flyer and completed the U.S. Army trials. A few months later, Wilbur flew before over a million spectators in New York Harbour – his first public flight in his native land. All of these flights stunned and captivated the world. The Wright brothers became the first great celebrities of the twentieth century.[18]

As their fame grew, orders for aircraft poured in. The Wrights established the Wright Company as their commercial aviation business venture on 22 November 1909, in conjunction with several prominent industrialists from New York and Detroit to capitalize on their invention of the practical airplane. The company maintained its headquarters in New York City and built its first factory in Dayton, Ohio, with others following; they also set up flight schools on both sides of the Atlantic.[19, 20]

The brothers' efforts became more concentrated on protecting the company's patent rights, as after they had demonstrated their aircraft in public, it was easy for competitors to copy them. And they did. Time-consuming and energy-draining patent fights ensued in both Europe and America – the most bitter legal battle being with Glenn Hammond Curtiss, who, as part of his defence, borrowed Samuel Pierpont Langley's unsuccessful aircraft from the Smithsonian Institution, and rebuilt it to prove that the 'Aerodrome' could have flown before the Wright Flyer. However, too many modifications had to be made to get Langley's aircraft into the air, and the courts ruled in favour of the Wrights.

Soon after the historic one-kilometre flight by Curtiss in the AEA June Bug on 4 July 1908, the Wright brothers warned him not to infringe their patent by profiting from flying or selling aircraft that used ailerons. Curtiss refused to pay licence fees to the Wrights and sold an airplane equipped with ailerons to the Aeronautic Society of New York in 1909. The Wrights filed a lawsuit, beginning a year-long legal conflict. They also sued foreign aviators who flew at U.S. exhibitions, including the leading French aviator, Louis Paulhan. The Curtiss people derisively suggested that if someone jumped in the air and waved his arms, the Wrights would sue. Despite a pro-Wright ruling in France, legal manoeuvring dragged on until the patent expired in 1917. A German court ruled the patent invalid because of prior disclosure in speeches by Wilbur Wright in 1901 and Chanute in 1903. In the U.S. the Wrights made an agreement with the Aero Club of America to license air shows which the club approved, freeing participating pilots from a legal threat. Promoters of approved shows paid fees to the Wrights. The Wright brothers won their initial case against Curtiss in February 1913 when a judge ruled that ailerons were covered under the patent. The Curtiss Company appealed the decision.[21]

The world outside the courtroom seemed no friendlier towards the brothers. The aircraft business was uncertain, dangerous and very expensive, with most of the money being made in exhibition flying. Audiences wanted to see more than just an airborne plane; they wanted death-defying feats of airmanship. The Wrights sent out teams of pilots who had to fly increasingly higher, faster and more recklessly to satisfy the crowds. Inevitably, pilots began to die in accidents, and the stress began to tell on the Wrights. Additionally, their legal troubles distracted them from what they were best at – invention and innovation – and by 1911, Wright aircraft were no longer the best machines flying. In 1912, Wilbur Wright, worn out from legal and business problems, contracted typhoid and died. Orville, his heart no longer in the airplane business, sold the Wright Company in 1916 and went back to inventing.[22]

The Wright Exhibition Team

A group of early aviators, led by Walter Brookins, who had trained with the Wright brothers at the Wright Flying School in Montgomery, Alabama, formed a group called The Wright Exhibition Team in March 1910, at the suggestion of the aeronautical engineer and balloonist Augustus Roy Knabenshue.[23] The team made its first public appearance from 13–19 June 1910, at the Indianapolis Motor Speedway. There, they performed aerial shows and set records for endurance and altitude (4,939 feet). Knabenshue at the time was involved in demonstrating dirigibles at state fairs and was knowledgeable about the exhibition business.[24] The Wright pilots were hesitant about what they termed the 'carnival-like atmosphere' at the air meets and the 'fancy flying-daredevil' aspect of it but were eventually swayed by Knabenshue with the opportunity to showcase their technology and the opportunity to make some money and keep the company profitable. The pilots were paid $20 per week, plus $50 a day when flying, and by August, five separate teams were flying at one time with $186,000 in receipts.

The team's rival Glenn Curtiss had won the Gordon Bennett speed competition, which was part of the International Aviation Tournament at Long Island's Belmont Park, in the previous year, and the Wrights wanted to enter it to demonstrate to the world the superiority of the Wright airplanes. They decided to design a new airplane for the race that was built for speed. They named it the *Baby Grand*. Orville Wright flew it in a test before the big race and attained a speed of 78mph. Brookins was chosen to fly the airplane for the actual race, but on the first pass before the grandstand with Wilbur, Orville and the entire racing team intently watching, the engine started making a strange sound. The airplane began coming down too fast and although Brookins was able to level the machine, it hit the ground hard. The *Baby Grand* was destroyed. Brookins was badly bruised, but not seriously injured. The winner of the race, it turns out, flew 10mph slower than the Wrights' machine had flown before the race.

The Wright airplanes were attracting a lot of publicity with their daredevil stunts, but Wilbur and Orville were becoming concerned about the dangerous showmanship. Misfortune and tragedy soon began to plague the team. Ralph Johnson was the first of the team to be killed after attempting another altitude record over Denver's Overland Park in November 1910. Johnstone put his plane into a 'spiral dip' dive but never recovered. The plane plummeted to the ground, and Johnstone was crushed.

A month later, on New Year's Eve, 1910, in an almost identical incident, Archibald 'Arch' Hoxsey was killed after crashing from 7,000 feet (2,100 metres) while attempting to set a new altitude record. Although the team had lost its star fliers, newer pilots, trained by Welsh, joined the team and continued performing around the country at twenty-five locations.[25]

Leonard Warden Bonney was killed on 4 May 1928 during the maiden flight of the *Bonney Gull* when the aircraft nosedived into the ground from about fifty feet, seconds after taking off from Curtiss Field, Long Island.[26] Howard W. Gill, flying a Wright Model Ex single-seater, collided with George Mestach's Morane-Borel monoplane, and crashed, dying later of his injuries. Mestach sustained cuts and bruises but survived.[27] Philip Orin Parmelee was piloting an airplane at various altitudes at an air show in Yakima, Washington, on 1 June 1912, when air turbulence caused him to crash, killing him instantly. Arthur L. Welsh was killed in a crash while demonstrating a Wright Model C airplane for the U.S. Army on 11 June 1912. Troubled by the deaths of the pilots, the group was disbanded in November.[28]

Early Aviators

Almost as soon as early aviators had mastered the feat of staying aloft in straight and level flight, they wanted to experience manoeuvring in all three dimensions and to explore the unique freedom allowed by flight. The crowds who flocked to the first air shows were also eager to see daring exhibitions of flying. It was these twin incentives of curiosity and crowd-pleasing that spurred pilots forward to experiment with ever more difficult manoeuvres.

Probably the first 'stunt' pilot was the French aviation pioneer Eugène Lefebvre (1878–1909), who thrilled the crowds as a participant in the first international air race during the eight-day Grande Semaine d'Aviation at Reims between 22 and 29 August 1909, piloting a Wright Flyer.[29] Lefebvre had only learned to fly that summer, and despite being selected along with Louis Blériot and Hubert Latham as France's representatives for the Gordon Bennett Trophy on 22 August, he quickly found to his disappointment that his new Type A was no match for the Antoinette, Blériot or Curtiss types in terms of speed.

Hampered by gusty winds and rain which turned the grass flying-field to glutinous mud, many of the twenty entrants in the race on 22 August were unable to take off, and none managed to complete the necessary two laps. Eugène Lefebvre, flying his Wright Type A, put up the best performance, almost completing the course; Louis Blériot, who had managed to fly about two and a half kilometres in a Blériot XI, put up the next best performance, and it was decided that third place would be given based on performance in the speed competition to be held that afternoon – and it was taken by Hubert Latham.[30] Due to the Wright brothers' concern for control rather than inherent stability, the Flyer could be handled with great precision, and Lefebvre showed that off to full advantage. At this stage in flight's development, aerobatics consisted of no more than steeply banked turns and swooping dives, but to an audience that had never set eyes on an airplane before, this was thrilling enough. Eugène Lefebvre's untimely death in an air crash while testing an airplane at Juvisy-sur-Orge in northern France on 7 September undoubtedly added to the aura of daring surrounding aerobatic pilots. He was the first pilot to be killed in the era of powered flight.

The art of aerobatics did not develop much beyond swooping and diving for the next few years; air racing was far more popular. But in 1913, a young French pilot named Adolphe Pégoud (1889–1915) suddenly brought it very much to the world's attention. Despite having only gained his pilot's licence on 8 February, on 19 August 1913, Pégoud made the world's second parachute jump from an airplane (the first had been made by an American, Berry, in March 1912). Because it was thought at the time that the change in balance as a man jumped out would make a plane uncontrollable, Pégoud chose to jump from a single-seater Blériot XI piloted by himself. Whatever else happened, the experiment would be expensive. With his rudimentary parachute packed on the fuselage behind him, Pégoud climbed to about 2,000 feet (700 metres) over Buc, near Versailles, and then left the airplane. The parachute opened perfectly but Pégoud remained at some considerable risk as the pilotless Blériot spectacularly reared and somersaulted its way down to earth nearby. The Frenchman landed safely in a tree not far from the wreckage of his plane.

The feat brought Adolphe Pégoud to the notice of Louis Blériot, who decided that such a daring young aviator was just the man he needed to demonstrate the aerobatic qualities of his Blériot XI design. Blériot was keen to demonstrate that his airplanes were safer than his competitors' because they could be recovered to level flight from almost any attitude, however extreme. Pégoud was employed as a test pilot, and on 1 September 1913, he conducted a series of experiments at Juvisy, near Paris, on a somewhat modified 50hp machine which included 90-degree banked turns. The exhibition culminated with the world's first inverted flight, which confounded critics who said that an airplane could not possibly fly upside down. Pégoud was held in by a strong shoulder harness. On the ground, he told how it had not been an entirely pleasant experience as petrol had started to drizzle out of the air hole in the top of his petrol tank while he was upside down and blow back over him in the air stream.

Then, on 21 September 1913, he went up again and attempted 'flick turns', tail slides, a vertical figure 'S', and finally a brand-new trick: over the past few weeks, he had experimented with a different way of getting back to normal flight. Instead of rolling over, he would put the Blériot's nose down to vertical and then continue to pull back on the control stick until he came out of his dive flying in the opposite direction. Pégoud had realized he could improve on this trick by making a full circle in the air rather than just a half-circle. On that day, starting right way up and in a moderate dive to gain speed, he pulled back on the stick to bring the nose up to vertical and then kept the stick back into his stomach until he was inverted. The horizon appeared upside down. Pégoud held his nerve and kept the stick back until the ground was below again and he was back in level flight. He had looped the loop.[31]

Pégoud was credited with having achieved the first loop in the world, but it emerged later that he had been beaten to it by a matter of days. On 9 September (27 August by the calendar then used in Russia), Lieutenant Pyotr Nikolayevich Nesterov had looped his Russian Army 70hp Nieuport monoplane at Kiev in the Ukraine. At the time he was placed under arrest by his commanding officer for risking army property, but when it emerged that he was a hero he was promoted to captain.[32]

Between 25–27 September, Pégoud demonstrated his skills to amazed English crowds at Brooklands aerodrome near Weybridge, Surrey.[33] and before the year was out, several English pilots had learned the loop themselves. The first British pilot to loop was Bentfield 'Charles' Hucks, which he performed in his Blériot at Hendon airfield in September 1913.[34] followed by George Lee Temple (although it was actually as a result of trying to recover control of his 50hp Bleriot monoplane) at Hendon on 24 November. Temple was popularly known as the 'Baby Airman' because he was only 21 years old. To prepare themselves for inverted flight, both he and Pégoud bizarrely took to hanging upside down from chairs suspended from beams in their hangars like bats!

George Lee Temple attempted to perform a loop in his 50hp Bleriot monoplane which was thought to be unsuitable for looping the loop and, indeed, whilst upside down and a mile high on 24 November 1913, his machine began to plummet earthwards; but, when it was about 1,200 feet from the ground, it righted itself, and Temple made a safe landing. Later, he explained that he had been unable to make the machine respond to the controls and that, for a time, he had been falling at 100mph. He had calculated that, after flying upside down, it would require a dive of 500 feet to get the right way up. In fact, it took him nearly 1,500 feet.[35]

In the brief flying season before the First World War, aerobatics, and especially the loop, became enormously popular at air shows. On 13 March, Hucks and Gustav Wilhelm Hamel gave a looping and inverted flight display together at Hendon, and as well as flying inverted, Hamel in his 70hp Morane-Saulnier monoplane demonstrated what was described as 'a pirouette on the tip of a wing' which was probably a stall-turn, while Hucks in a 50hp Blériot performed a tailslide, looped at 800 feet (250 metres) and then executed eight consecutive loops from 2,000 feet (600 metres).

The French continued to lead the way, with a pilot named Pierre Chanteloup pulling off some particularly impressive new 'stunts' to demonstrate that the airplane was no longer an unknown quantity but a machine that could be mastered and controlled. On Christmas Day 1913, he performed to pilots and the press a 'cartwheel loop', in which the wings remain vertical throughout, in a Caudron biplane at Hendon. Then on 27 December, he went up and performed an outside loop, steep 'side-dives' (side slips) from 800 feet (250 metres), and then an inverted dive from 4,000 feet (1,200 metres), and finally a 'tourbillon dive' in which his machine corkscrewed around its axis whilst diving headlong for the ground. The pilot recovered at the last minute and landed to riotous applause.[36]

Henry Walden

Dr Henry William Walden, who was born in Massachusetts in 1883, had an intense interest in aeronautics as a youth; he built kites and balloon models while living in Europe. Returning to the United States, he studied dentistry at Columbia University and, on graduation in 1906, opened a dental practice in Manhattan. Two years later, Walden joined the Aeronautical Society of New York, which at the time was based at the Morris Park racetrack in the Bronx. There, he became interested in designing and building his own planes, the first two of which – both biplanes – were failures. For his third, he decided to try a different tack, and to avoid long trips to Morris Park, he rented a loft near his dental practice and, with the help of a cousin and a mechanic, began work on a monoplane. Before Walden's work, the double-wing models had held all attention, but in 1909, he built the first successful American monoplane. About the same time, Blériot perfected a French monoplane.

During a test run on 9 December 1909, Walden's fragile wood-and-fabric craft rose a few feet off the ground and travelled just over ten yards before the plane's one-gallon fuel tank ran dry, but it had become the first American monoplane to fly. However, this flight was discounted because of its brevity. So, on 3 August 1910, with a ten-gallon tank installed, Walden tried again and became airborne for a longer, albeit still brief, time. The flight ended in a crash, with Walden breaking several ribs and fracturing his collarbone. This epic flight made headlines in a New York City newspaper and the record books. The characteristic of Walden's monoplane was the 'ears' mounted above the wing for lateral balance control. These surfaces were mounted on brackets above the wingtips, hinged at the rear, and spring-held at the front. These controls were also a way to get round the Wright brothers' patents.

In late 1910, he teamed up with English flier George Dyott to establish the Walden-Dyott Aeronautic Company at Hempstead Plains field in New York, to build monoplanes, but business was very slow and, early in 1911, the two disbanded their company. (The Blériot and Deperdussin designs of 1909–12 were the true forerunners of the modern monoplane.) Dyott received two of the monoplanes in compensation, which he later sold in South America, and Walden got the hangar and an unfinished third plane. Returning to his dental practice, he would put in a whole day there, then motorcycle out to the hangar to spend most of the night working on his planes, a gruelling pace at best. In the following years, Walden built nine more ships, performed at air shows, and survived at least a dozen more crashes. It came to an end in 1912 when a flight student crashed in one of his planes and, while injuries were relatively minor, the accident so unnerved Walden that he quit flying to concentrate on laboratory work.[37]

The *Daily Mail* Prizes

In 1906, the British newspaper the *Daily Mail* offered a prize of £10,000 for the first aviator to fly the 185 miles (298 kilometres) from London to Manchester within twenty-four hours, with the strict rule that they made no more than two landings en route, and that the aviator must start and finish within five miles of the *Daily Mail*'s London and Manchester offices. Powered flight was a relatively new invention, and the newspaper's proprietor, Alfred Harmsworth, 1st Viscount Northcliffe,[38] was keen to stimulate the industry's growth. In the United States, Wilbur Wright had flown as far as twenty-four miles by October 1905, but in Europe, little progress had been made; on 23 October 1906, the Brazilian-born, French-educated airplane designer Santos-Dumont performed the first successful flight of nearly 220 yards (200 metres). Given the limitations of airplanes at the time, the prize money seemed unwinnable.

Chapter 2

The Races

The English Channel had been crossed by balloon by Jean-Pierre Blanchard and John Jeffries in 1785, but in 1908, the *Daily Mail* confidently offered £500 for the first powered heavier-than-air flight across the Channel before the end of the year. However, the year passed with no serious attempt being made, so the prize was doubled to £1,000, and the offer extended to the end of 1909. The pace of aeronautical progress meant that such a flight would be within the grasp of a bold aviator with a reliable machine. Flight instrumentation at the time was limited, and there were no airborne radios to call for help, but on 19 July 1909, Hubert Latham (one of the two leading contenders to attempt such a feat, Charles de Lambert being the other) was the first person in his Antoinette IV monoplane to attempt to cross the English Channel in an airplane, but due to an engine failure, he was forced to ditch in the Channel. Six days later, on Sunday, 25 July, the French aviator Louis Charles Joseph Blériot took off at 4.41 am from the cliffs at Les Baraques, near Calais, and 37 minutes later landed at North Foreland Meadow, behind Dover Castle in England. At Dover, the wind nearly caused him to crash, and his landing gear and propeller were damaged. But he had made it, and he was declared the winner.[39]

The conquest of the Channel by air was a media sensation, and brought Blériot instant fame, becoming a hero who was celebrated on both sides of the Channel. His Type XI monoplane, which had been designed primarily by Raymond Saulnier, was the eleventh flying machine he had constructed (he crashed four of them in test flights), and became a bestseller – probably the most successful monoplane of the pioneer era designed and built before the First World War.[40]

Claude Grahame-White, who had been running a successful motor car dealership in London's exclusive Mayfair district, was fascinated by the flight and went to see Blériot's aircraft which had been placed on display at Selfridges department store, in nearby Oxford Street. It prompted him to go to the Reims Aviation Meeting which ran from 22–29 August 1909, and, after meeting Louis Blériot in person and buying a Blériot XII from him, ended up staying for eight weeks at the new factory, Blériot Aeronautique, while his machine was constructed. Once completed, he made a few taxiing tests along the ground and then, without any air experience, took off on his first flight.

After setting up a flying school in Pau, which overlooked the Pyrenees in south-west France, the draw of the prize money offered by the *Daily Mail* gave Grahame-White the excuse he needed to move the flying school to England, amid the burst of publicity he would receive by winning the London–Manchester prize. He realized that his Anzani-powered Blériot XI would not be capable of making the flight in only three legs, and so he bought a Farman III, which had been fitted with one of the new 50hp Gnome rotary engines. After shipping it to Britain, he proceeded to survey the route. He planned to follow the London & North Western Railway all the way and persuaded the company to whitewash its sleepers for 100 yards to the north of every junction so that he might stay on the right line. He was helped in the attempt by Henri Farman himself and a team of French mechanics, who came over from France.

On Saturday, 23 April 1910, with the weather looking favourable, Grahame-White began readying his aircraft while it was still dark at Park Royal, in north London. Despite the early hour, several hundred people had come to see him go as well as members of the Royal Aero Club and Henri Farman himself. At 5.19 am, the Farman took to the air after a run of fewer than 100 yards and, to the relief of the onlookers, climbed over the factory chimneys, before becoming lost in the haze.

It had been agreed in advance that the landmark of a gas-holder near Wormwood Scrubs was within five miles of the *Daily Mail* offices in Fleet Street, and this was his first target: to get the time logged by an official from the Royal Aero Club, who was stationed there. Grahame-White passed over the heads of more cheering spectators on the Scrubs, circled the gas-holder, and then set course north to pick up the London & North Western Railway at Willesden Junction. His mechanics and friends, in the meantime, ran for their cars to give chase, although at times they struggled to keep up with the changes of terrain. The line took him over Harrow, Watford and through the Chiltern Hills at Berkhampstead. He emerged onto the flatter country of Buckinghamshire and pressed on up to Northampton. All along the route, people thronged the railway bridges and vantage points to cheer him on his way. His was the first airplane to be seen in some of the counties he crossed.

Two hours later, he was circling the treetops over the village of Hillmorton, near Rugby, locating the correct field in which to land. Mechanics ran out into the middle, shouting and carrying white sheets. Mr Harold Ernest, the secretary of the Royal Aero Club, who had driven like a demon from London to beat the airplane, awaited him along with some of Grahame-White's friends (most of the other cars arrived sometime later). He saw them below, cut the engine and glided down. The landing was fairly smooth, but he broke an undercarriage strut on a small hillock. When he clambered down from the plane, he was numb with cold and shaking. It was 7.20 am and he had covered 75 miles – more than a third of the distance. His speed had been between 30 and 50mph, depending on whether the section of the railway track he was following was pointing into or away from the wind.

He set off again at 8.15 am on the next leg to Crewe, in Cheshire, passing low over the roof of Rugby station, his wave answered by a cacophony of whistles from the engine drivers. This was a harder leg as the wind picked up and turbulence from hills and woods affected the low-flying aircraft and became head-on as he entered the Trent Valley. The Farman was spun around so that it was facing towards London on two occasions, the Gnome engine struggling to produce the power necessary to keep the aircraft under Grahame-White's control. The engine cut out completely when over a wood near Tamworth, fifteen miles north-east of Birmingham, but restarted as Grahame-White glided the airplane down in preparation for a forced landing. He realized that the engine was clearly in need of attention, and decided to land early, and came down near the village of Hademore, a couple of miles from Lichfield, and this time broke an undercarriage skid. The time was 9.20 am. The engine problem was traced to a defective valve, and Grahame-White took the opportunity to have some breakfast and a nap while the valve was being fixed by the mechanics. The high winds kept him grounded longer than he had anticipated, and Henri Farman agreed that the present conditions were dangerous even with a good engine. Things didn't improve as the afternoon went on, with the winds becoming even stronger. A crowd had started to gather as word spread that the plane was on the ground, and the enterprising owner of the field began to charge 2d for admission. At 7 pm they decided to give up for the day and try again at 3 am the next morning.

A storm appeared to be on its way early the next morning, and the wind was still too strong at 3 am, so Grahame-White climbed onto the Farman's seat and announced to the patient crowd that the attempt was off. He would go to Manchester and try to fly from there to London within twenty-four hours instead.

However, the bad fortune was not about to change; the mechanics forgot to tie the Farman down with the stakes and ropes, and during the night of Sunday, 24 April, it was blown over onto its back by the gale. The top wing was torn in several places and numerous struts were broken. Grahame-White was forced to return to London for major repairs. By the time he had arrived in London, he found that attempt had roused other aviators to the possibility of winning the £10,000 prize and that he faced a competitor.

The pioneering French aviator Isidore Auguste Marie Louis Paulhan was in Cologne and had been contemplating the prize himself, but upon hearing of Grahame-White's exploit, he immediately departed for England. He was similarly equipped with a Gnome-engined Farman and received equal help from Henri Farman. Worryingly for Grahame-White, Paulhan had set a record when he made a flight flying ninety-one miles (146 kilometres) in a straight route from Orleans to Troyes a few weeks earlier, on 14 March. The prospect of a head-to-head race between Frenchman and Englishman, on virtually identical aircraft, created a great deal of patriotic excitement in both countries.

Louis Paulhan's machine differed from Grahame-White's in that it had two rudders at the tail, forming a box shape with the tailplanes, while Grahame-White's only had one, making an 'T' shape. Paulhan's machine also had shortened lower wings to give it greater speed.

The challenge was on; Paulhan set up base in some flat open fields at Hendon in north London and proceeded to erect his plane, which had arrived some days after him on Wednesday, 27 April. His Farman had had to travel by road from Folkestone because the railway tunnels on the way were too narrow for its large crate. Meanwhile, Grahame-White worked flat out at the *Daily Mail* garages to repair his battered plane. Henri Farman spent Wednesday morning with Grahame-White, helping ready it for a test flight at Wormwood Scrubs, and the afternoon with Paulhan at Hendon. In the morning, the Englishman paid a courtesy visit to Hendon to discuss the problems of the flight with Paulhan. Grahame-White made a test flight at 2 pm, which was satisfactory, but the wind was still too strong (in his opinion) for an attempt at the prize, and he had to disappoint the 15,000-strong crowd who had gathered to see him off. He put his Farman into its hangar and went back to his hotel.

At 5.30pm, Paulhan and his team had finally finished putting together his Farman under the supervision of Henri Farman. Audaciously, he saw that he had a chance to snatch the prize there and then. Grahame-White expected him to start tomorrow morning, and so, without even a test flight, Paulhan took off, banked round back over the 4,000 madly cheering spectators, and headed south for Hampstead Cemetery (which was his agreed five-mile landmark). He came back into view, flying north, 400 or 500 feet up, and disappeared out of sight. Not long afterward, Grahame-White was wakened and told that his rival was already in the air. Immediately he jumped into a car and drove back to Wormwood Scrubs. He knew that there was always a chance that he could suffer engine problems that would delay him, but he was determined to try and catch Paulhan if he could.

Only a few hundred stragglers from the crowd of thousands remained on the ground to witness him take off at 6.30 pm. The Farman climbed shakily to the gas-holder against the strong wind, and then banked round to come back downwind over the crowd, and then away into the sky. By the time night fell, Paulhan was still as far ahead as ever; Grahame-White had made sixty miles and was at Roade, in Northamptonshire, while Paulhan had reached Lichfield, 117 miles (188 kilometres) from London. Along the route, even greater crowds turned out than at the weekend to see the Frenchman pass over, followed by the Englishman in pursuit an hour or so later. At Roade, after having a cup of tea in a signal box, Grahame-White returned to his airplane to find the field full of well-wishers. He was carried aloft and then made to sign autographs by the light of a bicycle lamp.

He was forced to resort to desperate measures to close the gap between him and Paulhan – he would fly through the night (making it the first night flight in England). The large clouds that accompanied the fine drizzle started to clear at just after 2.30 am, and the light of the moon provided a guide. The field was a tricky one to get out of even in daylight, surrounded by hedges and trees on three sides and by telegraph poles and a railway bridge on the fourth. Lamps had been placed at either end, so Grahame-White could see how much room he had. Watched by a sizeable crowd, the Farman bumped across the field, its thin wings seeming luminous against the dark ground, and took off over the line of parked cars in the road beyond the trees. The crowd breathed a sigh of relief. Unfortunately, as he disappeared north into the darkness, his crew on the ground could hear from its note that his engine was not developing full power.

A short distance away, a couple of Grahame-White's friends were waiting at a crossroads in a car to show him the right direction. When he flew over, they were to drive down the road with headlights burning. He was making good progress and passed Nuneaton at 3.50am, but the Gnome became weaker and weaker, while a headwind began to pick up as dawn approached. His ground speed dropped to a crawl. Once more into the Trent valley, he was forced to give up again with a faltering engine and landed at the village of Polesworth, around ten miles from Lichfield – and his rival. It was 4.13am when he jumped out and attempted to keep the airplane from being turned over in the gusty wind until his friends could come and help. Paulhan, in the meantime, had taken off from Lichfield at 4.09am and passed Stafford at 4:45 and Crewe at 5.20am.

At the landing ground at Burnage, near Didsbury on the outskirts of Manchester, the official timekeeper and other Royal Aero Club members had slept the night at a nearby inn on chairs. By 4 o'clock they were back on the field, and by 5 am a crowd of several thousand had gathered, made up of workers, tradesmen, farmers and country gentlemen. The roads were full of cars and the platform of the nearby elevated station was packed. At 5.25 am a buzz went round the crowd as they learned that a signalman had phoned up the line to say an airplane was only five miles away.

Every eye was directed to the skyline of the houses and the trees to the south. The eastern horizon was crimson with the light of a threatening sunrise; overhead the sky was dull and grey, and a light, cold drizzle was driving along on a south-westerly wind, which at times blew at about 15mph.

Suddenly there was a scattered volley of breathless exclamations: 'Here he is!', 'Paulhan is coming!' Over the tops of the trees appeared, small and faint at first, but rapidly increasing in size, the now familiar outline of an airplane. From the crowd there arose cheer after cheer. No one cared then whether the aviator who approached was Frenchman or Englishman. It was enough that he was a hero of the air.

Paulhan landed at 5.32 am, and climbed stiffly down from his painful seat, and vowed never to undertake such a flight again, 'Even for twice £10,000!' He was mobbed by the crowd and had to be escorted to the station, where his train had pulled in, by two policemen. He had succeeded in flying from London to Manchester in just over twelve hours – four hours, twelve minutes of which had been spent in the air. Grahame-White had been let down by his unreliable engine for a second time, but when he heard of Paulhan's success he climbed onto his machine to announce the news to the crowd which had gathered in the field, and to call for three cheers for Paulhan. He telegraphed congratulations to Manchester. But as it was still early, he decided to carry on and complete the course even if it meant coming second. He could still do it within twenty-four hours so long as he arrived before the evening. It was not to be, however. The Gnome was still playing up and the headwind blowing down the Trent valley was as fierce as ever. He battled on for a while but it was hopeless. It took him half an hour to cover the eight miles to Whittington, where he landed.[41]

Louis Paulhan was duly certified by a committee of the Royal Aero Club as having abided by the rules on Saturday, 30 April, and he drove straight from the club in Piccadilly to the luncheon given in his honour at the Savoy Hotel in the Strand. Claude Grahame-White was also present, and he received a 100-guinea cup as consolation. The lunch was also made the occasion for the announcement of another *Daily Mail* competition – a 1,000-mile race around Great Britain![42]

Heavier than Air

The first 'heavier-than-air' air race was the Prix de Lagatinerie (named after its financier, Baron Charles de Lagatinerie), which was held on 23 May 1909 at the Port-Aviation airport south of Paris. Nine entered and paid their 100 francs entry fee, but only four showed up on the day:

Léon Delagrange on the Voisin Delagrange No. 3, Henri Rougier on a Voisin, Alfred de Pischof on a 1907 de Pischoff et Koechlin (the first known example of a tractor biplane), and 'F. de Rue' (pseudonym for Capitaine Ferdinand Ferber) on a Voisin (a pusher biplane, powered by a 50hp Antoinette water-cooled V8 engine). As they were called one by one to start the race in the late afternoon, Pischoff could not lift off and stopped after only a couple of hundred yards, and decided to withdraw. Delagrange had to abandon his effort altogether due to broken elevator controls during the rollout. Rougier took off, but on the back straight of the first lap, flying very low, he had to veer to avoid a couple of spectators who had been lying in the tall grass and suddenly stood up. He hit the ground and put his plane on the nose, luckily without any injuries and, thanks to the plane being a pusher, with only minor damage. De Rue, by this time, has also withdrawn. Of the four pilots who entered the race, two managed to start, but nobody completed the full race distance. This wasn't completely unexpected, as the rules specified that whoever travelled farthest would be the winner if no one completed the race. Léon Delagrange, who covered slightly more than half of the ten three-quarter-mile (ten 1.2-kilometre) laps was declared the winner.

Some other minor events were held before the eight-day Grande Semaine d'Aviation de la Champagne (so named because it was sponsored by the major local champagne growers) from 22–29 August 1909 at Reims, France. This was the first major international flying event, which, as well as confirming the viability of heavier-than-air flight, drew the most important aircraft makers and pilots of the era, and attracted some 500,000 people including prominent figures such as Armand Fallières, the President of the French Republic and the British Chancellor of the Exchequer, David Lloyd George.[43, 44]

The premier event – the first Gordon Bennett Trophy competition (sponsored by Gordon Bennett, publisher of *The New York Herald*) – was won by Glenn Curtiss, who beat second-place finisher Louis Blériot by only five seconds. Curtiss was named 'Champion Air Racer of the World'. The meeting also saw the breaking of the world record for distance, a flight of 110 miles (180 kilometres) by Henri Farman, as well as the debut of the lightweight Gnome engine, which would achieve much acclaim.

Dominguez Field, a mesa just south of the plaza at the pueblo of Los Angeles, was the setting for the 1910 Los Angeles International Air Meet

– the first air race in the United States, which was held between 10–20 January 1910. It was organized by pilots Augustus Roy Knabenshue and Charles Foster Willard, who raised funding from railroad magnate Henry Edwards Huntington, and the Los Angeles Merchants & Manufacturers Association. William Randolph Hearst carried coverage of the event in his *Los Angeles Examiner* and hired a hot air balloon with a promotional parse touting his newspaper. Of the forty-three entrants who were attracted by the event, only sixteen enthusiasts appeared – Glenn Curtiss, Roy Knabenshue, Charles Willard, Lincoln Beachey, Charles K. Hamilton, Howard Warfield Gill and Clifford B. Harmon among them. The Wright brothers were there with their lawyers, but only to prevent Paulhan and Curtiss from flying (the Wrights claimed that the ailerons on their aircraft infringed patents), but notwithstanding their allegations, Paulhan and Curtiss still made flights.

As many new airplane designs were in the works, the early models of the 1908 and 1909 period, such as the Antoinette types, were being surpassed by newer, more powerful planes. Aviation meets were steadily expanding – there were fourteen meetings held in 1909 – and amidst the numerous exhibitions and demonstrations flights, challenges like the *Daily Mail*'s flights around Britain and rewards for the first to fly across the English Channel attracted great interest both among pilots and the general public, and which Louis Charles Joseph Blériot accomplished on 25 July 1909, winning the £1,000 prize money.[45] When the French announced the Circuit de l'Est, which was sponsored by the French news magazine *Le Matin*, it generated great interest, with thirty-five pilots signing up for the challenge. The only problem was that the race covered 500 miles (805 kilometres) as the long-distance circular race from Paris in a counterclockwise route to the borders of Germany, Luxembourg and Belgium and back again. It was unexpected that all of the pilots would finish – if any at all, and so the rules allowed that the pilot who completed the greatest number of legs along the way would be declared the winner. The prize awaiting if a winner could complete the entire circuit was huge – 100,000 francs – but half of that if it was not. Georges Legagneux in a Henri Farman biplane, Otto Lindpaintner with his Sommer biplane, Charles Terres 'C.T.' Weymann in a Henri Farman biplane, Juan Bielovucic Cavalié on a Voisin, Emile Aubrun, Alfred Leblanc and Julien Mamet, all flying Blériot monoplanes, and Arthur Charles Hubert Latham in an Antoinette, arrived at Issi, near Paris, on the day, Sunday 7 August. What might have been a disaster for the planners was instead taken in stride – aviation was a new field, after all.[46] The race was won by Alfred Leblanc in a Gnome-engined Blériot XI, and covered the whole course in twelve hours and one minute, averaging a speed of 41.6mph (66.99kph). Emile Aubrun arrived around ninety minutes later in his Blériot to take second place. None of the other aviators completed the circuit.

The First International Aviation Meeting at Reims

The first international aviation meeting was held from 22–29 August 1909, at a racetrack on the Bétheny Plain, outside Reims, France. Officially known as Le Grande Semaine d'Aviation de la Champagne (The Champagne Region's Great Aviation Week), the event was sponsored by the great French champagne houses, and intended to be a showcase of man's conquest of the air and progress in aeronautics. There would be display flights, record attempts and races. Public, as well as political and military interest in aviation, was at a fever pitch during the summer of 1909, and with Louis Blériot's successful crossing of the English Channel the previous month, the meeting was eagerly anticipated.

Lucrative cash prizes and impressive trophies enticed competitors to set new records in categories including those for the best flights of distance, altitude, and speed. A rectangular course of six miles (ten kilometres) was marked out on a large plain near the village of Bétheny, three miles (five kilometres) from Reims; the course was marked by tall pylons at each corner. Grandstands, public enclosures (sufficient for 5,000 people) and aircraft sheds were erected, and a take-off area was designated in front of the sheds so that the airplanes could become airborne before they joined the course. Special trains were laid on to bring the crowds of spectators from Paris. Around thirty-eight airplanes were entered for the competitions to be held throughout the week.

The first race was the most prestigious of the competition: The Gordon Bennett International Aviation Cup, of which both the trophy and prize money were provided by James Gordon Bennett, proprietor of *The New York Herald* and *Paris Herald*. It would become an annual competition in which pilots would represent their countries in speed trials over 12.4 miles (20 kilometres). While the Wright brothers dismissed the event as an 'amusement', six of their machines were flown. Twenty-two aviators arrived to compete, including Paul Albert Gaston Tissandier, Charles de Lambert, Louis Blériot, Henri Farman and Hubert Latham, and it was Glenn Hammond Curtiss who represented the U.S. in the race. Captain Louis Ferdinand Ferber, a serving French army officer, was forced to fly under the pseudonym of 'Monsieur de Rue' to satisfy his superiors, and the British were represented by George Cockburn, a Scot and founding member of the Aero Club of Great Britain.

While the competitors had been assured that the Bétheny Plain would be clear of crops to facilitate any forced landing, they were in dismay to find that there were still some fields of standing crops, and many more full of sheaves of wheat and barley drying in the sun.

The first man to complete a circuit of the course was Eugène Lefebvre, who flew for the Société Ariel, the company formed to market the Wrights' designs in Europe. He took eight minutes and forty-five seconds to complete the course, and in doing so set the first time in the Prix de Tour du Piste, the contest for the fastest time over one lap (ten kilometres). Farman thrilled his fellow citizens by winning the distance contest (the richest cash prize of the meet at 50,000 francs), covering 112 miles (180 kilometres) in a plane of his own design in three hours, four minutes and fifty-six seconds. During the week, he won the Prix des Passengers for carrying two spectators for a total of six miles in ten minutes. Latham won the altitude prize by guiding his plane to a height of 508.5 feet (155 metres), and Lefebvre put on a daring display of aerial acrobatics and quickly gained a reputation as a daredevil.

On the second day, Latham's Antoinette suffered some damage to its propeller when the Frenchman stalled and hit the ground just after crossing the start line. Fournier was up next and, not wanting to suffer the same way Latham did, made sure he had plenty of speed before getting airborne in his Voisin. However, the judges decided that his wheels had not left the ground before he crossed the starting line, and despite completing a lap, only realized his mistake when he passed the judges' box. Furious with himself, he wheeled around and came in for a fast landing in front of the sheds, but only compounded his problems by smashing one wing into the ground in his haste.

Curtiss beat the world record in his Golden Flyer with a time of eight minutes and thirty-seven seconds, and afterward would only compete in the speed competitions throughout the week. Despite receiving criticism for his decision, he had considered that he was the only representative of his country, had only one airplane and few spare parts with him, and was using an engine that had only run previously on the test bench. He also believed, despite Blériot having a more powerful engine, that he still stood a fighting chance.

On Tuesday, 24 August, Blériot regained the speed record with his Type XI completing the circuit in eight minutes and four seconds, at an average speed of 46mph (74.3kph), and Latham amazed everyone by flying at the height of 300 feet (90 metres) while he completed three circuits on his Antoinette in thirty minutes and three seconds. Lefebvre continued to delight the crowds with some daring 'aerobatic' manoeuvres, such as steep turns and dives.

The field of competitors had narrowed considerably by Saturday, 28 August, due to several crashes. The weather had become very bad by the fourth day (25 August) and Fournier was forced down with engine trouble, but the wheels of his Voisin touched a haystack and somersaulted it onto its back. While Latham suffered engine trouble after 18.5 miles (30 kilometres) as he attempted to break the distance record, Paulhan went on and set a new distance record of 81 miles (131 kilometres) in a flight lasting two hours, forty-three minutes and twenty-four seconds. The flight only ended because of his supply of petrol being exhausted and was made all the more dramatic when he continued through a rain shower, which swept the course towards the end of the flight. It also meant that a Frenchman had beaten Wilbur Wright's endurance record of 78 miles (125 kilometres), a feat of huge significance to the French spectators. Paulhan received a hero's welcome on landing and the flight did much to cement his reputation as one of the best French pilots.

The weather improved slightly the next day. Although Latham was able to improve his distance record to 96 miles (154 kilometres) in two hours, seventeen minutes and twenty-one seconds and Blériot practised on his two-seater Type XII for the passenger-carrying competition (the Prix des Passagers) by taking up his friend Leblanc. Cockburn damaged his Farman's tail unit on one of the ubiquitous sheaves of wheat and had to make repairs. Tissandier, Sommer and Cockburn all took their turns retrieving their planes from the fields after engine failure. On target to win the 50,000 francs, Paulhan immediately set to work fitting a twenty-gallon- (ninety-litre-) tank to his Voisin. The Comte de Lambert was not far behind and made a good flight for the Grand Prix on his Wright of 72 miles (116 kilometres) in just under two hours.

Blériot experienced a freak accident in the evening as he was flying in his Type XII with another passenger, a Mr Rath, the designer of his 60hp ENV engine, when he experienced engine trouble. He headed at once for the landing area, but gliding in, found his path suddenly blocked by a troop of cavalry whose duty it was to keep the course clear of spectators! Blériot was forced to swerve and his new landing run now ended at the crowd barrier of the public enclosure. The spectators saw him coming and quickly scattered in all directions. The Blériot XII burst through the barrier and finished its run in the middle of the enclosure in a somewhat bent condition. Fortunately, the crowd had been able to flee in time and no one was hurt.

Many pilots had to stay up late on Thursday night preparing their machines for a final attempt to snatch the Grand Prix de la Champagne prize. The weather on Friday (27 August) continued to be gloomy with an early mist. During early morning practice runs, a near collision between Delagrange's Blériot XI and Paulhan's Voisin caught the Voisin and tipped it into the ground, nose-first. It suffered a broken propeller and crumpled left wing. Paulhan received a cut to his hand and was badly shaken. It quickly became clear that Paulhan would not be improving on his existing time. By the end of the day, Sommer, Farman, Blériot and Latham were all in the circuit trying to outdo each other. Sommer and Blériot dropped out with engine trouble. Farman was left alone circling on endlessly around the course and relentlessly on into the night. By 7.30pm, the judges flagged that they could no longer time him because of the gloom and rising mist. Farman completed one more lap and then came into land, whereupon, according to *The Times*, he 'was seized upon by the enthusiastic crowd and carried in triumph to the restaurant where a scene of almost delirious excitement was witnessed'. He had officially covered 112 miles (180 kilometres) in three hours, four minutes and fifty-six seconds – and had won the Grand Prix de la Champagne.

The rules were simple for the competitors for the Gordon Bennett International Aviation Cup on Saturday (28 August). Each country could enter up to three competitors, and each of those competitors would have one opportunity (and only one) to fly 12.4 miles (20 kilometres) in the fastest time they could. The winner would receive the trophy worth £500 and £1,000 in prize money; the next year's competition would then be defended in the winner's home country. Latham, Blériot and Lefebvre had been chosen earlier in the week to represent the French Aero Club. George Cockburn represented the Aero Club of Great Britain and Glen Curtiss the Aero Club of America.

Curtiss flew first, and gained height relatively easily in his Reims Racer, and then completed the course in a shallow dive to maximize speed. There was nothing in the rules against this. He crossed the line about 65 feet (20 metres) up in the time of fifteen minutes and fifty seconds. 'I made the turns as tightly as I dared,' he recounted, 'and banked the machine up steeply. The bumps were so violent that I was lifted out of my seat and could only stay in by jamming my feet against the framework.'[47] Cockburn followed on his 50hp Gnome-powered Farman, but engine trouble soon forced him to make an emergency landing in a field. Once again, he collided with a sheaf of wheat on landing but was unhurt.

Of the three Frenchmen who remained, Lefebvre, who had a 20hp Wright-designed engine, realized he had little chance and went next, completing his two laps of the course in twenty minutes and forty-seven seconds, which, considering the relatively low horsepower he had available, was a credit to the aerodynamic efficiency of the Wright and his piloting skills. Latham followed next in his 50hp Antoinette and crossed the line seventeen minutes and thirty-two seconds after taking off. But it was not good enough. Blériot and his rebuilt Type XII, and specifically installed heavy British 60hp ENV engine in the hope of creating a fast 'racing machine', took off and made what was a very fast couple of laps. On landing, he was greeted by rapturous applause from his countrymen, and Curtiss feared the worst. All eyes were on the judges' box. The scoreboard showed that Curtiss had been just six seconds faster than Blériot, whose time was fifteen minutes and fifty-six seconds. Curtiss had made history by winning the first-ever airplane race. Blériot's 'consolation' was that he was able to win the speed prize over ten kilometres, the Prix de Tour du Piste, later that evening, completing a lap in seven minutes and forty-seven seconds and so created a new world speed record of 48mph (77kph). Farman won the Prix de Passagers afterward, beating the only other competitor, Eugène Lefebvre, by carrying not one but two people around the circuit (an extra weight of 20 stone/132 kilograms).

The last day of the meeting (Sunday, 29 August) drew around 250,000 people – the largest crowd of the entire week – into the stands and public enclosures. The main event was the altitude contest (Prix de l'Altitude); this was also the last day of the speed contests – the Prix de la Vitesse and the Prix de Tour du Piste.

Curtiss challenged Blériot again for the fastest lap but was unable to beat the Frenchman's time. However, while trying for the thirty-kilometre prize, Blériot was unlucky to experience another accident in his Type XII monoplane. His propeller suffered structural failure in midair and the resulting vibration threatened to rip the aircraft apart. Blériot had to throttle back and make an immediate forced landing. With insufficient time to choose his landing spot, the XII's wheels caught in rough ground, causing the airplane to somersault onto its back. The petrol tank was split open in the crash and fuel poured out onto the hot engine, starting a fire from which Blériot was lucky to escape. Once clear of the airplane, he had to roll on the ground to put out the flames consuming his clothes. The machine was destroyed apart from the metal parts. Remarkably, Blériot was not seriously hurt. The experience likely hastened his retirement from competitive flying – he flew little after Reims. The thirty-kilometre prize ultimately fell to Curtiss and his Reims Racer, in which he broke the '50mph barrier' and set a new speed record of 52.6mph (84.7kph).

Twenty-three out of the thirty-eight original entrants went aloft, and of those, fifteen were biplanes and eight were monoplanes. In all, the pilots completed eighty-seven flights during the competition. The air meet showed that aviation competitions were a tremendously exciting form of entertainment for most of the people who attended. As one spectator, David Lloyd George, the future prime minister of Great Britain, noted, the meet also proved that 'flying machines are no longer toys and dreams … they are a fact'. For those who had any doubts about the future of aviation, the Reims Air Show not only legitimized the importance and significance of flight but also set the standard by which people would measure all future air meets.

The 1927 Dole Air Race

Charles Lindbergh's flight across the Atlantic in May 1927 generated sensational reporting in the U.S. press, and shrewd businessmen saw the PR potential in sponsoring record flights. The first to seize the opportunity was James D. Dole, founder of the Hawaiian Pineapple Company (HAPCO, now the Dole Foods Company, Inc., Westlake Village, California), who offered a prize of $25,000 to the first pilot to fly from Oakland Field, Oakland, California, to Wheeler Field, Honolulu, Oahu, Territory of Hawaii, a great circle distance of 2,406.05 miles (3,872.16 kilometres). A $10,000 prize was offered for a second-place finisher.

The Dole Derby (as it is also known) was an unprecedented air race that took place on 16 August 1927, and out of 33 entrants, only 14 were selected for starting positions, and following accidents and inspections by the race committee, finalists were whittled down to eight. Accidents had begun to claim the lives of entrants before the race even began. On 10 August, a Pacific Aircraft Company J-30 Tremaine Hummingbird named *The Spirit of John Rodgers*, and flown by U.S. Navy Lieutenants George D. Covell and Richard S. Waggener, crashed into a cliff on the fog-enshrouded Point Loma, fifteen minutes into its initial climb from North Island Naval Air Station, San Diego, California, en route to Oakland Field. Both officers were killed. They had drawn starting position 13.[48] On the following day, Captain Arthur Vickers Rogers was killed on approach to Vail Field, Montebello, San Gabriel Valley, California, following a test flight in his Bryant Monoplane (NX705) *Angel of Los Angeles*. Rogers was reported to have attempted to bail out but died as either his foot or parachute snagged on the aircraft as it crashed.[49,50] One airplane, *Miss Doran*, made an emergency landing in a farm field, and a fourth, an International Aircraft Corporation F-10 triplane, *Pride of Los Angeles*, flown by the movie star, Edmund Richard 'Hoot' Gibson, crashed into San Francisco Bay while on approach to Oakland Field. The occupants of those two airplanes were unhurt.[51]

The starting positions for the remaining eight entrants for the race had been selected by random draw. Spectators at the event helped to push the planes to assist with take-off since they were so overloaded with fuel. Just before 11 am, the first airplane, a Travel Air 5000 (NX911) *Oklahoma*, took off but soon had to abort the flight because of engine trouble. *El Encanto*, a Goddard Special (NX5074), crashed on take-off, and the Breese-Wilde Monoplane, *Pabco Pacific Flyer* (NX646), also crashed on take-off. The crews of these three airplanes were unhurt. The next airplane to take off was the prototype Lockheed Vega 1, *Golden Eagle* (NX913), sponsored by Hearst Newspapers and flown by Jack Frost with Gordon Scott as the navigator. It never reached Honolulu, disappearing without a trace.[52]

The Lockheed was followed by the Buhl CA-5 Air Sedan (NX2915), named *Miss Doran*, which had undergone repairs from its unscheduled landing in the farmer's field. It was flown by John 'Auggy' Pedlar, a stunt flier with the Lincoln Standard Circus (an adjunct of the Lincoln Standard Aircraft Company), with Lieutenant Vilas Raymond Knope, U.S. Navy, as navigator.[53] Also aboard was a passenger, Miss Mildred Alice Doran, the airplane's namesake, who was a 23-year-old fifth-grade schoolteacher from Flint, Michigan, who knew William Malloska, owner of the Lincoln Petroleum Company (later CITGO) and convinced him to enter the airplane in the Dole Air Race and allow her to fly along. Two local air circus pilots reportedly flipped a coin for the chance to fly the airplane. Pedlar won the toss. Just ten minutes after take-off from Oakland Field, *Miss Doran* returned with engine problems.

Next off was a Swallow Special, *Dallas Spirit* (NX941), with William Portwood Erwin, pilot, and Alvin Hanford Eichwaldt, navigator. It also quickly returned to Oakland. Next was a Breese-Wilde 5 Monoplane *Aloha* (NX914), with Martin Jensen as the pilot, and Master Mariner Captain Paul Henry Schlüter as navigator, The Travel Air 5000 *Woolaroc* (XN869) took off without difficulty. *Miss Doran* made a second attempt and took off successfully. *Pabco Pacific Flyer* also tried again, but crashed for the second time.[54] *Woolaroc*, with Arthur Cornelius Goebel as the pilot and William Virginius Davis, Jr, as navigator, flew across the Pacific and arrived at Honolulu after twenty-six hours and seventeen minutes, to win the race. *Aloha* arrived after twenty-eight hours and sixteen minutes. *Golden Eagle* and *Miss Doran* never arrived. Information of some belief that the missing Dole flyers might have come down just outside the Farallones (off the coast of San Francisco) was contained in a message intercepted in the afternoon on navy radio, ordering destroyers to proceed from San Diego.

Forty-two navy vessels, including submarines, destroyers and aircraft carriers, were involved in the search, and a fleet of 100 sampans of experienced Japanese fisherman, scattered through the various island ports and fishing grounds, was ordered in a radio organization to make every effort to assist the searchers. The *Aloha*, winner of second place in the Dole Race, left Honolulu immediately on a cruise of the islands in hope of finding clues about the two missing planes. *Dallas Spirit* was repaired and Erwin and Eichwaldt took off to join the search for their competitors. They, too, were never seen again. George Hearst, the owner of *Dallas Spirit*, told reporters that, 'they had provisions on board that would be sufficient for two weeks, and also, the plane was equipped with every possible device to sustain life in the event it was forced down. If they had any time at all before they landed, they could have inflated the flotation bags, and the ship would float indefinitely'.[55]

James Dole offered $20,000 to find the missing planes. Malloska added $10,000 to find his friend and the others. William Randolph Hearst, Sr, also added a reward.[56] There were many tributes after the death of Mildred Doran. Doran Lake, in Simcoe County, Ontario, Canada, was named in her honour and Lincoln Oil dedicated a memorial and shrine to Mildred Doran. It was a windmill-shaped gas station with an upstairs apartment named 'Doran Tower', located on the south-east corner of Maple Avenue and Saginaw Street at the Lincoln airport property. A large boulder with a bronze tablet was installed just south of the tower with an inscription: 'Only those are fit to live who are not afraid to die.' In 1932, Lincoln airport gave way to the Lincoln Manor subdivision. The plaque was lost during relocation due to road construction. The Doran Tower Restaurant which occupied the building closed in 1966 giving way to several other businesses. The tower was destroyed in 1973 because the owner could no longer afford the taxes.[57]

Chapter 3

The 13 Black Cats

The members of the 13 Black Cats defied both superstition and death in their performances for newsreels and motion pictures. The earliest well-known organization of Hollywood aviators that set rates and aerial standards for the movie industry, the group was based at Burdette airfield, located at Western Avenue and 102nd Street, Los Angeles, California.

The first event of the aviators who formed the Black Cats was performed before several thousand people at an early air show on 5 July 1925 at Burdette airfield. The famous Hollywood stunt man Dick Grace had been hired to provide the entertainment that day, but he failed to show up, and as a result of the gap it created in the entertainment schedule, the Burdett pilots decided that they could provide the aerial entertainment themselves (without the professionals). The pre-publicity for the event had encouraged a large crowd to pay to watch, and they would soon start demanding what was promised. According to one of the original members, Kenneth Nichols, it would be have been 'destructive' if what was promised was not delivered. On this day the Black Cat stunt team was born.

The original members of the Black Cat group were Ronald G. 'Bon' MacDougall; Kenneth 'Fronty' Nichols; William 'Spider' Matlock; Jerry Tabnac, who was head of Cross Aerial Photo Service and one of the best cameramen of the day; Heard 'Herd' McClellan, who specialized in delayed jumps; Paul E. Richter, Jr, who went on to become general manager of Trans-World Airlines; Lieutenant William John 'Jack' Frye, co-owner of the Burdette airport with Burdette Fuller and MacDougall, who went on to become president of Aero Corporation of California, Standard Airlines, Transcontinental Western Air and Trans-World Airlines, as well as chairman of the board of Ansco Film Corporation and Dyestuffs Inc.; Al Johnson; Ivan 'Bugs' Unger, a well-publicized daredevil who danced with his sister on top of flight balloons; Major

Sanford 'Sam' Greenwald, who was a cameraman for forty-five years, much of that time with International Newsreel: he was one of the first men ashore at Normandy on 6 June 1945, and later went on to become a head cameraman for the Columbia Broadcasting System (CBS); Colonel Arthur 'Art' Goebel, an actor known for *Won in the Clouds* (1928), *Three Miles Up* (1927) and *The Air Patrol* (1928), the winner of the Oakland to Honolulu Dole Air Race on 19/20 August 1927, and the pilot of the Lockheed Vega (NX4789) *Yankee Doodle* on its record non-stop (eighteen hours and fifty-five minutes) transcontinental flight on 23 June 1924 from Los Angeles to Garden City, New York; William 'Bill' Stapp, a professional aerial photographer; and Gladys Ingle, who was the first to perform target shooting and archery on an airplane: she completed over 300 airplane transfers without a parachute, yet she was only an honourary member because the group didn't accept girls.

There were many members of the 13 Black Cats who were never officially photographed with the group because they were an evolving group of participants who came and went, with some even dying in accidents. For that reason, there were many members involved with the group that never received well-earned credit let alone being recognized as official members. A few individuals who are thought to have been official Black Cat members at various times (including honourary) were as follows: Burdett Fuller, Frank Helfing, Reginald Denny, Elbert 'Babe' Stapp, 'Wild Billy' Lind, Wayne Allies, Theodore 'Ted' A. Woolsey, Gerald Phillips, Howard Batt, Frank Lockhart, Native American member Chief White Eagle and Gladys Roy. There were associates of the Black Cats who assisted in stunts but did not seek membership such as Joe Campi, Frank Tomac, Bobby Chase, Frank Clarke, Dick Grace and Philip Johnson.

Reginald Denny, who was often referred to in the press as the 'thirteenth member' of the Black Cats, was a Hollywood actor of the day, but allegedly, because he was under studio contract, he was never allowed by studio moguls to become an 'official' member of the daredevil group. William Stapp and Sam Greenwald were also professional aerial photographers, and Jerry Tabnac was one of the best cameramen in the country, along with Sam Greenwald.

The Black Cats' 'uniform' was a black sweater with a cat and number 13 emblem patch on the front, and their names on the back. The logo showed a black cat perched on a fence with its back up ready for a fight, and a full moon shining over its shoulder (inspired by the sacred cat of Bubastes from an Egyptian tale); it had been used previously by Bon MacDougall on his own plane for several years before the formation of the group, and because a great many people had a superstition about both black cats and the number 13 and – corresponding to 13 men at The Last Supper – the trademark was a natural for these daredevils who on an almost daily basis, seemed to spit in the eye of fate. It was also played up by the press when it was found that nine of the thirteen members signed their names using thirteen letters.

In the business, Frye, who was married, was always the leader and the vision behind the operations he headed and this kept him walking the fine line of responsibility; he was never careless with the safety of spectators or passengers. Despite suffering from acrophobia (although he was not afraid of flying), he was responsible for every decision made at Burdette airport in its early days, so in the circumstance where the entertainment failed to show up, Frye and Fuller had to quickly find a solution to keep the crowd appeased, and that would invariably include stepping up to perform some of the stunts themselves – the 'can-do' attitude was a trait Frye instilled in his pilots. Being more cautious than the death-defying daredevils of the group, he was counted on for his navigation skills to provide a stable platform from which they could perform their parachute jumps, wing-walking and loops. Frye's modus operandi became an intricate part of the fabric of Standard Air Lines and TWA.

If a Black Cat Can't Do It, It Can't Be Done

The Black Cats performed many stunts, some relatively tame, but others extremely dangerous. Many of its members flew with a lack of caution, planning or preparation, this being evident by their mishaps which is something that would be unheard of today with professional stunt pilots. Four of the most visible Black Cats – 'Spider' Matlock, Al Johnson, 'Fronty' Nichols and Bon MacDougall – heartily endorsed the group's creed, 'We'll Do Anything', for a price, and there was a fixed fee for all of the stunts. A delayed parachute jump with a thousand-foot freefall was standard at $150. A plane-to-car or plane-to-boat or plane-to-plane transfer cost the same (and was almost always executed without a parachute). A double parachute jump – both men using the same parachute – was $180. A loop, with men standing on the wingtips, cost up to $450. And a fight tableau on the upper wing, where one man got knocked off, which became one of the specialities, went for $225. It seemed to be a very lucrative business to be in considering that one could live on $100 a month in those days.

A sample of the most commonly performed Black Cat stunts, although they did a little bit of everything, is outlined here:

- Wing-walking
- Flying through a building – or crashing into a building, ocean, trees or objects, etc.
- Transfer from various moving objects to and from planes, including trains
- Blowing up planes in the air; passengers and pilot eject
- Spinning airplanes (engulfed by fire) toward the ground but not crashing
- Loops, while men or women stand on the tips of each wing
- Flying low and picking up hats with wingtips
- Handing hats from the ground to men on the wingtips of low-flying planes
- Playing (faux) tennis on wing tops
- Hanging from rope ladders and dangling upside down by ropes (nooses)
- Changing tyres in the air
- Intricate spins and loops (as under the famous Pasadena Colorado Street Bridge)
- Wide variety of parachute performances
- Flying inverted for extended periods
- Riding a bicycle dangling from a rope and then parachuting down to the ground
- Landing upside down
- Saloon brawls on wing tops (not regular feats)
- Staging a fight on the wing with one man getting knocked off with a punch

Within seven months, based on stunts like these, the fame of the Black Cats had spread worldwide. They began to pick up new members and more new stunts. They originated the stunt of picking a hat off the ground with a plane's wingtip. They would crash into anything for $1,200, and they would even blow a plane up in midair as the pilot parachuted out, for $1,500. But things became harder over time as the movie and newsreel companies built up a library of stunt footage that they could use and re-use as required. Then the Department of Commerce, which preceded the Civil Aeronautics Authority, passed stringent laws against dangerous air stunts. The new rules, which involved a lot of red tape, created long delays in getting stunts approved when the hiring companies usually wanted them on a day's notice and would become the main reason that the Black Cats were so short-lived.

One Black Cat trip seemed to have been haunted by bad luck. Spider and Nichols took off with MacDougall for Bakersfield racetrack to do a show. Because of the weight of an additional passenger in a two-passenger plane, the Jenny could not gain enough altitude to clear Tehachapi Pass. Only by jettisoning everything not bolted down, including their shoes, did they clear the mountains. They had no compass on the trip but instead followed the highway which was typical of this (pre-navigation chart) era. A 'gravity string' thumb-tacked to the dash told the pilot if they were flying upside down or right side up in clouds. After the performance in Bakersfield, they landed the plane in a limited clearance area with no brakes. The only way they were able to stop was by Spider and Fronty hanging from the wings and dragging their feet on the turf.

They were unable to lift off again with a short runway so fifteen men held on to the wings while Bon revved the engine to full throttle. After he signalled the men to let go, he roared off, just barely clearing a fence and trees. Bon had to set the Jenny down again, though, in a big field to pick up Nichols and Matlock, after which, they finally took off for Los Angeles. Unfortunately, on the way, the three got caught in the ever-present coastal evening fog. They decided to descend below the soup to get their bearings, regarding Los Angeles, but what they found instead was an endless ocean. Luckily, they had enough fuel to turn and head back to the coast where they soon exhausted their fuel and were forced down in a beet field. A farmer was able to help them locate some gasoline but had no funnel. The funnel was necessary to fuel the plane through the underwing filler pipe. The only solution was filling a whiskey bottle with gasoline and dumping it into the plane over and over. After several hours of this procedure, the ship finally had enough fuel to take off for Los Angeles. By now, though, it was dark, but despite this, they still managed to find Burdett Airport. On approach, descending in the darkness, Bon MacDougall tried to use the (closed) office nightlight for a bearing. Not surprisingly, they ended up in a ditch and tore off the landing gear of the Jenny. Seems the only good omen of the cursed trip was they made it home without any deaths.

On another performance, Al Johnson, Spider and Fronty took off to do the 'first' multiple parachute jump in the country. The plane was again overloaded and Al desperately fought the machine to gain altitude. Spider fell off the plane and plummeted to the ground while desperately trying to pull his parachute ripcord which ripped off the pack. Finally, within 200 feet over a tomato field, the 'chute deployed and his life was spared. Al and Fronty landed, repaired and repacked the parachute, took off again, and performed for the waiting Pathé and International newsreel cameras. This was, perhaps, the same tale oft-told when Ivan Unger was a part of the group that did the first quadruple parachute jump, all under the same 'chute. Johnson knocked Spider off the wing, dazing him, at which he fell to the ground in a tangle, but miraculously survived the fall. The crowning element was that it was Matlock's first jump, something he was not forthcoming about at the time. Another time, Al Johnson's 'chute deployed while he was on the wing, which in turn, yanked him against the tail whence he fell from the plane in a half-conscious tangle. An aircraft hangar miraculously appeared below him and helped break his fall, but he ended up hanging from the side of the building, where his head harshly contacted the wall.

Bon MacDougall would pilot a Jenny, with passengers Nichols and Spider performing a wing-walking dance for the crowd, with the finale of the two parachuting from the plane. On 20 November 1925, the newsreels cranked away, as Spider, Fronty and Al Nichols, expanded the feat with all three men cavorting on the upper wing of MacDougall's plane – a stunt unheard of before then.

In another publicized event, Art Goebel flew a loop under the Colorado Street Bridge with Kalisihek and Gladys Ingle standing on the top end of each wing for newsreel cameras. Goebel performed with, and independent of, the Black Cats at times, with his own act. The Pasadena Bridge was a regular haunt for Black Cats who would perform the stunt – a hair-raising feat, as there were trees at the bottom of the loop, which would often brush the undercarriage of the planes. Gladys Ingle was highly skilled at transferring from one plane to another in flight and without a parachute – over 300 times without incident – often purportedly to save another airplane that had a wheel fall off on take-off.

At the air show at Clover Field, Santa Monica, on 19 September 1926, Art Goebel, in his famous Jenny No. 27, soared 2,000 feet above Clover Field, merrily performing his aerial escapades over an excited crowd, which was estimated to have been 10,000 people, when suddenly one of his wheels fell off and plummeted to the ground. Rather than land and damage the ship, or himself, Art continued to slowly circle the air show waving frantically toward the ground. Gladys Ingel and Jack Frye were watching closely from the sidelines and jumped up to save the day. Frye quickly darted to his Jenny and started it whilst Gladys ran to a hangar and grabbed a spare tyre for Goebel's stricken ship. In no time, Gladys scrambled into the passenger seat while Frye gunned the engine and, in a flash, they were off the ground and in pursuit of number 27.

Frye expertly navigated his ship close enough for Ingle to lower herself down onto the wing, with the spare tyre strapped to her back. As the Frye plane maintained a close vigil nearby, Ingle climbed down below the fuselage of 27 and proceeded to replace the wheel. The axle had also slipped, so she had to secure the wheel to the ship and climb down to wrestle with the axle. She encountered quite a struggle sliding it back in but she was finally successful. Ingle quickly slipped the wheel on and anchored it with an axle nut and cotter pin – the whole feat carried out with nothing under her but 2,000 feet of empty air.

Nicked up, bleeding, and covered with axle grease, the shaken Ingle clambered for the cockpit after which the two planes quickly descended and landed. Once safely on the ground, Goebel heartily thanked Gladys and Frye, with a lot of back-slapping, while the two planes and heroes were inundated by a pressing crowd of over 500 impressed spectators. The back story suggested that the event was staged – and it seemed likely. After all, all three were members of the 13 Black Cat aerial stunt team, and Goebel's plane seemed to lose its wheel quite often. Either these 'in-air tyre-changing episodes' were an act, or a ground crew member needed to be fired for faulty repairs. The axle problem, however, was unplanned and added a little anxiety to an otherwise well-orchestrated feat. Just another notch though in a thrilling Black Cat performance for unsuspecting air show participants. Ingle was well known as Goebel's partner in many aerial misadventures and was a highly skilled licensed pilot.

Gladys Ingle was also adept at shooting an arrow at a target from the top of one wing to the other side (same plane) while at cruise elevation – let alone her knack for shooting back over her shoulder at a target while looking in a mirror. Yes, of course, again, all on the wing of a sputtering Jenny. If a plane experienced a flat (or staged flat) in the air nobody wasted time calling Triple-A, but instead called Gladys Ingle, who would appear, jack the plane up – well, that wasn't necessary at 1,000 feet – and wrestle that 'ole flat tire loose', and mount a new one for the pilot and audience.

Changing planes at high elevations was becoming an everyday occurrence for a Black Cat. However, on 1 May 1926, Spider and passenger Howard Batt suffered a disaster, unlike anything the 13 Black Cat aerial team would ever have dreamed up. They departed Bakersfield at 4.10pm and started west to Burdett airport at Los Angeles. However, as they neared Los Angeles, fog surrounded them and dusk descended over their small, sputtering plane. In the foggy soup, unbeknown to the two, they overshot Los Angeles and ended up 25 miles west off the coast, far above the Pacific Ocean, and far from land. Running out of gas they had to ditch in the sea. As luck would have it, before the plane sank to the bottom of a very deep ocean, the two cold and wet fliers were spotted, and subsequently hauled on board the SS *Hamlin F. McCormick*, the largest lumber freighter on the West Coast, which happened by on its journey from Portland, Oregon, to Los Angeles with a full load of Northwest lumber.

Anyone for Tennis?

Gladys Roy and Ivan Unger played tennis regularly at 3,000 feet, where it was assumed, the air was crisper. Of course, sans tennis balls, retrieving an 'out of bounds' tennis ball meant landing the aircraft first. Frank Tomac was the pilot on many of these matches, and one was recorded on 25 October 1925, for the cinema newsreels.

Al Johnson held the unusual record of riding a bicycle at 3,000 feet over Los Angeles, while suspended below a plane – all with a climax of parachuting to the ground with a bike (one would assume, so he could pedal his way back to the airport). Photographers gasped at this feat on 12 November 1925.

A staged poker game performance on top of the upper wing of a Jenny went awry after Al Johnson passed out. Bon MacDougall was the pilot of a plane with two chairs strapped to the upper wing surfaces. Once in the air, Al and Fronty were supposed to play cards and pretend to start arguing. Fronty was to then pull out a gun and shoot Al who would proceed to fall off the plane and parachute to the ground. This all for the Pathé News cameras set up in Art Goebel's ship which shadowed Bon's plane. Because Pathé didn't want the parachutes to show on camera, Fronty didn't wear one but Al did. However, because of the camera angle, Al's 'chute did not show on camera. Once in the air, Art gave the signal to start playing cards, when suddenly Al fainted and started to slip off the wing. Fronty, in a flash, quickly grabbed him by the ankle. This positioned Fronty against the hot engine where he desperately tried to hold on to Al's lifeless body in the wind. At this point, Bon stood up in the cockpit and tried to save Al by grabbing his parachute ripcord. As the parachute deployed, Fronty released Al and let him slide off the wing into the air. Bon immediately followed Al down to the ground with the plane, watching as Al floated down into a daisy field, limp as a rag doll. After they landed, Bon and Fronty rushed to Johnson and revived the passed-out Kitty Cat. Pertinently, the reason Al passed out was that he hadn't eaten in two days before the event and as a result was very weak. This alone reveals that times were hard (the Great Depression) and the Black Cat saga was not all glamour and glory.

Thrills galore featured in the sky-high manoeuvres of a flock of airmen in their first attempt to establish commercial airplane records on the Pacific Coast. The *Los Angeles Times* covered the event that took place on 8 November 1926, when thousands of spectators converged on Clover Field, Santa Monica, to watch as stunt pilots performed death-defying acts, and got an unexpected thrill during an unscheduled event when Miss 'Bobby' Chase forgot to cut the safety cord of a parachute from which she leapt. She dangled for about twenty minutes caught in the undergear of the plane until her 'chute was cut away by Fred Osborne, who went to her assistance in a rescuing plane. According to the *Los Angeles Times*, Osborne wing-walked to Chase's plane, several hundred feet up in the air, so he could cut the safety line that kept her dangling. She deployed her parachute, landed on a street near Venice Beach and sprained her ankle on a curb.

Another thrill came when Johnson was attempting to change from one plane to another, which was speeding beneath the ship on which he was stationed. The wings of the upper plane struck those of the plane beneath it, and when Johnson landed it was discovered that a foot of fabric from one wing had been torn away. The spectators could distinctly hear the two planes make contact. Johnson succeeded in changing planes while he was 125 feet in the air, although he was forced to circle the airfield seven times before he accomplished the transfer.

In a second stunt, Al Johnson leaped from an altitude of 150 feet in a parachute in an attempt to land on a target marked out on the ground, but his 'chute didn't open until he had nearly reached the ground, and he landed flat on his back. The spectators, horror-stricken, rushed onto the field, the police having a hard time in dispersing them. Ambulances took both stunt flyers to the army emergency hospital, where it was said that neither of them had been seriously injured. Before Johnson's accident, Miss Jackie Dare had successfully jumped from a plane and landed 138 feet from the mark. She was a 17-year-old high-school girl from Los Angeles and won the first prize for a parachute landing.

Pilots in the altitude contest selected to make the final test were Paul Richter in an Alexander 'Eaglerock', Arthur C. Burns in a Weaver Aircraft Company (Waco) and Jack Frye in an M-14 Thunderbird. According to Lieutenant Charles Harding Babb, of the National Aeronautic Association, it would take about two days to make a complete calibration of the 18,000-feet altitude thought to have been attained according to the barographs attached to the planes.

Frank E. Samuels, the manager of *Aero Digest* magazine, interviewed Johnson:

> I had been doubling for movie actors since I was big enough to ride a motorcycle, and have done almost every known ground stunt for them. I can't say that I was ever nervous. I generally have it all figured out as to how I am going to do the trick and am usually very careful to see that everything is prepared in advance to assure me the minimum danger. The carelessness of detail is the cause of most accidents.

While preparing to make a parachute jump recently, I was in such haste that I did not properly fasten my ripcord. We took off, Bon MacDougall flying the ship. When we reached an altitude of 1,500 feet, Bon signalled me to get out of the cockpit. I went out on the wing, and as we were circling for position, my ripcord came loose and blew back over my shoulder. I was sitting on the edge of the wing at the time. The pilot immediately noticed it and pointed to it. I thought that he was motioning for me to look down which I did, and noticed a ship looping close to the ground, and thought that Bon was watching it too. When I looked at the pilot again, he motioned to me frantically, pointing to my pack. Again, I looked down toward the earth. I didn't see anything, so leaned away out to get a good view under the wing. As I did so, my ripcord became entangled around the incidence wire, pulled and opened my pack. Bon immediately signalled for me to come to the cockpit, but just as I gained my feet, the parachute flew through the wires and opened, dragging me through with it before I had the chance to think.

The force of the 'chute pulled me through the wires, broke parts of my harness, and strained my back. The jar on the ship was terrific. It tore the streamline of the wires and threw the whole ship out of line. The last thing that I remembered was the look on the pilot's face as I shot by him.

When I landed, at last, I was partially conscious, but was okay a few minutes later, minus about eight square inches of good tough hide. That was when Bon MacDougall got his revenge for a busted ship, and he took great pleasure in acting as my doctor, using an entire pint of Iodine on my raw flesh at one painting. I have a full quart of Iodine that I am saving in case I ever have the chance to return the compliment.

Chapter 4

Post-First World War and Barnstorming

The First World War ended on 11 November 1918, and America's economic boom quickly faded. U.S. officials found themselves in a bleak position. Factories began to ramp down production lines in the summer of 1918, leading to job losses and fewer opportunities for returning soldiers. The federal debt exploded because of wartime expenditures, and annual consumer price inflation rates jumped well above 20 per cent by the end of the war. This led to a short recession in 1918/19, followed by a sharper deflationary recession in 1920 /1.[58, 59] In the United States, United Kingdom and other countries, despite the economy showing signs that it had started to grow, many major adjustments that were required for the transition from a wartime to a peacetime economy had not been completed. The resulting downturn was further complicated by the millions of returning troops, who created a surge in the civilian labour force, changes in fiscal and monetary policy, and changes in price expectations. Unemployment rose sharply, and the climate was terrible for businesses. From 1919 to 1922 the rate of business failures tripled, climbing from 37 failures to 120 failures per every 10,000 businesses. Businesses that avoided bankruptcy saw a 75 per cent decline in profits.[60] Further economic dislocation was caused by the Spanish flu pandemic in the United States, which began in spring 1918 and returned in waves into 1920, killing about 675,000 Americans. After the depression, the United States proceeded to enjoy the 'Roaring Twenties' – flappers danced the Charleston, and behind the doors of the 'speakeasies' – underground clubs that offered illegal alcohol, so it was important to speak softly or 'easy' – everyone lived like they were immortal. It brought a period of economic prosperity between August 1921 and August 1929, but in September 1929, the American stock market crashed, triggering the start of the Great Depression.[61]

Few Americans owned a car before the war, and even fewer had seen an airplane, which had been invented just over a decade earlier. Outside the big cities, people were more accustomed to the pace of horses and bicycles than of trains or cars. Americans had enthusiastically mass-produced planes for the war but found when they got to the Western Front that the British, French and Germans were far ahead of them when it came to cutting-edge flight technology. The post-war solution by the U.S. government for all of the surplus flying machines was to sell them off for as low as $200 each. Ex-military fighter pilots returned from battle to find the country was ravaged by unemployment and faced an uncertain future in the economic hard times. Still flushed with adrenaline from living life on the edge, it was an offer that a great many of them could not turn down.

Despite people needing to have a licence to drive a car since 1903 (although there was no requirement to pass a test to obtain one until a decade later), there were already rules of the road and strict standards for drivers. Yet as aviation came into its own after the First World War as a reliable, affordable technology, pilots were not required to have a licence to fly an airplane – or have to have taken any lessons, which meant that they were free to develop this new American pastime in the spirit of opportunity and without restriction. Aviation evolved dramatically following the war. The dual-winged wood, fabric and wire contraptions that could hedge-hop and puddle-jump and land in any farm field that presented itself, gave way to sleek metal monoplanes fitted with powerful engines and capable of travelling great distances.

'Barnstorming' become something of a phenomenon, especially in the U.S. The appeal was an age-old one, but barnstormers had an attraction no predecessor could beat: the thrill of brand-new, superfast technology. This loud, dangerous machine was addictive, and barnstormers quickly created their unique acts to stand out. Part entertainers and part thrill-seekers, they made their way across the country. Some were racers, flying customized planes that roared around pylons at speeds that had broken set records just weeks earlier. Most of the entertainers, however, modelled their acts on old-time Western shows like Buffalo Bill Cody, and practised target shooting, or even danced on the wings of planes, combining circus flair with impossible stunts. These public displays of aerobatics were often called 'flying circuses,' and were common during the late 1920s up until the mid-1940s. To let everyone in town know they were there, they created little dramas such as flying low down the main street, 'looping the loop' and the big attraction – flying with a wing-walker out on the wing, often one of the pilots themselves. Aerobatic pilots would often land at local farms to drum up business. They would offer locals rides in their planes and would put on air shows. Farmers' fields would double up as runways and barns would become impromptu venues – from which stunt pilots and wing-walkers became known as 'barnstormers'. (Barnstorming was the first major form of civil aviation in the history of aviation, and many pilots began providing flight training, charter flights, opened up FBOs (fixed base operations) and other services, which brought in the age of commercial aviation.)

Some barnstormers did quite well both financially and socially. Several towns across the nation paid them quite handsomely for their shows and held parties and dances in their honour. Some pilots and aerialists also obtained free room and board when they travelled. Nevertheless, the nomadic existence of barnstorming could also cause serious problems. Sometimes it was difficult for pilots to find fuel or the right parts for their planes. Other times, they could go several days without attracting a large enough crowd to make a profit. And if those factors were not problematic enough, as Jessie Woods of the Flying Aces Air Circus declared: 'Don't let them kid you – it wasn't romantic. I slept on the bottom wing of an airplane. I learned how to sleep there without falling off. I've gone through as much as three days without sleep. There's nothing romantic about that.'

Barnstorming thrived in North America during the first half of the 1920s, but by 1927, new safety regulations forced the demise of this very popular entertainment. The federal government – spurred by a perceived need to protect the public after several aircraft accidents, and responding to local pilots who were upset that barnstormers were stealing their customers – enacted several laws that began to regulate the fledgling civil aviation business. Such laws made it nearly impossible for barnstormers to keep their already fragile Jennys up to specifications (let alone in the air), and outlawed several forms of aerial stunts, at least at a low enough altitude where crowds could easily view them. When these factors were coupled with the fact that the military stopped selling Jennys in the late 1920s, barnstormers found it too difficult to continue to make a living stunting and they abandoned the art. Although some modern pilots such as the famous airmen Joseph Kittinger continued to put on barnstorming exhibitions, nothing can compare to the magnitude of that period in the 1920s, when itinerant aerial shows sprung up throughout North America day after day and made audiences gasp with excitement.[62, 63]

Many pilots were killed performing their dangerous feats and performing aerobatics that many of them had learned during the war, but property damage had become commonplace as they entertained audiences to earn money, with some of the pilots flying through the open doors of a barn hoping that it wasn't their last flight.

Chapter 5

The Flying Circuses

Some of the early flying circuses included the Gates Flying Circus (Gates was an old-time promoter of early exhibition fliers), Jimmy Angel (Eddie Angel's brother), the 13 Black Cats, the Flying Aces Air Circus (Jimmy and Jessie Woods, a husband-and-wife team from Kansas), the Five Blackbirds (an all African American team), Mabel Cody's Flying Circus, and a troop run by Douglas Davis (the future winner of the 1934 Bendix Race).

The Gates Flying Circus

The Gates Flying Circus was probably the organization that made the greatest impression on the public. At its peak, it had thirteen planes on the apron at Teterboro airport, in Bergen County, New Jersey. In one day alone they were reported to have flown 980 passengers.[64] This was done by pilot Bill Brooks at the Stuebenville Air Show in Ohio, where the 'One Dollar Joy-Ride' was a sensation. One of Gates's best-known fliers was Clyde 'Upside-Down' Pangborn, an ex-army pilot.[65] 'Pang' was part owner of the Gates circus and its chief pilot and operating manager. As his nickname suggests, he specialized in flying upside down. Another key stunt he performed was to change planes in midair; he held the world record for the feat. In 1924, he also performed a newsworthy deed when he rescued Rosalie Gordon, a stuntwoman, in midair when her parachute got tangled in his plane's landing gear. Gates paid his pilots anywhere between $400 and $1,500 per month, which is the main reason his circus attracted the best pilots.

In 1925, four planes from the Gates Circus 'attacked' New York City. They stunted, wing-walked, plane-changed, and dived within 100 feet of the sidewalk. They flew around and through the canyons between the skyscrapers and worked up a tremendous amount of publicity. Of the 'old bunch' of Gates's pilots, three of the members later flew across the

Atlantic Ocean: Walter Stewart 'Billy' Brock, Sr. with Edward F. Schlee, Wilmer Lower Shultz with Amelia Mary Earhart and Clyde Edward Pangborn with Hugh Herndon, Jr. William Menefee and Shultz have airports named after them, and Pangborn has a street named after him in Hackensack, New Jersey.

The circus broke up in December 1928, and while a few stuntmen lost their lives during its operations, none of the pilots was killed until after it had disbanded. Eugene Cecil hit a fence and broke his neck after making a forced landing near Morgantown, West Virginia, in April 1929. On 28 June 1929, Jack Ashcraft plunged to his death at Roosevelt Field, New York, while engaged in an endurance test. McKinney was killed in the 1930 air race at Teterboro, New Jersey, as was Roy Ahearn, two months later at the same field, when he plunged 4,000 feet after attempting an outside loop. Freddie Lund was killed during an air race in 1931. Brock died of cancer and Gates committed suicide in 1932. Mason died at Hadley, New Jersey, and McMahon died in 1933, near Washington, D.C.[66]

The Mabel Cody Flying Circus

Mabel Cody, the niece of Buffalo Bill Cody, organized and promoted a flying circus even though she wasn't a pilot. She made her name by performing delayed parachute jumps, dancing on wings and on occasion grabbing the rope ladder under her Jenny while tearing across a lake in a speedboat. Her flying circus did many stunts including night flying, wing-walking, car-to-plane transfers both with and without the use of ladders, single and double parachute drops, wing-walking while the plane looped, and changing planes without the use of a ladder.

The flying circus performed at fairs as well as events organized by real estate developers to attract potential land and homebuyers to Coral Gables. Cody fell fifty feet while performing an auto-to-plane transfer stunt, suffering injuries, and the circus disbanded shortly after the accident. She went on to join the Doug Davis Baby Ruth Flying Circus after she recovered.

Women had recently won the vote and feminism, if not strident, was a-flutter. Cody, who wore pants, boots and goggles, was not in the mainstream of the movement, nor had she hitherto attracted the attention of her sisterhood.

Crowds were expected from miles around to watch the fearless Cody match the daring of the famous McGowan. It was late November 1921, and Cody was barely 20 years old and was the star attraction of one of four aerial 'circuses' that crisscrossed the South and hung out on Florida's east coast, especially Daytona Beach. McGowan was the actual star of the show, but in the opinion of the boss, Richard 'Curly' Burns, 'Bugs McGowan's Flying Circus' didn't have the cachet of 'Mabel Cody's Flying Circus'.

McGowan had been, up until that time, the only person to have carried off the auto-to-airplane; standing in a speeding car and grasping a swinging ladder from a passing plane. Cody, up to then, had been a wing-walking, loop-looping, parachuting daredevil who had yet to attempt the auto-to-plane trick. Her history-making attempt was planned for Pablo Beach, mainly because the Norwegian speed king, Sigurd Olson 'Sig' Haugdahl, was in Jacksonville for the races at the Florida State Fair. (Sig would go on to break the land speed record at Daytona Beach on 7 April 1922 by reaching 180mph in a car he built, named the *Wisconsin Special*.)

The newspapers reported that 'several thousand' people made the trip from Jacksonville to the scene of the show, about three miles south of Pablo Beach. It was a big day for Haugdahl and McGowan. Haugdahl had kicked up speeds of 115mph in the beach tests, and McGowan nipped up onto the wing skid of the passing plane. The pilot, who has only been identified as Herman or Heermanese, was given sustained applause for his steady handling of the plane in what the papers described as 'humpy' air. However, when it was Cody's turn, the clouds opened and her attempt was rained off. Adding to her disappointment, Heermanese turned the plane over on Anastasia Island a couple of days later, and Haugdahl was called to other things.

Three years later, Cody stood in the back seat of a car travelling at 70mph down the strand of Pablo Beach. Thousands cheered as she grabbed the ladder of a plane roaring inches above her head, but as the plane lifted Cody from the speeding car, the rung she was holding broke. Sickeningly, she fell to the beach, even before the applause had stopped. She landed on her feet and was 'swung into a series of somersaults by the impact', the newspaper reported. Cody was unconscious when

Burns reached her. She was taken by ambulance to St Luke's Hospital in Jacksonville while a stunned and anxious crowd returned somberly to Jacksonville. Luckily, a movie camera filmed the whole thing, and four weeks later, the film showed at the Imperial Theatre. Cody herself attended the premiere.

Some shows, such as the Gates Flying Circus, took spectators along for rides for a small price. By 1927, it was drawing as many as 30,000 spectators to each of its performances, and selling rides to 100,000 passengers a year. They had established themselves as 'The Daddy of the Air Circuses'. And their permanent headquarters was located in a wooden factory building were near Teterboro airport in New Jersey. As its success grew, Ivan Gates had Charles Healey Day of the New Standard Aircraft Corporation, Paterson, New Jersey, design an aircraft to accommodate four paying passengers in its front cockpit.

Gates and his fliers did not hold a monopoly on organized barnstorming. They shared the skies and farm fields of America with dozens of other aerial circuses. Most of these enterprises worked their way around the country from pasture to pasture, small town to small town, tacking up posters on barns and telephone poles, often advertising their arrival by buzzing rooftops along Main Street with a wing-walker out on one wing. The circuses learned that morbid curiosity could lure many reluctant bystanders to purchase a ticket. They often hired a local ambulance to drive into their pasture with its siren screaming. Another ruse was to send a plane aloft with a dummy in the front cockpit and allow it to fall to earth during a loop.

Big or small, circuses did their best to offer at least one unusual stunt. Eddie Angel of Jimmy Angel's Flying Circus specialized in a 'dive of death' – jumping out of a plane after dark with a flashlight in each hand and opening his 'chute only when he could see the ground. Walter Hunter of Oklahoma's Hunter Brothers Flying Circus hung by his knees from the undercarriage of a plane and dropped into a haystack without any 'chute at all. Cliff Rose of the Cliff Rose Death Angels fastened 'batman' wings to his arms and did spirals and other stunts before reaching for his ripcord.

The Coloured Flying Circus

On 6 December 1931, thousands of Angelenos filled the field of the Los Angeles Eastside airport in East Montebello Gardens. Although it was winter and the depths of the Great Depression, they paid their 50 cents to watch daredevils parachuting and airplanes flying in breathtaking formations. The Coloured Air Circus, a benefit for the city's unemployed, was one of the first air shows in the world piloted entirely by black aviators.

Even the *Los Angeles Times*, known for ignoring events by and for people of colour – to say nothing of its racist reporting on issues such as housing, segregation and police brutality – gave the air show a good review:

> The 'Black Eagle,' known in private life as Colonel Hugh Julian, and five other colored pilots kept nearly 10,000 necks craned skyward over Los Angeles Eastside airport yesterday afternoon during the colored air circus conducted under the auspices of the Associated City Employees Fund for the Unemployed. Along with the 'Black Eagle' flew the 'Five Blackbirds' stunt squadron of colored speed aces. Stunt and parachute leaps completed an afternoon of thrills.[67]

The real event was the brainchild of a lanky pilot and aviation educator named William J. Powell. A World War I veteran and successful owner of a chain of Chicago gas stations, Powell had become enthralled with flying in 1927, after taking his first spin above Paris.

This was the era of Jim Crow laws, which strictly enforced racial separation, especially in the South. Blacks had to sit in the back of the bus, or in the rear carriages of the train. Airlines wouldn't fly black passengers. 'I believe that with the proper leadership,' Powell wrote, 'Negroes can be systematically trained to the use of the airplane to such an extent that a great airplane industry might spring up.' Not only would blacks avoid the indignation of sitting in the back of the airliner, they could also pour thousands of dollars back into the black community.

After the American Legion convention, Powell returned to the United States in search of a flying school. He tried Chicago but was turned down because, he was told, the white students would walk out if a black man walked in. He tried to enlist in the Army Flying Corps, but the recruiter told him the War Department wouldn't accept 'colored men in the air corps'. After writing to schools everywhere, one in Los Angeles accepted him. The price was $1,000, then three times the average workingman's annual salary. But Powell had the money.[68]

He was finally accepted into the Warren School of Aeronautics, located at 120 West Slauson Avenue, in 1928. After earning his pilot's licence, Powell worked to convince other African Americans that the burgeoning aviation industry offered them the opportunities they had been denied in many other occupations[69] 'There is a better job and a better future in aviation for Negroes than in any other industry,' Powell wrote in his autobiographical novel, *Black Wings*, published in 1934. 'And the reason is this: aviation is just beginning its period of growth, and if we get into it now, while it is still uncrowded, we can grow as aviation grows.'[70]

To further his mission, Powell founded the Bessie Coleman Aero Club in 1928, which was sponsored by bandleader Duke Ellington and boxer Joe Louis.[71] The club was named after the world's first licensed African American pilot, Bessie Coleman, who had died in a plane crash near Jacksonville, Florida, in 1926. Under the auspices of the club, Powell, who had a degree in electrical engineering, began to teach aeronautics classes to men and women at Jefferson High School, South Los Angeles. Powell was inspired by the National Air Race held in Los Angeles in 1928 and decided to mount his own show, the All-Negro Air Show, at the Los Angeles Eastside Airfield on Labour Day, 1931.

The show attracted a crowd of around 15,000 people and featured the Negro Formation Flying Group, made up of Powell, William Aikens and a charismatic aviator named Irvin Wells. A blimp dropped flowers in honour of Bessie Coleman, and Lottie Theodore and Maxwell Love made parachute jumps. There were no accidents, which demonstrated to the public that blacks indeed had the skills to handle an airplane. Encouraged by the success of the event, Powell began to organize a larger show, the Coloured Air Circus.

He put together a flying team of five pilots, one of whom was a woman, Marie Dickerson Coker, and even came up with a name for them: the 'Five Blackbirds'. Powell also invited a friend and frequent collaborator, James Herman Banning, a famed aviator and the second licensed African American pilot, to headline the show. As for airplanes, Powell scrounged up a Challenger Commander, a Hisso-Eaglerock, a Waco 10, a Kari-Keen and a Wright J6 Travellaire.[72]

On 6 December, thousands of people crammed onto Eastside Airfield, and the show, which ended with parachute jumps by Maxwell Love and Marie Daughtry, received rave reviews in the Black press and demonstrated that Black Americans deserved their place in the skies. Powell planned to stage 100 air shows across the country, but in the meantime, he decided to enter the 1932 National Air Races' transcontinental competition with Irvin Wells – the first blacks to do so.

Powell and Wells qualified for the race in a Curtiss OX5-powered Lincoln-Page PT, flying at an average speed of 94.7mph. They joined 56 other teams that had entered airplanes in the competition. Two days before the race began, however, the pair learned that Banning was preparing to set out for New York on his own, determined to beat them for the honour of becoming the first black to fly across the country. Somewhat miffed but glad that another black pilot would be in the running, Powell and Wells took off, but never made it. Their engine failed as they went through the Sacramento Mountains and they crash-landed. Both walked away unhurt, and their airplane was salvageable. Making their way to a farmhouse that night, they decided not to disturb the farmer and instead fell asleep outside the house. The following morning a Texas Ranger woke the pair and accused them of murdering a milkman in El Paso two days earlier. They showed the Ranger their pilots' licences, also displaying them to a group of shotgun-wielding men who drove up a little later. Fortunately, one of those men was a pilot who confirmed that they were indeed entered in the National Air Races. In no time the locals pitched in and repaired their airplane, after which Powell and Wells managed to limp back to Los Angeles.

Although the Five Blackbirds only performed one show, they demonstrated their skill and talent to thousands of spectators. To blacks, they proved that their dreams of flying could be fulfilled; to any whites who saw them, they showed that a black man or woman could be just as competent in the cockpit as a white pilot. In the short haul, Powell and his Blackbirds opened the American skies to the race-busting pilots who followed. Powell died in 1942 at the Veterans Hospital in Sharon, Wyoming, of complications resulting from having been gassed more than two decades before. Wells died in 1973.[73]

Glenn Messer

Glenn Edmund Messer, from Henry County, Iowa, was responsible for major advances in the use and modification of existing aircraft as well as the design and construction of aircraft and aircraft instruments. He began his flying career in 1911 by taking lessons from aviator and exhibition flyer George Gustafson in a Wright biplane in Bay City, Michigan. He had also been doing some dirt track automobile racing for sports editor turned promoter John Alexander 'Alex' Sloan, so after taking flying lessons he persuaded Sloan to obtain a Wright biplane for exhibition work, and made his first solo flight and public exhibition at Streator, Illinois, on 13 May 1911.

He financed his training at the engineering school at the University of Illinois, by travelling backward and forward between engagements. Messer purchased a Kemp engine-powered Curtiss biplane in 1912 at a sheriff sale in Kansas City, Missouri, and although he performed with it at exhibition flights, he experienced considerable engine trouble, so he installed a Gnome rotary engine. Capitalizing later on the money he earned from some of the exhibition flying over the next three years, he replaced the Gnome with a Curtiss OX-2 engine.

Leaving college in 1916, Messer joined the Royal Flying Corps and served there until 1917, when he accepted a commission in the Aviation Section of the Signal Corps at Camp Kelly, Texas, where he served as an instructor, along with Edward Anderson Stinson, Jr, and several other early pilots. He was later transferred to the Royal Flying Corps mission to the United States, to install the Gosport system of instruction at the various flight training fields, where he remained until the summer of 1919 when he returned to Kelly Field and remained until he was discharged from the service later that year.

After forming a partnership with Stinson to operate a new flying field at Birmingham, Alabama, he left Stinson in charge to manage the field, while he formed the Messer Flying Circus to engage in more advanced exhibition stunt work consisting of acrobatic flying, wing-walking, parachuting and similar feats. Phoebe Jane Fairgrave Omlie soon became an active partner, and the name was changed to the Messer-Fairgrave Flying Circus.

Messer and fellow pilot Jack Turner completed a successful demonstration, a U.S. Air Mail flight from Birmingham's Roberts Field to Marr Field in Chattanooga, Tennessee, on 24 March 1925 under a temporary commission. (Messer recreated that flight on its fiftieth anniversary in 1975.)[74]

Messer was billed in *The Fairfield Tribune* as 'The World's Most Daring Aviator' for the Fairfield Aviation Meet on 5 August 1921, which promised 'Thrills! Thrills! Thrills!' with his 'death-defying acrobatic feats and stunts'. He started the ball rolling on that day by leaving his seat in the cockpit and going on the lower wing to the extreme tip of the wing, where he threw himself up to the top wing by the strength in his arms, landing squarely on the top wing.

His Moves: Backward Hand-spring
Here he stands upright, balancing himself and holding on to nothing whatsoever. From this position he does a backward hand-spring; then grasping the edge of the wing he raises and stands on his head with his feet straight in the air, depending entirely on his grip and sense of balance to hold this position and onto the plane as well.

From Top to Lower Wing, Head First
From this position he goes head-first down the front strut to the lower wing, depending entirely upon his grip and strength in his arms to hold him as he goes hand over hand, head-first down the strut to the lower wing. From there he goes to the wing skid beneath the lower wing on which he does several stunts, including hanging by one hand and by one foot and several other stunts of this type.

Stands Erect on Tail Unsupported
From here he goes up on the wing again and back on the fuselage to the tail, where he stands straight, balancing himself with his arms outstretched. Returning up the fuselage, he crawls over his pilot and then down to the undercarriage on which is attached a trapeze.

Hangs by His Teeth
On the trapeze, he does several stunts that are ordinarily done by trapeze performers close to the ground. Then he hangs by one hand to a rope attached to the trapeze. After hanging in this position for some time, he grasps a leather strap fastened to the end of the rope. With his arms

outstretched, he hangs by his teeth, while the plane makes one complete circuit of the field.

Hangs by His Toes
Completing this, he grasps the rope with his hands, and swings up, his toes over the bar of the trapeze. He then releases his grip and hangs head downward, supported only by his toes.

Does a Twenty-feet False Drop
Then, again sitting on the trapeze, he ties a twenty-foot-long rope to his ankle, and again hangs down by his toes for a few seconds, then allows his toes to slip clear of the bar. He drops head-first to the end of the rope which had been prepared up in a series of slip-knots, which pull out as his weight comes on the rope, giving the appearance of falling from the plane. Messer has been the only man who has successfully performed this daring feat, saving the late Tex McLaughlin, who used only five feet of rope in his drop.

Stands on the Top Wing While the Plane Does Loop
Climbing, hand over hand, back up the rope, Messer goes to the top wing, and there he stands, while the pilot does a loop, depending on the centrifugal force to hold him in position on top of the plane while the plane goes upside down. This completed, he stands on his head on the centre section of the wing while the pilot does another loop.

In 1927, Messer started the Southern Aircraft Corporation, which designed and built the 'Air Boss'. He later started the Glenn E. Messer Company of Birmingham, Alabama, and later the Municipal airport in Birmingham, with Edward Stinson. He later operated Messer Field.[75]

The Inman Brothers Flying Circus

The Inman Brothers (Roger 'Rolley', Arthur and Donald) Flying Circus was established in 1933 and was one of the largest airplane circuses and one of the few to survive the Great Depression, having developed one of the most successful aerial stunt acts during the inter-war period. Their sister Jenny, and Margie Lynn (Rolley's wife) were wing-walkers, and another of their featured performers was 'Kitty', a 2-year-old lion who had flown with the Inman brothers since it was a cub, and although the joint property of the three brothers, it slept in the bedroom occupied by Mr and Mrs Ora Rolley Inman.[76] A second act was parachute jumper Carl Hall, who featured on the Inman Brothers Flying Circus poster.

Various other pilots flew with the circus, including Alvin Melvin 'Tex' Johnston and Merle 'Mudhole' Smith. Smith taught himself how to fly as a teenager, and after flying with the Inmans for a few years, he felt the 'call of the wild' and headed for Alaska, where he hired on with the Cordova Air Service. After a mishap on a soggy, muddy bush field that caused him to nose over his Stearman (he reportedly got the plane running and flying again using nothing more than a screwdriver, putty knife and an old rag), he picked up the nickname 'Mudhole'. Smith eventually became the president of Cordova and led it into a merger with Alaska Airlines in 1968.[77]

The brothers operated a twenty-passenger Boeing 80-A Clipper and a smaller Ford Trimotor. The Boeing 80-A, dubbed the *Clipper*, was a three-engine biplane, and one of the first generation of airplanes designed for carrying passengers instead of mail, and had the distinction of being the largest plane used in a stunt circus in 1929–31.[78] The Inman brothers offered rides and parachuting trips. Rides were cheap at 50c each. Early American airlines embraced the Ford Trimotor. It was rugged, built of metal rather than wood and fabric; it was reliable, able to land safely with just one of its three engines. And it was versatile. Trimotors flew passengers and freight for public carriers and served as executive transports, travelling showrooms, and aerial delivery vans for private companies. Ford built around 200 Trimotors from 1926 to 1933. Passenger air travel was a completely new – and perhaps a fearsome – concept for most Americans in the 1920s. National advertisements for the Ford Trimotor promoted 'roomy and comfortable' wicker passenger chairs – one of the many advertised amenities used to convince a sceptical public of the appeal of flying in a Ford plane. Later models featured aluminum seats covered with leather.[79]

The death of Donald Inman in an airplane crash, on 10 February 1935, parted a strange aerial companionship – the Inman Brothers Flying Circus. Donald, who began his flying career as a ticket seller for his older brothers when they were giving performances, was 22 years old at the time of the crash, and gave his life in a gallant effort to protect a woman when the ship in which Inman and two others were riding, was smashed to bits in a take-off at Ellenton, Florida. Miss Corinne Edwards, aged 17, suffered a broken nose and internal injuries. The pilot, Charles Hoanes, 26, of Marshall, Michigan, suffered a fractured chin. According to reports from Ellenton, the plane had cleared the landing field when its motor stalled. The pilot was unable to prevent the aircraft from diving into a clump of trees. The wreckage was sprayed with gasoline but did not catch fire. Reports further said that Inman threw himself across Miss Edwards, to prevent her from being more seriously injured.[80]

Being multi-engine pilots, Art and Rolley ferried bombers to Africa and England in support of the war effort. Rolley died in upstate New York in 1944, when the plane in which he and several others were being transported back from England, lost its way at night while in weather, ultimately crashing into a mountainside. Art went on to fly commercial passenger planes as a captain.[81]

Local pilots and airport operators objected to the way circuses invaded their territory, skimming off the cream of the aviation business, and then leaving them to their year-round struggles to stay solvent. Federal regulations were tightened by 1936, with the result that wing-walking was only permitted above 1,500 feet – too high for anybody on the ground to see it. Wing-walkers were also required to wear parachutes. On the ground, additional fencing was mandated to contain the crowds, and various insurance requirements were drastically raised. The flying circus was essentially grounded, its rickety airplanes cracked up or unfit to fly, their pilots scattered or gone on their last flights.

Chapter 6

Across the Pond

The Round Britain Race 1911

The piece below is paraphrased from the *Grantham Journal* of Saturday 29 July 1911.The contest itself was held between Saturday, 22 July and Saturday, 5 August 1911. The race started at Brooklands on 22 July and the conditions of the race were that the competitors all finished back at Brooklands by 7.30pm on 5 August.

Great interest was shown in the Circuit of Britain airplane race, which commenced on Saturday and finished on Wednesday with André Beaumont (the racing name of Lieutenant Jean Louis Conneau) of the French Navy, the winner of the £10,000 prize offered by the *Daily Mail*. It culminated, so far as the Melton district (over which the 'course' lay) was concerned, in a most extraordinary display of enthusiasm and admiration on Monday. From vantage points a mile or two out of the town, spectators witnessed the unique and thrilling spectacle of airmen passing overhead (on their way to Harrogate in the second section of the contest), but also in no less than four instances, competitors landed for their refill of petrol or other instances.

Altogether, on Monday, ten of the seventeen competitors who set out from Hendon, either passed over or reached the vicinity (one who came down being, unfortunately, unable to make further progress), and, it may be convenient to give their names here in the order in which they were seen:

- No. 1, André Beaumont, Blériot Monoplane
- No. 9, Jules Charles Toussaint Védrine, Morane-Borel Monoplane
- No. 24, Gustav Wilhelm Hamel, Blériot Monoplane
- No. 14, James Valentine, Deperdousin Monoplane
- No. 20, Samuel Franklin Cowdery (Cody), Cody Biplane
- No. 19, Charles Howard Pixton, Bristol Biplane

- No. 17. Flight Lieutenant *Collyns Price Pizey*, Bristol Biplane
- No. 12, Lieutenant Reginald Archibald Cammell, R.E., Blériot Monoplane
- No. 23, Oliver de Montalent, Bréguet Biplane
- No. 25, Lieutenant Herbert Ramsay Playford Reynolds, R.E., Howard Wright Biplane.

In the early hours of Tuesday morning, No. 2, Henry Jacob *Delaval* Astley, on a Birdling Monoplane, flew over the district. The fact that arrangements had been made with the Melton Mowbray Polo Club for the use of their splendid ground at Brentingby, two and a half miles out of the town, for some of the airmen to land to replenish their fuel, made that particular vicinity the chief point of assembly for those who wished to witness the progress of the contest, and no better situation could have been selected.

The polo enclosure itself, as well as the immediate rising ground towards Wyfordby, just off the Saxby road, was invaded by sightseers numbering in the thousands, and several of the airplanes passed directly overhead, while those which landed not only enabled everyone to see this particular feat accomplished, but also allowed a closer inspection of the wonderful machines. From daybreak, the town of Melton was alive with passing motorcars, motorcycles, 'safeties' and brakes, which brought contingents from Leicester and the surrounding districts, making their way to Brentingby. The scene of the Saxby road from 4 am to 6 pm in some respects eclipsed the familiar sight of the Burton road on the occasion of the annual steeplechases at Burton Flats. The road was simply blocked with both wheeled and foot traffic, the town of Melton itself, of course, making up the large proportion of it.

It was certainly an unprecedented scene for so early an hour, and it is safe to say that to the great majority it was a very unusual time to be 'abroad'. There were an extraordinary number of motorcyclists, and motorcars were to be numbered by the score. There must have been thousands of people all told, all badly smitten with 'airplane fever' and all discussing what might or might not be seen. While many hundreds proceeded down to Brentingby and over the railway level-crossing on the polo ground, as many hundreds wended their way another half-mile farther to the Wyfordby turn; the field through which the road passes to that village was simply alive with people. Those who assembled there certainly had the advantage, for a distance of some miles could be seen in all directions, and two of the first three airmen passed directly over their heads, while the second one was also plainly visible. Later it came to the turn of the crowds on the polo grounds to have their anticipations fulfilled, by the descent of three competitors in their midst, at varying intervals, and, needless to say, the excitement was tremendous. Had either of the three accomplished something definitive in the contest, they could not have had a more enthusiastic reception. When it was seen from the Wyfordby hilltop that a landing was being made, there was a regular cross-country scramble to the polo ground, half a mile away. It may be mentioned here that the polo club made a charge for admission to the enclosure, and what with the large crowd and rows of motor cars, it looked a typical race meeting, that is, of course, in an equine sense.

One section of the large, level playing area had been roped off and the spectators were supposed to keep behind the barrier, but on the arrival of the airmen, each after a most graceful descent, their enthusiasm outdid all prevention, and the policemen on duty were powerless to prevent the crowd breaking into the centre of the ground; each competitor as he arrived was fairly mobbed in a display of delight and wonderment. Several officials of the Leicestershire Aero Club were present, and, with members of the polo club, saw to it that the arrangements made, as far as they could supervise them, were as they should be. A large repair truck belonging to the British & Colonial Airplane Company, Ltd., of Bristol, which had no less than seven airplanes entered in the race, was present and a large supply of petrol supplied by local firms was on the ground. In the centre of the field was a large white cross as a guide to the fliers and at the Brentingby end of the field was kindled a fire which gave off dense white smoke, also intended to attract the attention of the aviators. The weather before the sun got up was very foggy, especially in the valley, and the airmen had some difficulty during this part of the journey in discerning the landscape at all and had largely to rely on their maps, their compasses and their judgement to guide them.

It was considerably after six o'clock before the air became very clear, though the sky itself, to those on terra firma, was visible above the haze and enabled them to see the aviators, if the latter could not properly discern them. For the younger generation, the occasion was one which, in particular, will stamp itself on the memory, and hundreds of children were, of course, among the throng, as exuberant and excited as the rest. No doubt they had promised to be 'back in time for school', but they were not, and so a small number of scholars did present themselves at 9 am that it was decided to close the schools for the day. Naturally, there were other points of vantage in the neighbourhood beside those just dealt with from which a fine view of the airmen could be obtained on the north side of Melton, and these had a considerable quota of spectators, and those on the Scalford road had the opportunity of witnessing a descent, in this case, compulsorily, Hamel, one of the 'favourites' for the race, coming down owing to engine trouble and landing in what he described as a 'two-foot field'. It was, of course, of slightly larger dimensions than that, but his ascent from a very circumscribed space was probably the most thrilling of all.

When one arrived at the spot thought to be the best for viewing the competitors (alluding more particularly to the Brentingby side), one's eyes and thoughts naturally turned upwards, and in the direction from which the aviators might be expected to appear. It was anticipated that, barring accidents, the leading man might pass over the vicinity between 5–6 pm, and from 5 pm, not only naked eyes, but dozens of field glasses and telescopes were directed to the south and south-east. It was just three minutes to half past five when a steady floating object, no larger than the smallest of small birds, was observed, and the shout of 'here's one coming' caused everyone to look in the same direction. Gradually, slowly it almost seemed, the object in question assumed a shape that left no doubt it was the first of the flyers, and exactly at 5.30 pm, a monoplane which by the aid of glasses could easily be distinguished by 'the number' on each side of the plane as '9', passed straight over the heads of the people assembled in the field over the Wyfordby hilltop. This, from the reference, was seen to be the number of Védrine's airplane, and its progress was instantly watched, and a loud cheer was raised, as it went by 'the Broom' towards Scalford. The hum of the motor could be heard very distinctly, and the machine appeared to be gliding along (possibly at 50mph or 60mph) without the slightest trouble; in fact under perfect control.

It proceeded some miles, but was not out of range, when, suddenly as it were, at 5.32 pm, a second airplane came into view through the haze which still hung over the horizon. There were thus two in sight at once, and the second one appeared to be 'taking a corner' off from the first, with a line nearer Freeby than the leading one had done. Although its number could not be ascertained, there was no doubt in anybody's mind but that this was M. Beaumont on his Blériot Monoplane and he continued on a stern chase after his fellow countryman. At 5.35pm the now fully recognized 'song' of the airplane motor again broke on the air, and, flying at a very low altitude, there next sailed over the hilltop, No. 24, the figures being so plain that no glasses were needed to distinguish them. It came to everybody's mind that the airman, Mr Hamel, had some reason for being so low; not more than 200 feet high it was conjectured, and this surmise proved to be correct. Had he known, probably he would have brought his airplane to earth on the polo ground, half a mile away on his left, but he held a line which took him almost over the town of Melton itself to descend in a small field between the Great Northern Railway and the Isolation Hospital, of which more anon. Recognized as the first Englishman to cross over, he was accorded a particular hearty cheer, which could hardly have failed to penetrate the whirr of his motor.

Then came quite a lull, for one had by now begun to expect seeing airplanes every two or three minutes. However, suddenly there was descried going nearly over the town of Melton itself, going 'entirely on its own', an airplane, whose white tail flashed in the sunlight over the mist below and which proved to be Mr Valentine's monoplane. He was much too far off for any demonstration to be made, but the huge crowds above and below Brentingby were on exceedingly good terms with themselves, and only waited now for the first descent to be made that they could witness.

They had not very long to wait, for a minute or two after 6 pm, a 'speck' appeared on the horizon over the hill between Whissendine and Old Dalby, and the biplane which it in a few seconds resolved itself into was evidently for 'business' on the polo ground. As it came almost in a direct line for the assembled crowd behind the ropes, it perceptively slackened speed, and then took a delightful birdlike swerve, and the next minute Pixton's 'Bumble Bee' planed beautifully on to the level turf and with scarcely a tremor of the frame upon the running wheels touching the turf, it ran a dozen or so yards and came to a complete standstill. The whole thing had looked so simple and natural-like in its execution that for a moment or two everyone appeared lost in astonishment, but when the pilot himself, without any loss of time, sprang from his seat, which by the way, had a Union Jack cushion at the back of it, their wonderment gave way to a tremendous outburst of cheering, and everyone rushed across the intervening ground to not only congratulate the pilot himself but, as far as was possible, to examine the marvellous piece of mechanism which had dropped into their midst from a point between 80 and 90 miles away. Pixton readily acknowledged the greetings, but there was no time to be lost, and while everybody who could get anywhere close enough to admire the airplane itself did so, the mechanics of the Bristol form, whose machine it was, quickly replenished the fuel tanks, and saw to it that everything was for the safe continuation of the fateful flight. In the meanwhile, a sudden inspiration appeared to seize those within immediate proximity of the plane, and that was to inscribe their names, and in many instances addresses, on the canvas, and the airplane, when it left again, must have carried quite a lot of the lead away with it in addition to its ordinary weight.

By 6.20pm, all was in readiness for Pixton to resume his journey, and after a trial spin along the ground, apparently to test the engine, the airplane, with no seeming effort, soared into the air once more, and making a circle of the ground, was in a minute or two lost to sight beyond the trees, though the motor sounds could be heard for some time as the pilot got underway. It was rumoured that another airplane might be expected to alight on the ground in twenty minutes, and this proved to be so far correct that towards seven o'clock, the machine driven by Mr Pizey, also a 'Bristol', could be seen in the distance, though coming from the direction of Saxby Station. It appears that Pizey, on reaching Oakham, fancied he was at Melton, and, in searching around for a landing place, twice or thrice made a circuit of the Rutland County town, and then, finding he had mistaken the place, set off for Melton.

With the fog by now all cleared off, Pizey sighted the polo ground a mile or two away and bore straight for it. He came over the trees by the level-crossing, and, like his predecessor effected a landing which quite took the heart of the spectators, stopping plump in the middle of the field. Rousing cheers had been given all the time the aviator had been within hailing distance, and these were smilingly acknowledged by Pizey upon descending from his perch, which also had a Union Jack cushion at the back. Whether it was a cigarette or a cup of tea which first reached his lips we will not venture to say, but both were cordially welcomed. It transpired that one of Pizey's reason's for coming down was engine trouble, that great bane of all aviators, and, as events proved, this turned out to be so serious that not only was he unable to continue his flight there and then, but it eventually involved the practical destruction of the biplane, and put him out of the race altogether.

When Pizey had got all in readiness for a start, considerable trouble was experienced in getting the engine going, and when this was succeeded in the pilot did not attempt anything more than a run the length of the polo-playing piece. He had two more attempts before venturing to lift the machine into the air, and then he had not risen more than 20–30 feet before he hurriedly came down again, and before he could bring it to a standstill on the ground itself, the wheels and lower supports had crashed over the board which makes the polo 'touchline', and the concussion caused the upper plane to catch a propellor blade and rip it. It was then announced that Pizey would not attempt to start again without new parts to the engines being put in, and, as these had to be obtained from Bristol, a resumption of the flight was not possible before late in the afternoon in any case. The disappointment naturally experienced by the aviator himself was shared by the crowd, a large section of whom watched the partial dismantling of the machine with sympathetic interest. The propellors, it was noticed, were constructed of wood, presumably of teak and highly polished. Then ensued a considerable period of quiescence for the spectators and many of those who had journeyed from Leicester and other places took their departure.

It should be stated that Mr Cody, who, as previously stated, passed seventh in order over the district, took a course almost directly over Holwell Works, where his number could be easily distinguished, but he was not visible to those assembled at Brentingby. The time was about 6 pm. At 8.45 pm, Lieutenant Cammell flew at a great height straight across the centre of the polo ground from a south-easterly direction, and it was about this time the news was received by the officials at Brentingby that Mr Hamel had had to come down in a field in the occupation of Mr Freeborough, off the Scalford road between the town of Melton and the Isolation Hospital. He had, of course, then been down over three hours in a vain endeavour to put things right; but his own mechanics, expecting him to alight at Mansfield, had preceded him there and were, of course, anxiously awaiting him. At length, he motored over to

Brentingby and explained that he had broken an inlet valve, and at once a new one was placed at his disposal by the Bristol Company, and not only that but Pizey, being unable to 'help himself' for the time being, went back with Hamel to his damaged machine to assist in putting it right.

This action was a subject of considerable comment and showed that despite the great rivalry a race for such a prize must have engendered, still one competitor was quite willing to come to the assistance of another in the hour of need. Of course, Mr Hamel had been seen to come down in the field, and very soon several hundred people had congregated around his machine, which being of the monoplane type, differed very considerably from those which descended at Brentingby. By ten o'clock, the necessary repairs to Hamel's machine had been completed, and eight minutes later he was once more ready to set out upon his big undertaking. Before he left Mr F. R. Carter, the superintendent of the Great Northern and London & North Western Joint Railway, who had provided men, ropes, etc., for Hamel's accommodation, wished the aviator, on behalf of the spectators, all good luck on his journey, and called for three cheers, which were given with rousing effect.

Hamel having started his engine, gave the signal for 'let go' to those who were at the rear and almost instantly the machine took to the air, and in a few minutes was out of sight. The airplane was not far from the hedge, and Hamel took some little risk in getting off as he did, but the exigencies of the situation demanded it. It is of interest to know that Hamel is only 23 years of age. To return to the aerodrome, one might almost call it, at Brentingby after the passing of Lieutenant Cammell shortly before nine o'clock, the next aerial visitor was M Olivier de Montalent, who arrived shortly before eleven o'clock and alighted, his descent being quite as cleverly accomplished as those before. There still remained a large number of people on the ground, and de Montalent was given a hearty reception. Upon wishing to go up again, the Frenchman found that the air currents were not to his liking, and he decided to wait until later in the day.

He eventually made a start at 4.13 pm and got away brilliantly, and, when 'fairly on the wing' travelled very rapidly. Meanwhile, just after two o'clock Mr C. T. Weyman, the American aviator, on his Nieuport Monoplane, soared over the district, and he, too, was bent on making up for the lost time. Pizey, the stranded airman at Brentingby, had hopes of getting away early in the afternoon but found the injuries to his machine such that it was seven o'clock before he could essay another flight. It appears the chief cause of the trouble was the denting of one of the cylinders of the propellor. At 7.13 pm, he made an attempt to resume his flight to Harrogate, but the machine refused to rise properly, and, after a short circuit, came down with an alarming crash on to the polo ground again. This time the biplane was seriously damaged, the propellor being smashed off, and the chassis stanchions and several ribs broken. It was then too late to attempt to remedy the defects, and the machine was left on the ground all night. At a quarter to eight the same evening, Lieutenant Reynolds, who did not start from Hendon until after 6 pm, went over the east end of the town, and this was the last of the aviators to pass over the district that night. Between five and six o'clock, however, on Tuesday morning, Mr Astley, and his Birdling Monoplane, who had been fogbound at Irthlingborough, near Kettering, was reported by railway officials to have gone over, and he reached Harrogate at 7.35pm. On Tuesday evening, Pizey had once more got his damaged machine put right, and again attempted his flight, but unfortunately without success. He rose a short distance from the ground and cleared the hedge on the opposite side of the polo ground to the railway, but he had only gone a short distance when down crashed the airplane again, this time damaged in such a manner that Pizey decided to retire from the contest. He was unhurt and explained that his engine, which had given so much trouble, was affected by the weather.[82]

The Aerial Derby Race

The Aerial Derby Race around London began on 8 June 1912 and attracted around 45,000 people paying to watch the start and finish of the single circuit that started and finishing at Hendon Aerodrome with control points at Kempton Park, Esher, Purley and Purfleet. Seven of the original fifteen entrants started the race (the rest held up by poor weather on the day), during which they had to fly their machines low enough for the judges to be able to see the race number of their aircraft at these points. Thomas Sopwith, in his 70hp Blériot XI-2, was the first of four of the entrants to finish (one ran out of fuel, another experienced engine trouble and another didn't finish owing to getting lost in the clouds), and for his time of one hour, twenty-three minutes and eight seconds, he received the prize of £250 and a gold cup. William Barnard Rhodes-Moorhouse arrived second in his 50hp Radley-Moorhouse and James Valentine in a 50hp Bristol Prier Monoplane picked up the third prize of £50. Radley-Moorhouse had a chequered past: on a visit to New Zealand in 1907 while practising for a motorcycle race on New Brighton Beach, Christchurch, on 7 March, Moorhouse killed Kennett Frederick Gourlay, a 7-year-old child who had run out in front of him. He was charged with manslaughter and released on bail for £100, but acquitted by the Supreme Court in Christchurch in August that year. In 1912 he was again charged with manslaughter following the death of Arthur William Cheacker on a county road in Gloucestershire while driving his racing car. He changed his surname to Rhodes-Moorhouse in 1912.

The Aerial Derby on 20 September 1913 was flown over a slightly longer course of 94 miles (151 kilometres). The *Daily Mail* offered £200 and a trophy for the winner, and Shell added three prizes of £100, £70 and £25 for the winners of a handicap competition. Gustav Hamel was the overall winner in his 80hp Morane-Saulnier, and Bentfield Charles Hucks, in his 80hp Blériot, was the winner of the Shell trophy for the handicap competition. The following year, despite being postponed from 23 May to 6 June, the weather conditions caused six of the eleven entrants to retire. Walter Laurence Brock won first prize in his 80hp Morane-Saulnier G. His closest contestant was Louis Noël, who flew the same type of aircraft but was disqualified for missing two control points owing to poor visibility.

The race, having been suspended during the First World War, was restarted on 21 June 1919, and was tagged as the 'Victory Aerial Derby'. The race offered substantial prizes and trophies for outright speed, and performance versus a handicap: the *Daily Mail* Gold Trophy (value 200 guineas) and the Shell prize of £500 for the winner, a Shell trophy and £100 for second place, a Shell trophy and £100 for the winner in the Sealed Handicap, and a Shell trophy and £50 for second place, with a final prize of a Shell trophy and £25 for third place in the handicap. Queen Alexandria was there to present the prizes, with Claude Grahame-White.

While many of the leading aviators of the time competed, it was never quite enough to attract the intended overseas competitors. Hendon was the start and finish point for the race: two laps of 94.5 miles (153 kilometres) starting at 3.30 pm.

The first turning point of the circuit was the waterworks pumping station chimney at Kempton Park: a square chimney, 230 feet high, just north of Kempton railway station, of dark brown brick, low buildings, with filter beds and connecting reservoir. In the neighbourhood were a lower (round) chimney and two very large reservoirs. The second turning point was the Epsom Race Course grandstand which is at the top of Epsom Downs, making a conspicuous landmark. The third was the turning point at the Wouldham Court Cement Works, at West Thurrock, on the north bank of the river near the top of the bend a mile east of Purfleet and slightly to the east of West Thurrock Church. The actual point consisted of a long rectangular buff-coloured building with a large diagonal white cross on the roof. Five factory chimneys stood in line at equal distances behind the building flanked by two taller chimneys plus a high one farther to the right. The fourth turning point was Epping church tower in the centre of Epping village on the west side of London Road; 200 yards south of the church was a solitary water tower 120 feet high. The last turning point was a large white cross in Hartham Meadow, immediately north of the town adjoining the railway stations and enclosed on the north, east and west by streams.

The race results are given in speed/handicap: the twelve starters of the original sixteen competitors were:

- Racer No. 1: Mr Clifford B. Prodger in a British Aerial Transport Company Limited (BAT) F.K.23 Bantam (G-EACN) – he retired during the first lap, going down at Fairlop
- Racer No. 2: Captain Paul Richard Tankerville Chamberlayne in a Grahame-White GWE6 Bantam (G-EAFK) – he retired during the second lap, going down at Epsom
- Racer No. 3: Major Christopher Draper in a BAT F.K.23 Bantam (G-EACP) – he finished 4th/2nd
- Racer No. 4: Lieutenant-Colonel George L. P. Henderson in an Avro 504K– he finished 6th/7th
- Racer No. 5: Major Reginald Hugh Carr in a Grahame-White GWE6 Bantam (G-EAFL) – he was forced to retire with engine trouble during the first lap, landing at Hounslow

72 Barnstormers, Wing-Walking and Flying Circuses

- Racer No. 7: Captain Gerald Gathergood in an Airco DH.4R – he finished 1st/5th
- Racer No. 8: Mr Marcus Dyce Manton in an Airco DH.4 (G-EAEX) – he finished 2nd/4th
- Racer No. 9: Captain Howard John Thomas Saint, DSC, in an Airco DH.9 (G-EAAC) – he finished 5th/6th
- Racer No. 10: Lieutenant Robert Nisbet in a Martinsyde F.4 (G-EAES) – he finished 2nd/3rd
- Racer No. 11: Major Leslie Robert Tait-Cox in a Nieuport Nighthawk LC.1 (G-EAEQ) – he retired during lap two due to a punctured carburettor float and landed at West Thurrock
- Racer No. 12: Major Charles H. C. Smith, DSC, in a Bristol Type 20 M.1C (G-EAER) – he retired during the first lap, going down at Hendon
- Racer No. 14: Captain Harold Alan Hamersley, MC, in an Avro 534 Baby (G-EACQ) – he finished 7th/1st.

The Aerial Derby of 1920 took place on 24 July, again, starting and finishing at Hendon and with the same direction and route as the previous year, with the turning points at Brooklands, Epsom, West Thurrock, Epping and Hertford:

- Racer No. 1: Mr Herbert 'Bert' John Louis Hinkler in an Avro 534 Baby (G-EACQ) – he finished second
- Racer No. 2: Captain Harold Alan Hamersley, MC, in an Avro 534 Baby (G-EAUG) – he finished in first place
- Racer No. 4: Mr Frederick Sidney Cotton in an Airco DH.14a (G-EAPY) – he retired following a forced landing near Hertford after a petrol leak caused a fire but his passenger, Mr Harwood, was injured, and the aircraft suffered damage (it was subsequently repaired and renumbered J1940)
- Racer No. 5: Captain William Lancelot Jordan, DSC & Bar, DFC, in a Sopwith 7F1 Snipe (G-EAUW) – he finished in fifth place
- Racer No. 6: Flight Lieutenant Walter Hunt Longton, DFC & Bar, AFC, in a Sopwith 7F1 Snipe (G-EAUV) – he retired during the second lap

- Racer No. 7: Flight Lieutenant Joseph 'John' Stewart Temple Fall, DFC, AFC, in a Sopwith 7F1 Snipe (G-EAUU) – he retired after making a forced landing at Epping during the first lap
- Racer No. 8: Captain Denis George Westgarth-Heslam in an Avro 539 (G-EALG) – he was forced to land with fuel problems near Abridge
- Racer No. 10: Lieutenant John Herbert 'Jimmie' James in a Nieuport Nieuhawk LC.1 (G-EAJY) – he finished in third place
- Racer No. 11: Lieutenant Robert H. Nisbet in a Martinsyde F.6 (G-EAPI) – he finished in sixth place
- Racer No. 12: Squadron Leader Thomas O'Brien Hubbard, MC, AFC, in a Martinsyde F.4a (G-EAPP) – he finished in eighth place
- Racer No. 13: Mr Harry George Hawker, MBE, AFC, in a Sopwith Schneider Cup 'Rainbow' (G-EAKI) – he was disqualified
- Racer No. 14: Mr Cyril Frank 'Papa' Uwins, OBE, in a Bristol Type 32B Bullet (G-EATS) – he finished in seventh place
- Racer No. 15: Captain Frank Thomas Courtney in a Martinsyde 'Semi-Quaver' (G-EAPX) – he finished in fourth place (he finished first in the speed section, but then made a bad landing and overturned, fortunately without serious injury)
- Racer No. 16: Major Leslie Robert Tait-Cox in a Nieuport Goshawk (G-EASK) – he retired following a forced landing at Brooklands on the first lap.

Only twelve of the original competitors took part in the Aerial Derby on 16 July 1921 and took place at 3 pm at the same venue, with the same route and turning points as the previous year:

- Racer No. 1: Captain Terence Bernard Tully, AFC, in an Avro 534 Baby (G-EAUM) – he retired after a forced landing at Brooklands on lap two
- Racer No. 2: Mr Herbert 'Bert' John Louis Hinkler in an Avro 534C (G-EAXL) – he retired during the first lap
- Racer No. 4: Mr Dring Lester Forestier-Walker in a Sopwith Pup (G-EAVX) – he retired on lap one, feeling ill, then nosed over on landing at Hendon when the undercarriage collapsed
- Racer No. 5: Mr Alan Samuel Butler, J.P., in a Bristol 29 (G-EAWB) – he finished 4th/3rd

- Racer No. 6: Major Leslie Robert Tait-Cox in an Avro 552 (G-EAPR) – he finished 5th/5th
- Racer No. 7: Captain Hubert Stanford Broad, MBE, AFC, in a Sopwith Camel (G-EAWN) – he finished 6th/6th
- Racer No. 28: Captain Walter Hunt Longton in an S.E.5a (G-EAX_) – he finished 3rd/2nd
- Racer No. 30: Mr Frederick John Ortweiler, MC, in an S.E.5a (G-EAXU) – he was disqualified after an incorrect pylon turn at the end of the first lap
- Racer No. 12: Flight Lieutenant Jack Noakes in a Nieuport Nieuhawk LC.2 (G-EAJY) – he retired during lap two after running out of fuel
- Racer No. 15: Major Ernest Leslie Foot, MC, in a Martinsyde F.4 (G-EAXB) – he retired during the first lap with an oil-feed problem
- Racer No. 17: Captain Cyril Frank 'Papa' Uwins, OBE, in a Bristol Type 32B Bullet (G-EATS) – he finished 2nd/4th
- Racer No. 21: Mr John Herbert 'Jimmie' James in a Gloster Mars I (G-EAXZ) – he finished 1st/1st.

A change of direction was in place for the Aerial Derby of 1922, which took place on Saturday, 7 August. It started and finished at Waddon (Croydon), and started at 2 pm, and again covered two laps of 99.5 miles (160 kilometres), but going clockwise, with the turning points at Brooklands, Hertford, Epping, and West Thurrock. Nine of the ten original competitors took part in the race:

- Racer No. 1: Mr Herbert 'Bert' John Louis Hinkler in an Avro 534 Baby (G-EAUM) – he finished in fifth place
- Racer No. 2: Mr Larry L. Carter in a Bristol Type 77 (G-EAVP) – he finished 4th/1st
- Racer No. 3: Mr Frederick Philips Raynham in a Martinsyde F.6 (G-EBDK) – he finished in third place
- Racer No. 4: Mr Alan Samuel Butler, J.P. in a DH.37 (G-EBDO) – he retired after the first lap
- Racer No. 5: Captain Herbert Howard Perry in an S.E.5a (G-EAXQ) – he retired during lap two
- Racer No. 6: Flight Lieutenant Reginald Herbert Stocken in a Martinsyde F.4 (G-EATD) – he retired after the first lap with plug trouble

- Racer No. 7: Major Leslie Robert Tait-Cox in a Gloster Mars II (G-EAYN) – he retired after the first lap
- Racer No. 8: Mr Rollo Amyatt Wolseley de Haga Haig in a Bristol Type 32B Bullet (G-EATS) – he finished 2nd/2nd
- Racer No. 9: Lieutenant John Herbert 'Jimmie' James in a Gloster Mars I (G-EAXZ) – he finished 1st/3rd.

The Aerial Derby of 1923 took place at 1.45 pm on the bank holiday Monday, 6 August, and as in 1922, started and finished at Waddon (Croydon), with two laps as before. It produced a better show, with twelve of the original thirteen competitors taking part in the race:

- Racer No. 1: Dr Edward D. Whitehead Reid in an S.E.5a (G-EBCA) – he finished 9th/9th
- Racer No. 2: Mr Herbert 'Bert' John Louis Hinkler in an Avro 534 Baby (G-EAUM) – he retired on lap two following a forced landing at Hounslow.
- Racer No. 3: Mr John R. King in Sopwith Gnu (G-EADB) – he finished 8th/7th
- Racer No. 4: Flight Lieutenant John Whitaker Woodhouse in a Boulton & Paul P.9 (G-EBEQ) – he finished 7th/3rd
- Racer No. 6: Captain Harold Alan Hamersley, MC, in an Avro 553 (G-EAPR) – he finished 6th/1st Racer No. 7: Mr Frederick Philips Raynham in a Martinsyde F.6 (G-EBDK) – he finished 5th/4th
- Racer No. 8: Major Harold Hemming, AFC, in a DH.37 (G-EBDO) – he retired during lap two following a forced landing at Romford
- Racer No. 9: Mr Herbert Howard Perry in a DH.9A (G-EBCG) – he finished 4th/2nd
- Racer No. 10: Mr Frank Thomas Courtney in a DH.9A (G-EBGX) – he retired during lap one following a forced landing at Brooklands
- Racer No. 11: Captain Charles Douglas Barnard in a DH.9 (G-EBEZ) – he finished 3rd/6th
- Racer No. 12: Flight Lieutenant Walter Hunt Longton in a Sopwith Schneider Cup 'Rainbow' (G-EAKI) – he finished 2nd/8th
- Racer No. 13: Mr Larry L. Carter in a Gloster Mars I (G-EAXZ) – he finished 1st/5th.

Flight magazine had described in 1919, the Aerial Derby as being 'quite the most effective race of the year … It is no exaggeration to say that millions of people see the race, talk about it for days before it is flown, and discuss it for days after it has become a memory'. However, by 1922, thoughts had been reduced to 'this year's race was even duller than last year's'. The derby had degenerated into a purely national affair, and become rather predictable: the same aircraft won the speed race three years in a row, and in 1923, the nine machines finished in exactly the order predicted by the handicappers. The derby was abandoned in 1924 and effectively amalgamated with the King's Cup (which had started in 1922). Occasionally, the Royal Aero Club would float the idea of reviving it, but it never happened.

Two more significant tours were held in 1936. Aviator and solo flight record-holder Charles William Anderson Scott, who had taken over Sir Alan Cobham's National Air Displays, started his 'Flying for All' display on 8 April at the Ace of Spades open land aerodrome (1933–7) at Hook, Kingston upon Thames. The display, which showcased at least sixty-five venues, toured around Ireland and ended back at Weston-super-Mare in August, but it ran for just one season because, in the September of that year, Scott won another air race; he and Giles Guthrie flew a Percival Vega Gull and won the Schlesinger Air Race from Portsmouth to Johannesburg, South Africa.

In contrast, the British Empire Air Display Tour of the UK (Barker & McEwan King) started in Luton on 8 April and visited 111 venues in England, Wales and Scotland, and finished in Birmingham on 6 September. The last major flying circus tour was by Coronation Air Displays, another Barker & McEwan King enterprise, coupled with Aircraft Demonstrations Ltd., in 1937.

Flying Circuses

The *Daily Mail*-sponsored flying tours in the United Kingdom, with 'star' pilots such as Henri Salmet and Gustav Hamel even before the First World War, when crowds of thousands would converge just to see just one airplane flying. After the war, several enterprises set out to give joy-rides, mostly in the holiday season (spring to autumn) at seaside resorts.

The seeds for the flying circus type of operation were sown by the Berkshire Aviation Company, who conducted tours from 1919 to 1922. Their first tour in 1919 visited at least thirty venues, nearly all in England, but at least one in Edinburgh, Scotland. The tour ran from April until December and typically, unlike the bigger, later tours, they tended to stay at venues for several days at a time. The tour in the following year also appears to have focused on venues in England, the farthest north being Carlisle. Starting in January, it ran until December, which seems quite remarkable given the typical winter weather. But, typically a joy-ride lasted for about five minutes or so, with a short low-level circuit around the venue. The tour of 1921, which also started in January, didn't venture above Accrington in Lancashire or Huddersfield in Yorkshire. And indeed, it appears the 1922 tour didn't venture north of Cheshire.

The Cornwall Aviation Company, which operated from an area close to Sticker, near St Austell, and was, without too much doubt, the first to try to create something resembling the later large-scale flying circus: in effect, an air show filled with novelty flying acts, aerobatics and joy rides. They had also learned from the touring theatrical companies and circuses, the tremendous value of advance publicity; their pilots carried postcards depicting themselves and their airplanes, and produced drama pieces and short films showing flying demonstrations. They had three Avro 504Ks: G-AAAF, G-EBSE (ex-H2234) and G-EBIZ, with G-EBNR (ex-F8864) joining later. G-EBIZ was co-owned by Captain Percival Phillips, and was later sold to Cobham's Flying Circus, and became famous for carrying some 69,000 passengers during its time with them. Two engineers, Mr P. Swan and Cyril Poole were employed to maintain the planes, and a former Paignton beach photographer, 'Dick' Turpin, also assisted in mechanical servicing duties, provided the company with additional income from many hundreds of passengers seeking a souvenir of their flight.

Scottish-born aviator Oscar Garden, who had spent time from 1930 with John Tranum's Flying Circus, joined together with stunt pilot and parachutist John Tranum in October 1931 and formed Skywork Ltd., through which they, amongst other things, 'promoted, assisted, and encourage aerial navigation in all its forms'. This included flying four airplanes (one of which they crashed almost straight away) around South Africa, touring as 'The Spartan Circus' during the winter months. John

Tranum died from a heart attack on 7 March 1935, during an attempt to set a new parachute jumping record. The jump was from 30,000 feet, but as he was about to climb out of the aircraft, he suddenly signalled the pilot, Captain Laerun, to descend. The descent occupied an hour, and Tranum was found dead from heart failure.

The *Daily Express* correspondent said:

The pilot, Captain Laerun, said he had signalled to Tranum to get ready to drop. He received in reply three taps on the back, instead of the prearranged two. He turned and saw specks of blood on the glass of Tranum's helmet. Tranum signalled frantically to go down, and then dropped unconscious. Tranum was 18,000 feet up when he started to broadcast. Listeners heard his voice as he ascended, then there was a sudden silence. Tranum told me before the ascent that he underwent a gruelling test in a decompression chamber under the eyes of a doctor, and hoped that, except for earache and slight dizziness, he would suffer no ill effects. He added that when falling a normal man retained full possession of all his faculties.

Tranum's English wife, whom he married a fortnight ago, watched the vain attempts at respiration.

Alan Cobham

Nothing had been seen before on the scale of Sir Alan Cobham's 'Municipal Aerodrome Campaign Tour' of 1929. Most venues were only visited for a day, or two at the most, but the tour started in May and ended in October, with 107 towns and cities being visited, mostly in England, but with two in Wales and eight in Scotland. Cobham's ambitious plan was to persuade towns and cities to construct aerodromes fit for aero clubs and, in many cases to serve as regional airports, in the hope of drumming up business for his activities as an aviation consultant. Each of the flying sites had to be certified and regulated, and in practice, each proposed venue was notified and visited by ministry officials, who would drive in various directions across the field to ascertain its suitability, and quite often, put performance limitations in certain directions regarding the aircraft being operated. Later, when they realized that the better operators were quite capable of working these aspects out for themselves, they became largely self-regulating.

Once the success of the 1929 tour became known, Cobham became known, several other enterprises emerged, the first of which appears to be Aviation Tours Limited in 1931. They ventured as far north in Scotland as Inverness between April and September. Another venture was the North British Aviation Company Limited, which operated between April and September, reaching Glasgow for one venue. The Charles Douglas Barnard Air Tours enterprise was the only other venture in 1931 to try and compete with the scale and impact of Cobham's tour and operated around sixty-three venues between April and October. Barnard aimed to keep himself in the public eye with the hype that followed his long-distance flights with the Duchess of Bedford. With support from the *Daily Mail*, he cobbled together a somewhat motley collection of airplanes (the old *Spider*, a Spartan three-seater, and an autogiro) and flew in a different place practically every day

For his tours, Cobham commissioned aircraft designer Alfred Hessell Tiltman together with his former de Havilland colleague Nevil Shute Norway, who were working at the newly established Airspeed factory at York, to design and construct an 'airliner' specifically for his tours. Verging on short take-off and landing (STOL) capabilities, and capable of operating from unprepared fields, the result was the three-engined ten-seater Airspeed AS.4 Ferry. A design that defines the exception to the rule that if it 'looks right, it is right'. An interesting and unorthodox biplane in its design, it was powered by one 120hp Gipsy III inverted engine in the top centre section and two upright 120hp Gipsy IIs mounted on the lower mainplanes, and it featured cranked lower wings attached to the upper fuselage, affording maximum views to the passengers. A serious contender for the ugliest airliner ever, but it was exactly right for the job, and the two examples operated by Cobham safely carried some 92,000 passengers. The prototype, G-ABSI, *Youth of Britain II*, first flew on 10 April 1932, from Sherburn-in-Elmet, Yorkshire, followed by G-ABSJ *Youth of Britain III* (renamed *Youth of Africa* for the 1933 tour). Two more AS.4s were built for Midland and Scottish Air Ferries (G-ACBT & G-ACFB).

Cobham recalls:

A reconnaissance party was sent out months ahead to deal with local authorities, advance publicity and farmers: the utilization of likely fields might be dependent on crops, hay or the local annual Morris-dancers festival. This sort of thing could see us flying up to 200 miles between displays, and was hell on earth for the road transport people. They had to pack, travel overnight, and set up well in advance of the first show. The store truck was often having a problem which, on short transits, usually delayed its morning departure. No matter how many likely spare gaskets were kept in the tool-boxes, there was often a last-minute something that only the stores truck could supply.

The public programmes were very good, varied and slickly produced air displays, twice each day in the afternoon and evening. With British Summer Time, it was light until after 10 pm, and later still in the northern latitudes. The shows also ran seven days per week. 'The show goes on' really meant something, because the name of the game was selling joy-riding. The opening mass formation flight over the local town did not see an engine start-up until every available seat for the flight had been sold –excepting the complimentary seat for the beaming local Lord Mayor, oblivious that the pilot of the 'giant airliner' would cheerfully strangle him with his own heavy gold chain of office.

Tickets were colour coded at different prices, the ringmaster MC at the microphone being singularly adept at gauging the optimum starting price for any locality. There were times when the Avro 504s were down to three shillings and sixpence. Towards the conclusion of the evening shows it was customary to reduce prices, the fundamental function of the display being to produce the maximum revenue before the public departed the field. The aircraft loaders retained the public's tickets, for pilots were paid on a retainer plus ticket commission. At the end of the day, any sounds of disharmony could usually be traced to the balancing of money receipts with ticket returns. The business command post was the 'gate van', which was almost impregnable and thiefproof because that was where the revenue money was kept. A staff of four gentlemen could be kept extremely busy on a good day, selling entry tickets for people and cars.

The 'loudspeaker van' was the centrepiece of the show, parked just inside the barrier wire by the ticket tent. The driver of this van was one of the hardest-worked people on the show. He looked after the loudspeakers, constantly misbehaving microphones, the amplifier, the gramophone records and the charging of a massive array of batteries supplying public address power. A huge Leyland six-wheel tanker supplied by National Benzol was the refuelling wagon. All engines – vehicle or aircraft – as was frequently mentioned on the loudspeakers, ran on National Benzole, although some of the engines, such as the Jupiters and the Armstrong Siddeleys, had the carburettors jetted for an 80–20 petrol–benzole mix. Wings and wheels, on the same gratis basis, were lubricated by Castrol in various grades. To minimize the quantity of reserve oil carried by the stores truck, Castrol in four-gallon drums was delivered to each display site in vast quantities and stacked in pyramids by the local depot, who also collected unused drums the next morning. With the Castrol label to the fore, at car promotions and strategic places on the flight line, the Castrol sales promotion team's confidence in their marketing technique was well justified.

Cobham went on to organize the National Aviation Day display tours, which ran from 1932 to 1935, and nothing of this magnitude had ever been seen before. The 1932 tour of the UK started in April and ended in October, with 174 venues around the UK except for Northern Ireland. When the tour ended, another started in South Africa from 23 November to 17 February 1933. His 'Blockbuster' tour was launched in 1933 with two separate tours, both of which started in April and ended in October. The first tour visited 116 venues throughout the UK, Northern Ireland and the Republic of Ireland. The second tour visited 152 further venues on the UK mainland.

On 30 April 1934, Christchurch entertained Cobham's National Aviation Day display and attracted over 8,000 spectators. However, the noise of the display on Sunday morning was audible in Christchurch Priory during morning service, and disrupted Matins in the priory, to the displeasure of many local worthies, and had repercussions the following year when a formal application for planning permission for the future airport was made. It wasn't until 27 March 1934, that the application was finally allowed (on appeal) to the Ministry of Health at a public inquiry held in Christchurch, and the eventual outcome was that Fisher took over the running of the erstwhile Shamrock and Rambler Air Station. Bournemouth Airport Limited was formed with Alan Cobham as chairman and Francis Fisher as managing director, and from February 1935, Christchurch became known as Bournemouth Airport.

Competition to the Cobham Tours was minimal during 1933, except for the British Hospitals Air Pageant (BHAP) Tour of the UK, which had obtained the use of Cornwall Aviation Company's aircraft, which were normally used by Sir Alan Cobham, and which ran between April and October, and visited 150 venues. The 1934 tour was of a much lesser extent, but still impressive with 159 venues lasting from April until September. His rivals during the same season were the BHAP and Henry Barker and James McEwan King's 'Sky Devils Air Circus Tour', and the 'Flying Fair' (Ronald Dixie Gerran/Aviation Developments Ltd.). Cobham came bounding back with another tour in 1935, starting in April at Fareham, and after the first part ended at Gravesend, Kent, on 30 June, with 72 venues, it was then split into two tours, the No. 1 tour visiting 88 venues and the No. 2 tour 84 venues. The competition became more intense when Henry Barker and James McEwan 'King's Jubilee Air Displays' (who had previously traded as BHAP) launched a tour that lasted from April until September.

Sir Alan Cobham's Air Circus was disbanded in December 1935 in face of the growing competition, which included Jubilee Air Displays Limited and all the equipment was acquired by Charles William Anderson Scott, AFC, and became W. A. Scott's Flying Display Limited. Scott had gained great notoriety by winning the Macrobertson England-to-Australia air race in October 1934 in the scarlet de Havilland DH.88 Comet Racer (G-ACSS) *Grosvenor House*. They even took over the Airspeed Ferry that had been in hangar storage for a very long time. Cobham's Clive was also withdrawn from service after carrying 120,000 happy fare-paying passengers – he had lost all interest in hosting flying circus venues, and concentrated more on the development of air-to-air refuelling capabilities, where once again he was a pioneer and visionary. The concept eventually proving to be of enormous importance after the Second World War.

* * *

W. A. Scott's Flying Display Limited, led by Charles Scott, had a fleet of sixteen aircraft, including one or two airliners down to the smaller two- and three-seat types. The air show ran continuously from noon until dusk and included The Great Air Race, grand formation flight, wireless controlled flying (instructions to the pilot), aerobatic flying, aerial marksmanship, wing-walking, parachute descents, upside-down flying, and humorous events. Also on show was a single-engine high-wing monoplane ambulance aircraft. Thousands of people were attracted to the show and 15,000 people paid admission to it. The aircraft could hardly cope with the demand for flights and there was a surprisingly high number of women and children wanting flights, including aerobatic flights in open-cockpit aircraft. On Sunday, 30 April, the aircraft flew on to the next venue at Northampton. The aircraft took passengers on the one-way flight and a coach was laid on to take them back to Guildford afterwards.

On Easter Monday, 25 April 1935, the Jubilee Air Displays held another show at Harrow Hill Farm, with the then mayor of Guildford, W. G. L. Sheppard, accompanied by the mayoress, opening the display in the afternoon. Again, a large crowd attended the air display, and there was a high demand for flights, despite the uncertainty of the weather. These included six passengers who had an exhilarating experience when they were carried in an air race around a triangular course, the three machines roaring across the finishing line almost abreast. Spectators were not disappointed with the aerobatics, which included loops, rolls and spins. A paper streamer released at 2,000 feet was repeatedly cut by an aircraft as it fell to the ground. A simultaneous parachute jump was made by two parachutists who made a perfect landing together. The crowd had swelled in number throughout the afternoon and was watched by hundreds of motorists and others on the slopes of Newlands Corner.

Two more significant tours were held in 1936. The 'Flying for All' display on 8 April was held at the Ace of Spades open land aerodrome (1933–7) at Hook, Kingston upon Thames. The display, which showcased at least 65 venues, toured around Ireland and ended back at Weston-super-Mare in August, but it ran for just one season because, in the September of that year, Scott won another air race; he and Giles Guthrie flew a Percival Vega Gull and won the Schlesinger Air Race from Portsmouth to Johannesburg, South Africa.

Charles Barnard

Captain Charles Douglas Barnard, an ex-RFC pilot who took part in the air races during the 1920s, started an extensive tour of England on 1 April 1931 with his flying circus, C. D. Barnard Air Tours Ltd.,[83] which comprised of a Fokker F.VIIa (G-EBTS), a Spartan three-seater Mark 1 (G-ABJS), an Avro Avian Sports, a Desoutter II, Potez 36 (F-ALJC *Ladybird*), and a Cierva C.19 autogiro (G-AALA). Barnard and his pilots, who included E. D. Ayre, F. S. Crossley and Reginald Alfred Charles Brie[84] planned to visit 150 towns, though not staying for more than two days at any one of them, and at each town, a well-organized air pageant was held, providing a spectacular and instructive picture of air progress, including parachute descents, demonstrations of aerobatics by the autogiro, and passenger flights. By July, the circus had expanded with the addition of six machines of different types, three of which were fitted with Hermes Mark II engines, which stood up to the demanding work without trouble.

In contrast was the British Empire Air Display Tour of the UK by Barker & McEwan King, which started in Luton on 8 April, and visited 111 venues in England, Wales and Scotland, and finishing in Birmingham on 6 September. The last major flying circus tour was by Coronation Air Displays, another Barker & McEwan King enterprise, coupled with Aircraft Demonstrations Limited, in 1937. Terry Mace states:

> The whole field is littered with wrecks of 'Aviation' firms. Wrecked for the most part by rank rotten management, and spendthrift policies. The whole trouble has been that the majority of these firms have been inefficiently run by men with little or no business experience. They operated in the blissful belief that 'the weather tomorrow will be better', and spent their takings up to the limit. An error of judgment and a write off, or a spell of dud weather, and there was another joy-riding company up a gum tree. Few people can realize how precariously some of these firms exist, and what a struggle it is to see the winter through. Ask some of their engineers and pilots who are given holidays, sometimes lasting from September until the next March. Do we have to look far to see evidence of this? We do not. A great many of these people 'live on the posh' during

flying days, and then in the fall and 'til the next spring eke out an existence on bread and jam! Who wouldn't be an airman?

By April 1935, as reported in the Royal Aero Club, the general view about aviation from the stance of the public had

> for the most part, become inured to the sight of mere flying, or even of aerobatic flying, a modern team of display pilots must be beyond criticism, and a modern display must rival, even if in miniature, the great show at Hendon. Furthermore, Sir Alan Cobham's display, designed as it was to encourage people to use the air, had to blend the spectacular with the commonplace so that the 'circus' element was not too dominant.

One year later, the trend continued to fall, as indicated by Terry Mace:

> There is no doubt that the opening flying display of the year showed several distinctly new possibilities. Not only are the joy-riding rates lower, probably, than they have ever been before, so that more people will be encouraged to discover that there is nothing very terrifying about this flying business, but the general public is also being shown at least a few types which might eventually appeal to them as private owners, flying lessons are being given and scholarships are being awarded to those newcomers who show the greatest aptitude.

The death knell was sounded twelve months later in the same paper: 'Within the past two years, the novelty has worn off the circuses and receipts from this source have dropped considerably.'

In the immediate aftermath of the Great War, the federal government had virtually no engagement with aviation. The government had no power to license pilots, no regulatory mechanism to deem aircraft airworthy, no legislation to guide private and commercial operations, and no central authority to coordinate federal action. By the end of the 1930s, the situation had changed radically. A series of legislative actions culminated in the passage of the Civil Aeronautics Act in 1938. That bill created an independent Civil Aeronautics Administration tasked to oversee private and commercial aviation. The administration licensed pilots, approved the airworthiness of aircraft, investigated crashes, oversaw navigation aids, ran the nation's air traffic control network, and determined routes and rates for commercial carriers. In short, the CAA created an independent federal agency with power over all aspects of non-military aviation.

Chapter 7

The Pilots

Charles Lindbergh

Charles August Lindbergh was born on 4 February 1902 in Detroit, Michigan, and was the third son of Charles August Lindbergh (who was a U.S. Congressman from 1907 to 1917), and from an early age, had exhibited an interest in the mechanics of motorized transportation. He showed exceptional mechanical ability and entered the University of Wisconsin at the age of 18 to study engineering. However, he left during the second year after deciding to indulge a long-held curiosity – he wanted to learn how to fly a plane. In the young and exciting field of aviation, he had learned as much as he could about the mechanics of airplanes before he went to Ray Page's Flying School in Lincoln, Nebraska, where he enrolled for lessons on 1 April 1922. Eight days later, on 9 April, Lindbergh took to the sky for the first time.

In 1922, aviation was still in its infancy and was regarded by most with a mixture of awe and suspicion. The practice of barnstorming had been devised to impress people with the skill of pilots and the sturdiness of planes. They would fly over a region and drop leaflets down upon the locals announcing when the next air exhibition would take place. Daredevil stunts were promised, as were $5 plane rides. Lindbergh was hired by Erold Bahl as an assistant, and as a promotional stunt, Lindbergh volunteered to climb out onto the wing and wave to the crowds below.

Lindbergh also wanted to learn the then-novel practice of parachute jumping. For years, he had been tormented by nightmares of falling from a great height. Parachuting, he was certain, would allow him to face down that fear. For instruction, he went to Charles Hardin, who, along with his wife Kathryn, designed and demonstrated parachutes. On his very first attempt, Lindbergh barely, but successfully pulled off a 'double-jump'. This stunt involved wearing two parachutes, both attached to one another. After the first 'chute opened it was cut off, allowing the jumper to free-fall. Then, the second 'chute would burst open just before the jumper slammed into the ground. The crowds loved it. Hardin taught Lindbergh all the finer points of parachuting, including how to land in almost any condition and avoid injury. It was a skill that would serve Lindbergh well throughout his life as an aviator.

Lindbergh's reputation on the barnstorming circuit grew when he teamed up with Harold J. 'Shorty' Lynch in the summer of 1922. During a four-month tour of Colorado, Wyoming, Kansas and Montana, Lindbergh did a little of everything: parachute jumping, wing-walking and mechanics. Leaflets rained down on small towns and rural hamlets announcing that 'Daredevil Lindbergh' was going to be in the area. Crowds were entranced as Lindbergh stood on a plane's wings as it did a loop-to-loop, or hung from its underside, seemingly, by his teeth alone. As the months wore on, however, Lindbergh decided he wanted to be the one flying the plane, not just performing the stunts.[85]

Lindbergh's father arranged a bank loan of £900 for him to buy a surplus army airplane, and in March 1923, he purchased a war-surplus Curtiss Jenny for $500 from Souther Field, a former Air Service training camp 3.7 miles (6 kilometres) north-east of Americus, Georgia. It had been fitted with a brand-new OX-5 engine, had been given a fresh coat of olive drab dope, and an extra twenty-gallon fuel tank for the price. The auctions were continuous. Big-time buyer John Alden Wyche, owner of S&W Airplane Co. of Macon, Georgia, had snapped up all 160 of the aircraft at Souther Field for as little as $16 each and was auctioning them off. This at the time when altimeters could be bought in lots of 200 for around a dime each, and propellers were going for around twenty-six cents.

Wyche had his hangar full of crated Jennys. His young buyer had over a hundred from which to choose. The problem was that it left no room for the assembly of the plane. For that, they went to see the man who had sold Wyche the planes, Glenn Messer, down at hangar number seven. 'Glenn,' said Wyche, 'I've sold this airplane to this young man. Would you mind his setting it up here in the hangar?' 'No objections whatsoever,' Messer replied and he had his chief mechanic, Orville Walker, assist with the assembly. Curtis Patrick and Bill Paulsen, two local men employed by Wyche, also helped set up the Jenny. During the next week, Charles

Lincoln Beachey, seen here in his Curtiss biplane at Grant Park in 1911, was an early aviation daredevil who exhibited his prowess at an air show held at the park in August 1911. The *Chicago Tribune* reported that Beachey was the 'biggest star of the nine days'. (Chicago Tribune *historical photo*)

Lincoln Beachey seated at controls of his airplane, 1913.

Pioneer balloonist Thomas Scott Baldwin at the wheel of the 'Red Devil', an aircraft of his own design, which was similar to the basic Curtiss 'Pusher' design but was constructed of steel tubing instead of wood. It made the first airplane flight over the Mississippi River on 10 September 1910. (*Bain News Service*)

The first powered, controlled, sustained airplane flight in history was made by the Wright Brothers on 17 December 1903 near Kill Devil Hills, about four miles (six kilometres) south of Kitty Hawk, North Carolina. Orville Wright, 32, is at the controls of the machine, lying prone on the lower wing with hips in the cradle which operated the wing-warping mechanism. His brother, Wilbur Wright, 36, ran alongside to help balance the machine, having just released his hold on the forward upright of the right wing.

The design of the French Farman biplane (1909) was so widely imitated, that aircraft of similar layout were generally referred to as being of the 'Farman' type. (*From an illustration by A. Molynk*)

A Farman III airplane flown by Louis Paulhan at the Dominguez International Air Meet, Los Angeles, 10–20 January 1910. (*Bain News Service*)

Claude Grahame-White was the first to make a night flight in his Farman III biplane during the *Daily Mail*-sponsored 1910 London to Manchester air race. He finished second. (*Bain News Service*)

French aviator Isidore Auguste Marie Louis Paulhan (1883–1963) wass renowned for winning the first *Daily Mail* aviation prize for the first flight between London and Manchester in 1910. (*George Grantham/Bain Collection/Library of Congress*)

Frederick Rodman Law and Ruth B. Law in their Wright Model B Flyer c. 1910–15. (*National Air and Space Museum*)

French aviator Adolphe Célestin Pégoud was a test pilot for Louis Blériot.

Standard J-1 (N2124) with Hispano-Suiza engine, with other aircraft including other Standards and two Ryan Broughams in the background, 31 January 1922. (*SDASM Archives*)

Dole Air Race: James Dole (centre) awarding prizes to Arthur Goebel (left) and Martin Jensen (right) on 19 August 1927. (*SDASM Archives*)

Dole Air Race: Mildred Doran in front of the Buhl CA-5 Air Sedan (NX2915) *Miss Doran*. (*SDASM Archives*)

Dole Air Race: The Breese-Wilde monoplane (NX646) *Pabco Pacific Flyer*. (*SDASM Archives*)

Dole Air Race: The Breese-Wilde monoplane (NX646) Pabco *Pacific Flyer* with Vance Breese, Major Livingston Irving and family before the start of the race. (*SDASM Archives*)

Dole Air Race: The Swallow Special Monoplane (NX941) *Dallas Spirit*. (*SDASM Archives*)

The Travel Air 5000 *Woolaroc* (NX869) high-wing monoplane, winner of the ill-fated Dole Race in 1927. (*SDASM archive*)

The start of the Dole Air Race at Oakland Field, California, on 16 August 1927. In starting position is *Oklahoma*. Waiting, left to right, are *Aloha*, *Dallas Spirit*, *Miss Doran*, *Woolaroc*, *El Encanto*, *Golden Eagle*, *Air King* and *PABCO Pacific Flyer*. (*SDASM Archives*)

Raymonde de Laroche in August 1919. She was the first woman in the world to receive an airplane pilot's licence. (*Bain News Service*)

Vickers Vulcan Type 61 (G-EBET) – nicknamed 'The Flying Pig' – at the time of its evaluation by Qantas in 1923. (*State Library of Queensland*)

Official 1929 National Air Races programme cover. (*Author's collection*)

A pilot for the Mabel Cody Flying Circus flew her plane above Sig Haugdahl, in his Miller 8 Special automobile, on Daytona Beach on 1 December 1921, while Bugs McGowan transferred himself from the car to the plane. (*rc10415 & rc12187 courtesy of the State Archives of Florida*)

The part-original, part-replica of Jimmy Angel's El Rio Caroni exhibited in front of Ciudad Bolivar Airport, Venezuela. (*Guillermo Ramos Flamerich*)

Inman Brothers 1930 Flying Circus poster.

Harry Houdini in the Curtiss JN-4 'Jenny' for the silent film *The Grim Game* in 1919.

Posters for the 1919 six-reel silent American film *The Great Air Robbery* starring Ormer Locklear, Allan Forrest and Ray Ripley.

Poster for the 1919 American silent film *The Grim Game* starring Harry Houdini and Ann Forrest.

Poster for the 1920 American silent film *The Skywayman* starring the noted aerial stunt pilot Ormer Locklear and Louise Lovely.

Poster for the 1927 American silent war film *Wings* starring Clara Bow, Charles Rogers and Richard Arlen.

American daredevil stunt pilot and film actor Ormer Locklear in 1919. (*Bain New Service*)

Aviatrix Ruth Law. On 19 November 1916, Law set a new cross-America air speed record of 8 hours, 55 minutes and 35 seconds, for the 884 miles (1,422 kilometres) distance from Chicago to New York State. (*SDASM Archives*)

American wing-walker Lillian Boyer on 21 January 1922.

Lillian Boyer performing a stunt called 'The Breakaway' from a biplane on 21 January 1922.

Amelia Earhart in leather flying helmet for her pilot's licence photo in 1923.

Bessie Coleman on 24 January 1923. She was the first black person to earn an international pilot's licence.

Florence Lowe 'Pancho' Barnes with pilots (from left): Barnes, Mildred Morgan, Clema Granger, Patty Willis (Clover Field Register signer), Gladys O'Donnell and Mary Charles.

Georgia Ann 'Tiny' Thompson Broadwick was an American pioneering parachutist and the inventor of the ripcord. She was the first woman to jump from an airplane, the first person to jump from a seaplane and the first person to jump freefall (without a static line) with a modern parachute. (*State Archives of Raleigh, North Carolina*)

Iris Louise McPhetridge Thaden was the first female pilot to be licensed by the state of Ohio, and in 1936, became the first woman to win the Bendix trophy, alongside Blanche Noyes, in a Beechcraft Model C-17R Staggerwing.

Women pilots of the first Women's Transcontinental Air Race gather for photos at Parks Airport on 24 August 1929. From left: Mary Elizabeth von Mach, Jessie 'Chubbie' Miller, Gladys O'Donnell, Thea Rasche, Phoebe Omlie, Louise Thaden, Amelia Earhart, Blanche Noyes, Ruth Elder and Vera Walker. (*Henry Schnittger Photograph Collection/ Women Pioneers in Aviation, Parks College Photographs, Saint Louis University Archives*)

Louise Thaden (left), Gladys O'Donnell and Ruth Nichols (right) who participated in the All-Women's Transcontinental Air Race in August 1929. (*Henry Schnittger Photograph Collection/Women Pioneers in Aviation, Parks College Photographs, Saint Louis University Archives*)

Marjorie Stinson, the only woman to whom a pilot's licence was granted by the Army and Navy Committee of Aeronautics. (*U.S. National Archives and Records Administration*)

Miss Ruth Law at Daytona Beach, Florida, c. 1916. (*U.S. National Archives and Records Administration*)

Lillian Boyer standing on the wing of a plane, 21 January 1922.

19-year-old Katherine Stinson and her purpose-built Curtiss aerobatic airplane, c. 1910. (*Bain News Service*)

Jersey Ringel standing on top of an airplane wing, 7 July 1921. (*Library of Congress*)

Pilot Jimmy Doolittle standing in front of Travel Air Type 'R' Mystery Ship (NR482N) c. 1930s. Produced in secrecy prior to the 1929 Cleveland Air Races, a Wichita newspaper dubbed it the 'Mystery Ship' and the name stuck with 'R' (for its designer Herbert Rawdon) (*SDASM archive*)

A stunt flier performs for a mounted movie camera during a Calpet-sponsored air show in 1927. (*Author's collection*)

Flight Lieutenant Charles William Anderson Scott, AFC, in 1932. (*Scott Family photo album, 1931*)

The English aviation pioneer Sir Alan Cobham. (*Bain News Service*)

Frank Frakes crashing a plane through a house (Camel cigarette advertisement) in *The Saturday Evening Post*, 24 September 1938.

Airspeed Ferry AS.4 (G-ABSI) manufacturer's photo. (*Author's collection*)

Advertising poster – Ward Beams Champion Auto Dare Devils Show.

Jane Wicker, of Bristow, VA, rides on the wing of her biplane *Aurora*, piloted by her ex-husband Kurt Wicker, 12 May 2012. (*Jim Knapp*)

Synchronicity at the Kemble Air Show, 4 May 2014. (*Neil Maxfield*)

De Havilland DH.82a Tiger Moth (G-AIXD) over Sywell Aerodrome, Northamptonshire, in 1981, with the wing-walker using an early SOW (Stand On Wing) rig developed by Lewis Benjamin of the Tiger Club in 1962. The rig was banned by the CAA in 1999. (*Dick Gilbert*)

Antonov An-2R Colt (HA-MEP) of the Utterly Butterly display team at the Royal International Air Tattoo at RAF Fairford, Gloucestershire, July 1996. (*Author's collection*)

A daring wing-walker stands on the top wing whilst the pilot of the Aerosuperbatics Boeing Stearman Kaydet puts the aircraft through an exhilarating display of aerobatics including loops and rolls, creating smoke trails. (*Author's collection*)

Boeing A75N1 (PT-17) Stearman Kaydet (N54922) 'Team Guinot' (Breitling Wing-walkers) at Southend Airport, Essex, 24 May 2009. (*Author's collection*)

Boeing B75N2S-3 Kaydet (SE BOG) Breitling at Southend Airport, Essex, on 27 May 2012. (*Author's collection*)

A Breitling wing-walker in her routine at the Southend Air Show on 30 May 2010. (*Author's collection*)

Boeing A75N1 (PT-17) Stearman Kaydet (N707TJ) 'Car Magazine' at RAF Swanton Morley, Norfolk, July 1989. (*Author's collection*)

Aerosuperbatics' Boeing Stearman PT-13D Kaydet (N5057V) in 'Team Crunchie' livery, 1998. (*Author's collection*)

Boeing Stearman (N74189) of the Aerosuperbatics wing-walkers team displaying at the four-day Airbourne 2019 International Air Show at Eastbourne, Sussex. Here, that petite young lady is only attached by a clip wire. (*Rob Finch*)

Boeing Stearman PT-17 Kaydets of the Aerosuperbatics Flying Circus and their gutsy wing-walkers performing at the four-day Airbourne 2018 International Air Show at Eastbourne, Sussex. (*Rob Finch*)

'They go up, tiddly, up, up. They go down, diddly, down, down.' The Breitling Wing-walkers in action at Dunsfold, Surrey, 23 August 2014. (*Rob Finch*)

Perched atop a Boeing Stearman biplane, an acrobatic wing-walker of the Utterly Butterly stunt team limbers up as the plane taxies out for the display at the Shoreham RAFA Air Show, August 2002. (*Rob Finch*)

Wing-walker Todd Green moments before he lost his grip while transferring from the top wing of a biplane to the skid of a helicopter. He fell to his death during the air show on 21 August 2011, at the Selfridge Air National Guard Base, Michigan. (*Larry Powell*)

De Havilland DH.82 Tiger Moth (G-AVPJ) of Barnstormers Ltd, Kettering, at Nottingham in 1979. It crashed into the River Trent during an air display on 17 June of the same year. (*Dick Gilbert*)

Boeing 'Super' Stearman (A75N1) (N4442N) during the air show at Cleveland, Ohio, on 1 September 2018. (*Jeff Scovronski*)

Boeing Stearman 'Crunchie' of the Aerosuperbatics wing-walkers team, July 1996. (*Jo Ware*)

Orville Wright in 1905, aged 34. He was the younger of the two Wright Brothers who invented the world's first successful airplane. (*Library of Congress*)

Wilbur Wright, aged 38 in 1905. (*Library of Congress*)

The Lincoln 'Standard L.S.5' on 1 March 1926. A modification of the 'Standard J' biplane, it could carry four passengers.

William Jenifer Powell served as a second lieutenant in the racially segregated 317th Engineers and the 365th Infantry Regiment in France in 1917.

A Curtiss JN-4 'Jenny' on a training flight in 1918. (*George Johnson, Aviation Section, US Army Signal Corps*)

Vickers Vulcan Type 61 (G-EBET) in 1923. (*National Library of Australia*)

Emiliano and Danielle Del Buono. (*46 Aviation*)

Danielle Del Buono doesn't require special hand holds as she's the perfect size to use what the aircraft already offers naturally. 13 November 2020 (*46 Aviation*)

Lindbergh slept in the deserted barracks and during the day he watched intently as his plane was assembled.

Once the job was done, Lindbergh took the plane out to the field and taxied around for a while, getting the feel of it. Although he had some dual instruction time to his credit, he did not advertise the fact that he had not actually soloed. After nearly dinging the plane with an attempted take-off, he taxied back to the hangars and asked Messer if he would ride with him. A few hours later, Messer exited the craft satisfied that his student would do fine but suggested that Lindbergh waited until later in the afternoon when the wind had calmed to do his first solo. Later that day, Lindbergh made his first solo flight above the cotton fields near Americus. He practised take-offs and landings for a week; then having filled up with forty gallons of gas, in May 1923, took off in his Jenny which he named *Lone Eagle*, and set course for Montgomery, Alabama, to start his barnstorming career.[86]

Four years later, in 1927, Lindbergh flew alone and non-stop in the *Spirit of St Louis* across the Atlantic from Roosevelt Field, close to New York, to Le Bourget Field, Paris, and into aviation history. He took off at 7:52 am on 20 May, and landed at 10.21 pm Paris time or 5.21pm New York time, on 21 May. Thousands of cheering people had gathered to meet him. He had flown more than 3,600 miles (5,790 kilometres) in thirty-three and a half hours. The first non-stop transatlantic flight had been made eight years earlier, in June 1919, when John Alcock and Arthur Whitten Brown flew a Vickers Vimy from Newfoundland to Ireland.[87]

Art Goebel

Like many others, Arthur Cornelius 'Art' Goebel turned to barnstorming after the end of the First World War, after trying his hand as a 'soldier of fortune' in South America to eke out some sort of a living (but finding no takers). A few lucky fliers managed to land paying positions with the U.S. Postal Service in its fledgling airmail programme, but Goebel found that there were few jobs in aviation for a man with his skills, but he did become associated with the Phillips Oil Company serving as a skywriter, which enabled him to exhibit his talents at Colorado county fairs, and later in other parts of the country.

By 1924, he was seemingly performing every trick that could be done with an airplane at the time. He carried wing-walkers such as Gladys Ingle and Ivan Unger, who wowed crowds with thrilling plane changes. He also performed hair-raising tricks such as diving under Pasadena's Colorado Street Bridge with women standing on the top wing of his biplane.

After the Atlantic flight of Charles Lindbergh in 1927, businessman James Drummond Dole (the Hawaii pineapple magnate) proposed a flight across the Pacific to pioneer commercial uses of aviation and incidentally, to publicize the Dole Pineapple Company. Although the Pacific had been crossed by airplane twice in the months before, the Dole Race was the first time prize money was offered. Of the pilots who entered this race, some were completely unequipped to the task, and others, like Goebel, had the background and skills to complete the journey. He was looking for a new challenge (and found it), entering the contest with the Clyde Cessna-designed prototype Travel Air 5000 cabin plane (NX869), the *Woolaroc*, the money for which had been loaned by Frank Phillips, president of Phillips Petroleum Company, and named the plane after Phillips's Oklahoma estate. Additionally, Goebel agreed to use a new aviation fuel developed by Phillips.

The preparations for the race were extensive, and all pilots were required to have a navigator. Each plane had additional fuel tanks fitted so that each aircraft could carry 15 percent more gas than was estimated as being needed for the trip. They were also required to be equipped with an air-to-ground radio. The American press had jumped on the story, and for weeks before the race, the newspapers covered every possible aspect of the contest, touting it as the greatest sporting event of the century.

There were eighteen official and unofficial entrants; fifteen of those drew for starting positions, and of those fifteen, two were disqualified, two withdrew and three aircraft crashed before the race, resulting in three deaths. On 14 August, the eleven remaining qualifying aircraft were lined up in a semicircle at the head of the dusty runway for the race. A crowd of 75,000 to 100,000 spectators had gathered along the wooden fences to witness this great day in the history of aviation, but the start was delayed by bad weather. Two days later, the weather had only improved slightly, and nine of the aircraft were lined up (two more had dropped out), ready to take off one at a time. Heavily laden with extra fuel, take-off was made doubly difficult by the wet, muddy field conditions. Two pilots didn't even attempt to take off, and two more couldn't get off the ground due to the excess weight and the conditions. This reduced the field to five. Once in the air, one plane, *Dallas Spirit* experienced engine trouble within a few miles of take-off, forcing its crew to Oakland for hurried repairs before returning to the contest. Two of the aircraft, *Golden Eagle* and *Miss Doran*, disappeared over the Pacific with no radio messages ever heard from the lost crews. The weather was so bad, that crews of the ships stationed along the route of the race never saw any of the planes. *Dallas Spirit* also took part in the search but vanished too over the ocean. All efforts to find the lost racers proved unsuccessful.[88]

When it was all over, only two planes had completed the flight. Goebel had won the race along with his navigator, Navy Lieutenant William Virginius Davis, Jr. in the time of twenty-six hours, seventeen minutes, and took the $25,000 prize. Martin Jensen and his navigator Paul Schluter in the Breese monoplane *Aloha*, arrived two hours later.[89] In all, before, during and after the race, ten lives were lost and six airplanes were lost or damaged beyond repair.

The *Woolaroc* was mounted in a place of honour in the Phillips Museum in Bartlesville, Oklahoma, after the race. Goebel's superior flying skills and training with the new radio systems were factors in his victory, as were his planning and attention to detail. The Dole race was the first time that a civilian pilot had flown the Pacific.

As www.coloradoaviationhistoricalsociety.org expands:

After the historic, though disastrous flight, Goebel became active in barnstorming and air show work, specializing in inverted flight, taking part in and winning many early air races, and becoming one of the best-known and respected flyers. It was at this time that he became associated with the famous 13 Black Cats, the pioneer professional acrobatic team working for the movies. He had performed in over a dozen movies, such as *Three Miles Up* (1927) starring Al Wilson, William Malan and Ethlyne Clair; *Won in the Clouds* (1928) starring Al Wilson, Helen Foster and Frank Rice; and *The Air Patrol* (1928) starring Al Wilson, Elsa Benham, and Jack Mower. He took part in dangerous plane-to-plane transfers and helped institute the system of standard fees for all 46 movie stunts.

Goebel set out on a goodwill tour of Japan with Ernest Robertson of the Fairchild Aviation Company in early 1928, and barnstormed their way around that nation, giving rides, performing, and selling the Japanese on the idea of flying. He was later called to service again in the Army Air Corps in the Second World War, retiring with the rank of colonel, having served over forty years.

Lincoln Beachey

Lincoln Beachey was born on 3 March 1887, in Mission Street, San Francisco, and, as a young man in his early teens, owned a bicycle shop and also repaired motorcycles and their engines. By the time the Wright brothers made their first flight, Beachey was already building and flying his own balloons. With this experience, he followed his brother, Hillary's, footsteps, and worked as a ground crewman for dirigible pilot Thomas Scott Baldwin, who, on 30 January 1885, made one of the earliest recorded parachute jumps from a balloon. Beachey also helped build the dirigible *California Arrow* which made its first flight on 3 August 1904, over San Francisco Bay. He went on to make his own flight in the dirigible in February 1905, at the age of 17, after convincing George Heaton, the pilot, to allow him to take the controls of the new machine. Beachey soon became the top aeronaut with the Baldwin troupe and travelled to East Asia and elsewhere showcasing their flying machine, the like of which had never been seen in most countries. He later helped to design a faster, more aerodynamic dirigible known as the 'Beachey-Baldwin'.

Beachey had initially received some early assistance from Roy Knabenshue but soon demonstrated his own ability to succeed by himself. With his home-built dirigible, which he named *The Rubber Cow*, he travelled across the country, participating in exhibition events where he found them. He was a daring and consummate performer who knew how to bring attention to his flights. In particular, Beachey's knack for contriving unique aerial feats to thrill the public gained him wide acclaim.

As a young dirigible aeronaut, he noticed the changing trends in exhibition flying, and although he was a recognized leader in lighter-than-air flight, after witnessing an impressive demonstration of the capability of airplanes at the Los Angeles Air Meet on 10 January 1910, which had drawn a crowd of 20,000 spectators to see Glenn Curtiss and Louis Paulhan race airplanes, he made the decision, to give it up in favour of the new heavier-than-air flying machines. It proved to be the right decision for him; after a few early mishaps in the new flying machines, Beachey became Glenn Curtiss's premier pilot, and in that role, he set the pace for American exhibition flying in the years preceding the First World War.[90]

The Los Angeles Air Meet of 1910 was as consequential to the progress of heavier-than-air technology in general as it was to Beachey's career in exhibition flying. An incredible new age was dawning when daredevil antics in the air thrilled thousands at fairgrounds, ballparks and farm pastures. The crowds watched in awe as pilots stunned them with their frail aircraft. But premature death haunted every pilot in those days. Flying was a new and dangerous, if exciting, endeavour and aviation knowledge was limited.

As the first large-scale American air meet to include numerous airplanes, the event created conflict between competing inventors. The same Glenn Curtiss who designed the motor for Thomas Baldwin's *California Arrow* organized the meet in Los Angeles.

In the autumn of 1910, Beachey began having flying lessons at the Curtiss Flying School. On his first attempt to solo, he stuck his plane's nose straight into the air, stalled and came down tail first. He walked away from the wreckage unscratched as Glenn Curtiss turned his back in disbelief. Curtiss thought he should go back to flying his *Rubber Cow*. The team manager, however, thought Beachey had potential and convinced Curtiss to give him another chance. After more instruction, he took off in another airplane and promptly crashed again. Curtiss, now angry, threatened dismissal, but the manager calmed the situation and for the third time, Beachey soloed. To the chagrin of Curtiss, by the end of 1911, Beachey had become his greatest moneymaker.[91]

After his early success as a managing member of the Aeronautical Experimentation Association, Curtiss incorporated the Curtiss Exhibition Company in 1910 and hired Jerome S. Fanciulli to manage it. At the time of the Los Angeles Air Meet, Curtiss was embroiled in litigation with the Wright brothers over their patent on heavier-than-air designs. Because of their patents, the Wrights viewed heavier-than-air technology as their own private industry. They feared exploitation of their heavier-than-air flying machines by Curtiss and other, smaller entrepreneurs. However, airplanes were causing great excitement across the country and the threat of legal action did little to impede engineers and pilots alike. Writer Martin Caidlin: 'Despite the threat of the heavy hand of the law, there was an enthusiastic new generation in America which wanted, more than anything else in the world, to fly. And it was willing to pay a heavy price to do so.' The fact that Curtiss went ahead with the Los Angeles Air Meet despite an injunction against him demonstrates his determination to assert himself as a leading airplane manufacturer.

The Wright brothers drew criticism from their former supporters for not divulging their methods. They did not receive a United States patent for their invention until 1906 and were thus very wary of revealing the design. They were so focused on maintaining a monopoly on heavier-than-air technology that they filed suit against a number of other aviation pioneers who exhibited flying machines for public audiences, including Curtiss. They even filed suit against foreign pilots who exhibited heavier-than-air flying machines in the United States. In one such incident in 1910, the Wrights filed suit against British aviator Claude Grahame-White, forcing him to either fly their airplane or pay heavy royalties if he exhibited other flying machines.[92]

The court battles only succeeded in polarizing the airplane industry. Starting in 1910, heavier-than-air technology was split between two controlling interests: the Wrights and Curtiss. By the end of 1909, Curtiss was a public figure ranking with the Wrights. He had flown from Albany to New York City, winning a $10,000 prize offered by the *New York World*; his trim pusher airplanes, with a ruggedly functional appearance, became as familiar to Americans as the distinctive Wright canard designs. Like the Wrights, Curtiss established an exhibition team to demonstrate the firm's aircraft.

Beachey knew that to be a part of the Curtiss team was to be at the forefront of exhibition flying. He was thus determined to convince Glenn Curtiss of his merits. Curtiss was only interested in hiring talented aviators to maximize public appeal for his product. Martin Caidlin: 'To pursue his goals with success, Curtiss assembled in one group the best pilots available. Impressing upon them the need for the desired impression with the public, he sent his men and airplanes off to barnstorm the circuits where there seemed the most likely prospects for airplane customers.'

Keeping Beachey on the Curtiss payroll soon paid off. Within one year of joining the Curtiss Exhibition Company, Beachey made national headlines by flying over Niagara Falls (and making $5,000 in the process) and under the suspension bridge connecting the United States and Canada. When he accomplished this feat on 27/28 June 1911, he established himself as a leading American aviator and set a precedent for performing inventive aerial stunts that were previously thought impossible. As America's most popular exhibition flyer, Beachey generated public enthusiasm for Curtiss's airplanes. Beachey's combination of daring and skill was the perfect complement to Curtiss's business strategy. Caidlin again: 'Curtiss was acutely aware that to sell, he must convince a torpid public and the nation at large that his flying machines were the finest made and that they had an almost limitless variety of thrills to offer.'

Between 1911 and 1915, Beachey dominated air exhibition in the United States by continually upping the ante on aerial stunt work. His Niagara Falls flight of 27 June 1911 defied the experts' belief that the air currents created in the gorge would batter his biplane. According to Beachey, people bet money that he would fail: 'When I flew over Niagara Falls and down the gorge, they were betting two to one that I would not attempt the feat and five to one that I would never get out of the gorge alive.'

Some 150,000 people held their breath as he passed safely underneath the steel bridge connecting the U.S. and Canada. The feat demonstrated his skilful piloting and testified to the strength of the Curtiss biplane. Caidlin: 'The space through which he flew was 168 feet in height and barely 100 feet from side to side. The distance from the brink of the falls to the bridge in which he made the dip [was] about 400 yards.'

Beachey did a repeat performance of the flight the next day in front of an equally amazed crowd. The public noted that Beachey was not afraid to take risks in his flying. If the Niagara Falls flight was not proof enough of his determination, Beachey's performance at the Chicago International Aviation Meet of late August 1911 cemented his identity as 'the greatest exponent of the flying age'.[93]

The one-week-long event was one of the largest aviation meets held before the First World War. It was attended by the world's leading aviators. Here, they competed for thousands of dollars in speed, precision control and altitude events. There was stiff competition, both from the pilots participating and the various airplanes that represented state-of-the-art in technology. Beachey was unsure that his Curtiss 'pusher' airplane was robust enough to stand a chance in a competition, but he was not one to concede defeat, and so he made up for the performance deficiencies of his airplane with his flying skill. He broke the altitude record by flying his airplane upward until he was completely out of fuel. While he was playing with fate as he glided back down to earth with a dead motor, he had attained an altitude of 11,642 feet. That day he impressed 500,000 spectators with his ability. Martin Caidlin: 'Here, against the cream of the world's aviators from France, England, and the United States, he demonstrated a mastery of control and daring that none could match.'[94]

In one year, seventeen million people saw him fly. At the time, the population of the United States was just ninety million. His achievements include inventing figure-eights and the vertical drop. He was also the first pilot to achieve terminal velocity by flying straight toward the ground. Several pilots died trying to imitate him.

Heavier-than-air flying came into vogue. Exhibition teams planned events throughout the country, demonstrated by the large public attendance of people from all around the Midwest at the Chicago International Aviation Meet in 1911. During the rest of the year and into 1912, Beachey performed in San Francisco, Boston, Los Angeles, Washington, D.C., Chicago, Niagara Falls, Elmira (New York), Hamilton (Ohio), Peoria (Illinois), Lawrence (Kansas), Milwaukee, Dubuque (Iowa), and towns in Florida, Georgia, Tennessee and Pennsylvania.[95]

Beachey performed in front of crowds of people who had never seen an airplane. At this time, the novelty of aviation was its main selling point, which was especially true in the Midwest, where people had no access to popular forms of entertainment such as vaudeville. Beachey commanded over $1,000 per flight during the peak of his success. It was estimated that between 1911 and 1915, Beachey performed in front of between seventeen and twenty million people.[96]

For two years, Beachey was considered far ahead of all the world's aviators at the fancy flying game. Then, on 9 September 1913 (27 August by the calendar then used in Russia), the Russian pilot, Captain Pyotr Nikolayevich Nesterov, made the first inside loop over Syretzk Aerodrome near Kiev. This was followed by the loop in France by Adolphe Pégoud. It was the bitterest moment of Beachey's life. He immediately became determined to outdo the rest and began to construct a machine sufficiently strong enough to stand the strain of the loop-the-loop effort. The 'scientific men' had predicted that not only would the biplane collapse when the full force of the loop strain was applied but that, without the use of one of the revolving engines used in France, the stunt was mechanically impossible. They said the upright motor would stop when the machine arrived at the top of the circle, and that the machine would then drop to earth. Such were the cheering words the wise men of science imparted to Beachey.

Captain Pyotr Nikolayevich Nesterov was disciplined after becoming the first pilot to ever perform an inside loop, with ten days of close arrest, ostensibly 'for risking government property'. His achievement made him famous overnight and when the feat was officially achieved by the famous French pilot Adolphe Pégoud on 21 September, Nesterov's punishment was reversed; he was promoted to staff captain and later awarded a medal.[97]

Beachey chose the time he thought would give him the most privacy in his trial at the loop. Scarcely a dozen army *attachés* and Curtiss people were on the field. If he failed in the effort, his failure and the awful consequences would be witnessed by but a few. Beachey thought nothing of the glory of success. He simply did not want to fail before a crowd. But the faithful watchers on boats and piers of San Diego were not to be eluded. Every day for the previous week hundreds of people had spent hours watching, waiting for the one great effort of the master birdman. And then they were rewarded. Half an hour later the entire city knew that Lincoln Beachey had won back the crown emblematic of aerial supremacy.

Beachey completed the first successful airplane loop the loop in America over San Diego on 25 November 1913. Famed for doing the unexpected, he fairly outdid himself after announcing that he would not fly for a couple of days and was giving his mechanical force a holiday, but he trundled his biplane out of a North Island shed at around 3 pm, and called to the army mechanics for a volunteer to twirl the propeller of his trick aircraft. Then he hurried off to the sky, and before the watchers could pass the word to those who had waited for days to be in at the first 'loop', Beachey had climbed to 1,000 feet and then sent his machine through two complete circles, as neat and dexterous loop-the-loops as were ever witnessed in a circus. His deft hand, alert brain and keen eye, which had made his past performances with the airplane the sensation of the aviation world, enabled him to do the thing no other aviator in America ever accomplished.

On the Thursday of that week, Beachey flew as the star of the Shriners' Sky Jubilee and put his machine through all the tricks and stunts he had mastered. He raced against an automobile driven by Olin Davis, and flew around the circular track, skimming close to the ground, to break the world's mile record held by Barney Oldfield.

Beachey carried out other low-flying stunts for around ten or fifteen minutes before the show closed. He ascended for his loop the loop and upside-down flying performances and performed the loop as low as the grounds allowed. The Shriners arranged for his great biplane, the last word in aerial construction, to be placed on exhibition where all the spectators might see it at close range and have the lecturer answer questions regarding it.

The jubilant Beachey stated that he was 'the happiest fellow in the world tonight. After a man works hard all his life and plans on accomplishing one great thing, the realization of his dream is about the sweetest thing that can come to him'. Regarding his wonderful flight:

> I do not want people to make a fuss over me for looping-the-loop today. Really, it was not the difficult task they thought. I deserve more praise for the repression of my desire to get up in the sky and slam into the loop regardless of everything, than for the actual accomplishment of the feat. But I knew that I must go about it methodically. That is the reason I have made a success of flying. All the time they have been saying, 'Beachey is a fool flyer and lucky to be alive.' I have been thinking, working, and studying. Constant practice and application to my task enabled me to get away with my feats.
>
> It will not be of much use to describe the sensations attending the loop, for anticipating sensations is about zero in looping-the-loop. I kept my head every second and could have looped half a dozen times before I came to earth, only I thought it wise to wait until I tested the wiring and ascertained if any damage had occurred to the machine.
>
> Now that I have started in, I am not going to quit until I make all the scientific fellows take to their holes. Those rocking chair aviators

who write articles on flying and try to run aviation are the worst menace to the sport. I used to pity those who came up and told me I was foolish to fly in an unusual manner, and I tolerated them. Now I am going to get angry at them. It is not a joke any longer. I am going to fly my head off for the Shriners Thursday, for I have been treated so royally by San Diegans that I owe them all a debt of gratitude. My stay here has been about the brightest spot of my career.

By the end of the year, Beachey had performed six consecutive loops and was soon setting records, performing as many as eighty loops in succession. He made a mock attack on the White House and the Capitol in 1914 to show the government that it was unprepared for the aviation age.

Beachey prepared for an extraordinary flight on Sunday, 14 March 1915, to showcase his new, more powerful monoplane. Gunning his engine and lifting off in less than 50 feet, Beachey made a loop, then flipped the plane over on its back for an inverted flight. So intent on exhibiting the ability of his new plane, he failed to realize he was now only 2,000 feet above the water, too low to complete his stunt. Pulling hard on the controls to bring the plane out of its sinking inverted flight, the strain on the plane caused the left wing to snap off, followed by the right one. The monoplane went into a screaming, twisting dive, and struck the water at high speed with Beachey strapped helplessly in the fuselage. The crash embedded the plane and Beachey in 30 feet of mud and water in San Francisco Bay. When the plane was raised after being freed by divers, Beachey was found still firmly strapped in his seat. Although the safety restraints had minimized his injuries from the impact of the crash, he had been unable to free himself from the wreckage and had drowned.

Beachey was the first man to fly upside-down; he performed the first loop-the-loop in America and later perfected it. Beachey was also the first to tailslide on purpose, the first to figure out how to pull out of a spin – a manoeuvre that had proved deadly for so many pilots.[98] A spin occurs when one wing of an airplane stalls while the other is still producing lift. This creates unequal pressure across the wings and causes the airplane to rotate (or 'spin') about its axis. Since less lift is being produced the machine also descends quickly. A spin can be vertical or 'flat'. The danger of a spin is that it is a stable state from which the machine will not recover unless the correct recovery action is taken by the pilot. To make matters worse, if the pilot instinctively tries to pull the nose up or roll the aircraft level, the spin will actually worsen. For this reason, the 'tail spin' was very dangerous to early aviators while it remained little understood. A spin can be entered by raising the nose of an airplane while performing a turn at low airspeed. Some accounts of Pierre Chanteloup's Caudron say that the wing-warping – an early system for lateral control of a fixed-wing aircraft – was linked to the elevator, rather than to the rudder which was more usual. If this was the case, Chanteloup could easily have entered a spin while turning with insufficient engine power on. Within just a few years, fighter pilots would be using aerobatic manoeuvres daily over the trenches in the swarming dogfights of the First World War.[99]

Clyde Edward 'Upside Down' Pangborn

Born in Bridgeport, Washington, near Lake Chelan, Pangborn worked briefly as an engineer for a mining company before joining the Air Service during the First World War. After completing his flight training, he was stationed at Ellington Field in Houston, Texas, as a flying instructor. While teaching cadets how to fly the Curtiss JN-4 'Jenny' biplane, Pangborn would roll his plane onto its back and fly upside down for extended periods, earning him the nickname 'Upside Down Pang'.

After the war, Pangborn took up barnstorming, exhibition flying and aerial acrobatics, which he did for the next nine years. He performed as a part of the Gates Flying Circus, of which he was a co-owner along with Ivan Gates. It performed internationally and made him famous for changing planes midair. Only once was he injured, when he fell out of a speeding car as he attempted to jump to a low-flying airplane; this was his only serious injury during his entire career in flying. He gained national fame after assisting in a midair rescue of stuntwoman Rosalie Gordon, who had got caught on Pangborn's landing gear while demonstrating a parachute jump, in Houston, Texas.[100]

During his time in the flying circus, Pangborn flew more than 12,500 miles and carried thousands of passengers. He met Hugh Herndon, who later became his co-pilot in the transpacific flight. The flying circus disbanded in 1929, but Pangborn continued flying with several other businesses he owned. The Great Depression, however, soon caused them all to go bankrupt, and as a result, Pangborn turned his attention to breaking world records in flight.

In 1931, Pangborn and co-pilot Hugh Herndon Jr, sought to fly around the world and break the current record of twenty days and four hours, set by the airship *Graf Zeppelin* in 1929. The record was broken by Wiley Post and Harold Gatty (while Pangborn and Herndon were still planning their flight) and re-established the record at eight days and fifteen hours. They flew their red Bellanca J-300 Long Distance Special, *Miss Veedol*, anyway, but were forced to abandon their effort due to poor weather while flying over Siberia.[101, 102]

With their eyes on a $25,000 prize, Pangborn and Herndon next decided to attempt the first non-stop transpacific flight. They flew from Siberia to Japan in preparation, and finally took off on 4 October 1931, from Sabishiro Beach, Misawa, Aomori, Japan. Their destination was Seattle, Washington, just under 5,500 miles. Three hours after take-off, a problem arose: the device intended to jettison the landing gear partially failed. The gear was ejected, but the two root struts remained, and Pangborn had to climb out onto the wing supports barefoot at 14,000 feet to remove them. They eventually belly-landed on a strip cut out of the sagebrush on Fancher Field, near what is now East Wenatchee, after a total flying time of forty-one hours and thirteen minutes. The regional airport, Pangborn Memorial (EAT) in East Wenatchee, also honours Pangborn's accomplishment.[103]

When the Second World War broke out in Europe, Pangborn joined the Royal Air Force (RAF) and assisted in organizing the RAF Ferry Command, and recruiting pilots throughout the United States and Canada.[104] From 1941 through the end of the war in 1945, Pangborn made around 170 trans-ocean flights (crossing both the Atlantic and the Pacific). In 1942, he flew the first Lancaster heavy bomber to the United States for tests, and later returned with the same aircraft and demonstrated it to the United States Army Air Forces, and major aircraft builders throughout the United States and Canada. Returning to commercial flying after the war, Pangborn had logged more than 24,000 flight hours over his forty years of piloting by the time of his death in 1958.

'Fearless' Frank Frakes

Bert Ward Beam was a small-time promoter and owner of an aerobatic flight school in Celina, Ohio. In 1922, he decided to put together a team of daredevil automobilists and started promoting 'wreck-it' races in which $50 jalopies would race to the finish, but crash along the way. Initially devising a set routine of car tricks consisting of precision driving and automotive endurance demonstration, the shows attracted more interest in the wrecks and smashes, autos colliding in head-on crashes, slamming into brick and flaming walls, leaping from ramps straight into other vehicles (known as the 'T-bone crash'), and running over human 'iron men'. Drivers' safety at the time relied on just how tightly they could grab onto the seat next to them. It was only a matter of time before staged airplane crashes joined the mix. The premier aviator-crasher was a stunt pilot by the name of Captain Frank Foster 'Bowser' Frakes, a native of Tennessee who performed scores of such spectacles at fairgrounds nationwide.

In 1913, Bowser had seen his uncle fly an old Curtiss-Wright pusher, and it was love at first sight. Through his uncle, Bowser learned everything he could about flying the flimsy planes from the infancy of aviation, but when he thought he had learned enough to help the Allies with the Great War, his uncle did not see it that way – he lacked the two years of college required to be a pilot in the early air force.

During an interview in 1955, Bowser said of his time during the war, 'The closest I came to flying was when a Maury County mule kicked me about thirty feet through the air.' Grounded by the army, Bowser's main objective was to transport mules to Europe to aid with the war effort. When the war was over, however, Bowser found himself in luck. The army had hundreds of surplus planes that they were all too happy to sell to would-be pilots like Frakes. Taking what he had learned from his uncle, he hit the road as a barnstormer, going on to become one of the best. His flying skills soon landed him with a job with Curtiss-Wright as a test pilot. But the Great Depression came along and, in its wake, Bowser's job was lost, forcing him back to barnstorming.

Bowser and his comrades in the 'air circus' quickly learned that things were tough all over the country: people were no longer paying to watch the old air acts with simulated dogfights and acrobatics that once brought in thousands of spectators. He had to come up with a completely new act. Bowser said, 'I got the idea of cracking up planes before a crowd which would pay admission to see me risk my fool neck.' In 1929, before a crowd of 30,000 spectators, he performed his first 'crack-up'. Jack Dealy, in a feature for *Flying* magazine, wrote, 'The crowd roared with approval – and Frakes was on his way to establishing a world record for walking away from crack-ups.' The title of the feature in the magazine was, 'He Walked Away from 99 Crashes.' Bowser had crashed into homes, barns, cars and, once, a body of water during his career spanning the 'ninety-nine' crashes.

Curtiss Jennys were famous for folding up on hard landings, and Frakes would travel to the show, check around for an old clunker airplane that he could pick up on the cheap. He would then do just enough work on it to get it to fly because his repertoire consisted of flying planes into trees, lakes, prefabricated houses and, occasionally, even straight into the ground.

Nine years later, Frakes was still dive-bombing houses. He told the newspaper *Reading Eagle* (Pennsylvania) that the house used in the stunt was specially built of two-by-fours and siding, and measured about 16 feet by 30 feet. 'I admit I fool the public,' he told them. 'Everybody who goes out there will expect to see me get killed, but I won't. Just the same, they won't be disappointed. I'll show them the most spectacular stunt they ever witnessed. The secret is that I never let that engine crankshaft hit anything solid. I don't care what happens to the rest of the plane. Let 'er rip.'[105]

All along this journey of cracking up planes, Bowser had to stay one step ahead of the law. The Civil Aeronautics Authority (CAA, the forerunner of today's Federal Aviation Administration) did not much care for Bowser's occupation. They disliked his stunts, and told him to stop, and that if he didn't, he'd lose his pilot's licence. Bob Duncan wrote that the CAA would watch the newspaper for advertisements for Frakes's shows, and as soon as it was announced Captain Frakes was going to perform a crack-up in a town, CAA agents would alert authorities with orders to nab him. But Frakes managed to stay a step ahead for years. 'As fast as they'd lift his flying licence in one state, he'd jump to another,' reported the *St. Petersburg Independent,* a Florida newspaper, in 1968.

Bowser was known to feign injuries after a performance and go straight from the crash site to the ambulance. Once away from the prying eyes of the spectators (and the police), he would have the medics drive the ambulance to either his hotel or the local train station. It may have been at the Florida State Fair that Frakes learned that CAA agents were in the audience. Duncan wrote: Bowser came into sight over the treetops, with his wings wagging, and slewing from side to side as if something was badly wrong with the airplane. He would cut the power, then pull on the choke to make the small engine cough and belch out puffs of smoke. Within seconds every eye in the stands was fixed on the struggling airplane. The crowd held its breath, and a few women screamed.' Frakes 'crashed his plane, and instead of jumping out and waving to the crowd, an ambulance came roaring onto the field. He would be slapped onto a stretcher, and with sirens wailing, the ambulance would roar out of the fairground toward the hospital. The federal agents watched it go. A few miles from the fairground, Frakes climbed out of the ambulance and hopped a freight train towards the next event over the state line.'[106]

'Fearless Frakes' had become a household name by the end of the 1930s and even became a pitchman for Camel cigarettes. In September 1938, Bowser knew the law was close, so he again played hurt. The medics threw Frakes in the back of the ambulance and before the car took off, two men climbed into the back with the 'patient'. Bowser looked at the men, but assumed they were doctors when one of them said they were going to the hospital. According to *The Lincoln Star*, 'No!' replied the flier, 'I'm all right, hurry up and get me to my hotel so I can get out of town.'

'Well,' retorted one of the men, 'If you're all right then we're going to the jail, not the hotel.'

That's when Bowser realized the two men were the town sheriff and one of his deputies.

The Wild West-era of air shows was coming to a close, but a new world war loomed on the horizon. Bowser decided to offer his services to the British by writing a letter to their embassy in Washington, D.C. According to Bowser, 'I told them if British intelligence would map out Adolf Hitler's residence for me I'd be glad to rid the world of his presence. I said I thought could fly a plane carrying high explosives right down his chimney.' The Brits thanked him for the offer but declined. That did not stop Bowser from enlisting in the Royal Air Force where he served honourably from 1941 until 1942 as a flight instructor, and after his service, he transferred to the United States Army Air Forces, where he finished out the war.

Having served through another world war, Bowser, now in his fifties, had to find a new show. Cracking up planes was out. He needed something a little easier to do in his golden years. So, Bowser developed the 'Casket of Death' routine, where he lined a coffin with dynamite, sealed himself inside, and had someone light the fuse. Then, BOOM! Later, at close to 60 years old, he started performing a rocket routine. Bowser would saddle onto a rocket and have it launched only to explode in midair. After the war, Frakes began to travel with an automobile thrill show, and never lost his love of spectacle, wrote Bob Duncan, in *The Tennessean* (Nashville): 'Neal Frakes, Bower's nephew, remembered that he was still concocting ideas for stunts into his old age. He tried to entice Neal into riding a homemade rocket into the air. The rocket would explode in the sky, and Neal was to float back to earth in a parachute. The lad had been previously warned by family members to "stay away from Uncle Bowser". Neal beat a hasty retreat.'

Frakes died in January 1970. Bowser is still considered an aviation legend. His story has been told in countless newspaper articles and magazines, including *Flying* and *Air & Space/Smithsonian*. He flew as a stuntman in thirty-four movies, including *Hell's Angels* and *Devil Dogs of the Air*, and was also featured in numerous newsreels during the 1930s.[107]

Ormer Locklear

Ormer Leslie 'Lock' Locklear is credited as being the first man to wingwalk. Having worked as a carpenter and mechanic in Fort Worth, Texas, he joined the U.S. Army Air Service in October 1917, just a few days before his 26th birthday. Having undergone training in Austin, at Camp Dick and Barron Field, Texas, Pilot Cadet Locklear started climbing out onto his Jenny biplane's lower wing while in midair to resolve certain problems. His first trip out onto his wing occurred when he could not see clearly enough some communications were being flashed at him from the ground because the plane's engine housing and wing were blocking his view. Because he needed to interpret the communication to pass one of his pilot's tests, Locklear decided to leave the plane in the hands of his instructor/co-pilot and climb out onto the wing and read the message. He passed the test, but his instructor was less than happy with him.

His instructor's displeasure did not keep him from continuing to wing-walk. On one occasion Locklear ventured out to fix a radiator cap that had come loose from his plane's engine, and another time he left the cockpit to fix a sparkplug wire. Although Locklear could have been court-martialled for such antics, his commanding officer encouraged him, instead, to perform more stunts because they boosted his colleagues' morale, and their confidence in the soundness of their Jenny biplanes, which were suffering a rash of accidents at the time. Once other pilots started watching Locklear's performances, several of them started developing their own stunts. As a result, the art of wing-walking took off.[108]

Locklear subsequently received an honourable discharge from the Army Air Service in May 1919, along with two of his military colleagues, Lieutenants Milton 'Skeets' Elliott and Shirley J. Short. Together with manager and promoter William Pickens, they soon obtained aircraft and formed the Locklear Flying Circus. Pickens had a great deal of experience promoting barnstormers, with Locklear being his greatest success. Both men became wealthy and lived in high style. County fairs throughout North America held special 'Locklear Days' in his honour. Sometimes he received as much as $3,000 a day for stunting, and that was usually only for about a half-hour of work, and he became an international star. Everyone wanted to see the enthralling man who claimed, 'Safety second is my motto.' As much of a daredevil he was, he did not have a fatalistic death wish and had a definite reason for what he was doing. As he clearly stated: 'I don't do these things because I want to run the risk of being killed. I do it to demonstrate what can be done. Somebody has got to show the way someday we will all be flying and the more things that are attempted and accomplished, the quicker we will get there.'[109] His trademark stunt of jumping from one aircraft to another led Locklear to perfect a transfer from a car, and then the 'Dance of Death', in which two pilots in two aircraft, would switch places in midair.[110]

Locklear developed most of the fundamental skills on which wing-walking rested. Contemporaries viewed him as the father of aviation acrobatics. He perfected such basic wing-walking stunts as handstands and hanging postures. He also helped develop the rather standard but impressive stunt of hanging from a plane by grasping only a trapeze bar or rope ladder with his teeth. He was the first person to 'transfer' from one plane to another while in midair, and also the first to transfer from a speeding vehicle onto an aircraft, specifically from a car via a suspended rope ladder. Both types of feats became standard stunts within the wing-walking repertory, and many aerialists copied Locklear's basic moves and poses, and built upon them. Clyde Edward 'Upside Down' Pangborn, another well-known barnstormer, who performed as a part of the Gates Flying Circus (which he co-owned with Ivan Gates), received a great deal of publicity for his own car-to-plane transfer, and several other wing-walkers developed other unique transfer stunts during the 1920s, including ones from speeding trains and boats.[111]

Locklear's popular flying circus performed throughout the United States and caught the attention of Hollywood. Pickens arranged for Locklear to appear as a stunt man in film work,[112] and that opened the way to a movie career in California for Locklear, who was considered the foremost 'aviation stunt man in the world'. Carl Laemmle, head of Universal Pictures, agreed to purchase all of Locklear's future air show dates in July 1919, to have him on contract for a proposed two-film series.[113] Locklear was signed for a starring role in *The Great Air Robbery* in 1919, a screenplay about the midair piracy of a U.S. airmail plane. Principal photography began in July at Cecil B. DeMille's Field No. 1, in Los Angeles, California, and for the filming of close-ups, the aircraft, a Curtiss JN-4 Jenny, was mounted on a raised wooden platform.

The film served as an opportunity to showcase the aerial stunts that had made Locklear famous, and its promotion was extensive, with Laemmle declaring that the film was 'the most amazing and unbelievable photodrama of all time.'[114] The promotional campaign included a premiere at the Superba Theatre in Los Angeles and a two-month personal appearance tour with Locklear. *The New York Times* review focused on the exciting elements of the film: 'Lieutenant Locklear swings from one airplane to another and crawls out on the tail of a flying machine several thousand feet, presumably, above the earth. The melodrama's use of airplanes for midnight mail deliveries, highway (or rather highair), robberies, and battles between the forces of law and lawlessness adds excitement.'[115]

DeMille Field No. 2 was the main base for filming in his next film, *The Skywayman*, which began on 11 June 1920. Despite Locklear's public claim that new stunts 'more daring ever filmed' would be involved, the production would rely heavily on models and less on actual stunt flying. Two stunts, a church steeple being toppled by Locklear's aircraft and an aircraft-to-train transfer were both problematic and nearly ended in disaster. The last stunt scheduled for filming for *The Skywayman* was a nighttime spin, initially to take place in daylight with cameras fitted with red filters to simulate darkness. Locklear, having learned that the studio head, William Fox, was not going to extend his contract beyond this film, insisted that he be allowed to fly at night. The studio relented, and on 2 August 1920, the publicity surrounding the stunt led to a large crowd gathering to witness the filming of the unusual stunt.[116]

Large studio arc lights were set up to illuminate the Jenny on its dive towards some oil derricks to make it appear that the airplane crashed beside the oil well. The lights were to be doused as the aircraft entered its final spin. As arranged, Locklear had forewarned the lighting crew to douse their lights when he got near the derricks so that he could see to pull out of the dive, saying that, 'When you take the lights off, I'll know where I am and I can come out of it.'[117] After completing a series of aerial manoeuvres, Locklear signaled that he would descend.[118] In front of spectators and film crew, Locklear and his long-time flying partner Milton 'Skeets' Elliot crashed heavily into the sludge pool of an oil well, never pulling out of the incipient spin. The crash resulted in a massive explosion and fire, with Locklear and Elliot dying instantly.[119]

With the entire film already completed except for the night scene, Fox decided to capitalize on the fatal crash by rushing *The Skywayman* into post-production and release. With notices proclaiming, 'Every inch of film showing Locklear's spectacular (and fatal) last flight,' and his 'Death-defying feats and a close up of his spectacular crash to Earth,' the film premiered in Los Angeles on 5 September 1920.[120] The advertising campaign that accompanied the film was very similar to that of Locklear's first feature film, focusing on his earlier exploits and combining model displays and exhibition flights across North America to coincide with the film's release.[121] Upon the film's release, Fox Film Corporation publicly announced that 10 per cent of the profits would go to the families of Locklear and Elliot.[122]

Paul Mantz

From a young boy fabricating wings out of canvas to try to fly from a tree in his backyard at home to attend the Panama Pacific Exposition in San Francisco at the age of 12, where he watched the world-famous Lincoln Beachey make his first-ever flight in his new monoplane, the Lincoln Beachey Special – which proved also to be his last flight as the airplane disintegrated as he performed his finale, the Dive of Death – Paul Mantz has done it all: air shows, flying in movies, air racing and competition flying, skywriting, air charters and flight instruction.

Mantz took his first flying lesson at the age is 16, using money that he made from driving a hearse during the influenza epidemic of 1919, but following the death of his father, any further thoughts about flying were put aside as he had to work full-time to help support the rest of the family. Then on 24 September 1924, he went to Cressy Field in San Francisco with a friend to join thousands of other people giving a hero's welcome to the army's round-the-world flyers as they neared the end of their flight in their Douglas World Cruisers (a modified variant of their DT torpedo bomber).[123]

One of the airplanes had to make a dead-stick landing in a field, its engine dead. Mantz disconnected the battery from his car and took it with haste across to the airplane for fitting so that it could quickly rejoin the other two in the sky. He was invited as a thank-you to join them in the festivities in Cressy Field. There, Mantz was introduced to the top aviators of the day and was asked by several of them if he had ever thought of becoming a military pilot himself. Upon learning that he had to sit at least two years in college to be eligible, he subsequently started to produce a forged transcript using Stanford University stationery to join the service as a pilot. He subsequently gained admission with the false documents and became a successful cadet, never having had to disclose to any officials about his previous flying experience.

Shortly before his graduation at March Field in 1927, Mantz was flying solo over the Coachella Valley when he spotted a train heading west over the empty desert floor up the long grade from Indio. He rolled over into a dive, leveled off a few feet above the track, and flew head-on towards the train as the engineer repeatedly sounded the whistle. At the last moment, Mantz pulled up, performed a 'victory roll' and flew away. Unfortunately, the passengers on the train included some high-ranking brass who were on their way to March Field to participate in the graduation ceremonies and had witnessed the dangerous stunt, and subsequently, Mantz was dismissed from the service. His instructor had (reportedly) made it clear to Mantz that he had the makings of an exceptional pilot and encouraged him to continue a career in aviation. He realized that the only way that he could do it would be to do something to make a name for himself. After working briefly in commercial aviation, he went to Hollywood, attracted by the large sums of money movie stunt pilots were making at the time.

Mantz decided that he would set a new record for consecutive outside loops, and for such an attempt, he had to design and build a special carburettor. Once perfected, on 6 July 1930, flying under NAA licence no. 5011, signed by Orville Wright, and with National Aviation Academy observers on hand, he climbed to 3,000 feet over San Mateo. He lost count and was on what he thought was his twenty-third outside loop and was just about to stop when he noticed that an airplane was flying close to him with a sign that said '36' on it. He assumed that meant that someone had just done that many loops elsewhere and he had to beat it. He kept going. By the time he finished, he was dizzy and sick, but he had a new record – forty-six consecutive outside loops. He had his headlines and now he hoped to get his foot in the door in Hollywood.

The Motion Picture Pilots' Association (MPPA) was a closed shop at the time and had a monopoly on movie flying. Paul planned to change all that; he wanted to give the studios what they wanted at a fair price. He wanted to form his own Hollywood air force. But first, he needed money. He was hopping rides at an air show in Fresno to make some extra money. His fourth passenger, however, was a man who weighed 275 pounds and could barely fit into the plane. During the ride, a snap roll went terribly wrong due to the altered centre of gravity, and the plane entered a deadly flat spin. Up until then, no person had ever recovered from a flat spin and lived to tell about it. Mantz tried everything and finally got it out of the spin.

Shortly after that, he was back at March Field teaching his spin recovery to his old instructors in the Army Air Corps. It was a sweet return for him. He befriended 'Pancho' Barnes and Roscoe Turner in his quest to become a movie pilot, but he couldn't get past the casting offices – nobody would hire him without an MPPA card, which at that time cost $100. Finally, he heard of a climactic stunt that nobody else would attempt for the film *The Galloping Ghost*, which involved flying through a canyon and just missing a prominent sycamore tree with a man on his top wing. On the day of filming, he barely made it past the tree, but once back on the ground, he was 'officially' made a movie pilot. His next big assignment was for the Howard Hughes film *Air Mail*, which involved Mantz flying a Curtis-Wright CW-16K through the hangar at Bishop airport during very turbulent conditions, with only a few feet to spare on either wingtip. Word quickly got around after he completed that flight, and he became known to be a pilot who could pull off the jobs that no other pilot would try. He was on his way. Mantz took most of the lucrative work away from the top dog of the time, Frank Clarke, who eventually went to work for Mantz.[124]

The calls now began coming in. Some were from young women, wanting to take lessons from the dashing stunt pilot. One student was a girl named Myrtle 'Red' Harvey, whom he married on 2 May 1932. But Mantz was dedicated to his career, and it didn't help that his work meant associations with glamorous women; the marriage ended in 1935. One name that would come up during divorce proceedings was that of Amelia Earhart. On the stand, Mantz testified that his relationship with Earhart, who had been a house guest of the couple on two occasions and who was married to George Putnam, was that she employed him as a technical adviser for her flights, and had bought some stock in his company.[125] Mantz remarried two years later, to Theresa 'Terry' Mae Minor, and had a son, Paul, Jr by her.

In 1933, Mantz attended the National Air Races when they were brought to Mines Field, Los Angeles, by Cliff Henderson. Some 48,000 spectators watched the four days of pylon and cross-country racing, sky diving and aerobatics. He was very aware that many people considered Hollywood pilots not up to par with the other aviators in the event that day, but at 4 pm that afternoon, he showed them differently when he took to the sky with Howard Batt and Franke Clarke and put on a spectacular show of formation aerobatics, while trailing red, white and blue smoke from their three different types of aircraft: a Stearman, a Travel Air, and Paul's Boeing P-12. Their show finished with Clarke and Mantz making a head-to-head pass and narrowly missing each other. At the last second, they then pulled into half loops and did the same thing at the top. The crowd went crazy.

The Hollywood Trio was immediately signed to perform at the rest of the races that year by Cliff Henderson. For a brief while, Paul was also the West Coast representative for the Skywriting Corporation of America. Not only did he sell the patented chemical used to make smoke, but he also did some skywriting. Paul did a large amount of benevolent flying that most people were never aware of. He took particular pleasure in flying doctors to critically ill patients or vice versa. One mission involved him flying a deep-sea diver who was stricken with the bends a distance of over 220 miles. He flew the entire flight at wavetop height to not worsen the diver's condition. When he landed, his plane was soaked. In 1935, Paul and Amelia Earhart raced her red Lockheed Vega in the National Air Races from Burbank to Cleveland. Before departure, he correctly predicted the finishing order of all of the contestants in the race. They finished in fifth place. In November 1936, he started the world's first advanced acrobatic flying course and hired Tex Rankin to run it. Rankin is the man who shattered Paul's record of consecutive outside loops: he did 131 of them in 131 minutes.

When not teaching, Rankin was practising almost daily for the international aerobatic competition being held in St Louis the following spring. Paul was amazed at his skill. Paul was trying to win a contract with 20th Century Fox Studios to make a picture about the contest. To get the contact, Paul had to enter the competition and asked Rankin to teach him his hardest manoeuvre. Paul had it figured out on the second attempt. When it was time for the contest, Rankin finished first, beating the former champion by thirteen points. When it was Paul's turn, he did a loop, slow roll, a bunt, an outside loop and a Cuban 8. Then he pulled out the manoeuvre that Rankin had shown him. Halfway through, the crowd cried out that his plane was on fire. He calmly finished the manoeuvre, unaware of the danger. Once finished, he dove at the ground to put out the flames and landed as a hero. Little did the judges know that the smoke was created by a smoke pot used in movie-making. Mantz later told Tex Rankin that he had only practised for half an hour!

Paul is largely known as Amelia Earhart's technical advisor. He trained her in all aspects of her flight and oversaw the design and construction of her Lockheed Electra. He was with her on the first leg of her first failed attempt. After crashing the plane on take-off, Paul had it returned to California for reconstruction. He was never totally at ease with her skill or the motives of her promoter-husband. She departed on her ill-fated flight against his wishes. He felt quite certain that he knew what happened to her, even though many theories to the contrary evolved.

Mantz was commissioned as a major during the Second World War, and eventually commanded the first motion picture unit for the army. Under his direction were some of the top stars in Hollywood, including Clarke Gable and Ronald Reagan. During his time there, Mantz was also involved in the production of hundreds of films used for morale-boosting and training that were credited by many as helping save the lives of thousands of soldiers and airmen. He even flew several missions over Europe in Boeing B-17s, winning a Bronze Battle Star for his European Theatre of Operations ribbon.[126]

Motion picture flying, charter flying, forest patrol work and air ambulance flights filled Mantz's days. His charter service was popular with the Hollywood crowd, and his legendary *Honeymoon Express* was in almost continual use by stars heading for Las Vegas marriage chapels.

Through most of 1941, Mantz's efforts went into making war films. For Warner Brothers, he flew aerial scenes for *International Squadron*, *Dive Bomber* and *Captains of the Clouds*. MGM called him to make *Stand By for Action* and *Flight Command*. Republic needed him for *Flying Tigers*, Paramount for *I Wanted Wings*, Universal for *Flying Cadets* and Fox for *A Yank in the RAF*. Pearl Harbor ended his lucrative commercial work.[127] His work on such films as *Test Pilot* (1938), *I Wanted Wings* (1941) and *Air Force* (1943) concentrated on designing intricate aerial scenes and then working with key aerial cinematographers to capture on film what the directors needed for their movies.

After the war, Mantz made the deal of a lifetime. In 1946, he paid the Reconstruction Finance Corporation $55,000 for what amounted to a whole airport full of airplanes. The airport at Stillwater, Oklahoma, was home to 75 Boeing B-17s, 228 Boeing B-24s, 10 Boeing B-25s, 22 Boeing B-26s, 8 North American P-51 Mustangs, 6 Bell P-39 Airacobras, 90 Curtiss P-40 Warhawks, 31 Republic P-47 Thunderbolts, and 30 other planes that the government had paid over $117 million for. Mantz estimated that the fuel contained in the planes alone was worth more than he paid for the lot. He was now the owner of the seventh-largest air force in the world. The only problem was that he had to get them off the field by a certain deadline. This turned out to be impossible. He settled on a dozen of the best planes and sold the rest for scrap.

Mantz turned to cross-country air racing, and developed a method of carrying fuel internally in the wings of his Mustangs, called 'wet wings'. This allowed him to carry enough fuel for the long flights from Los Angeles to Cleveland without having to worry about losing time for a fuel stop or the drag created by external drop tanks. He ended up winning the famous Bendix race three consecutive times, a feat never duplicated. On the night before his fourth attempt, he stepped aside and decided to let one of his other pilots fly his plane. He had accomplished what he had set out to. In addition to the Bendix trophy, Mantz set many inter-city speed records as well. One of his favorite aircraft was his modified B-25 (obtained in the government sale) that was used for movie work. He called this aircraft *The Smasher*.

Towards the end of his career, he did a tremendous amount of flying and directing from this aircraft. Television began to put a huge dent into his movie work. Once the Cinerama style of camera was developed, Mantz was back in business full time. He spent many months with Lowell Thomas flying *The Smasher* across almost every part of the globe, filming some of the most fascinating, picturesque scenery ever seen. The most famous of these productions were *America the Beautiful* and *The Seven Wonders of the World*. Some might recall seeing them played in the huge domed theatres at Disneyland and many fairs.

In 1961, Mantz joined forces with another of the big names in Hollywood aviation, Frank Tallman. They added Tallman's extensive aviation collection, combined their hangars at Orange County airport, and created Tallmantz Aviation, Incorporated. Tallman, sixteen years his junior, took a lead role, becoming president of the new corporation. They worked closely together to develop the billboard stunt for the United Artists's 1962 film *It's a Mad Mad Mad Mad World*; Mantz also helped film the final Cinerama production for Metro-Goldwyn-Mayer's *How the West Was Won* the same year. They had created something that Mantz had always dreamed of: The Movieland of the Air Museum opened to the public on 14 December 1963, and what made it especially impressive was that all of the aircraft in the museum were airworthy and were flown regularly.[128]

The Mantz family lived on Balboa Island, off Newport Beach, California, where Mantz had a yacht. After years of successful ventures in both air racing and movie work, he had accumulated more than $10 million in profits, and by 1965, was planning his retirement, although he continued to contribute towards various Tallmantz projects.[129]

His Hollywood connections were invaluable and still played a behind-the-scenes role even though he took on fewer and fewer actual filming roles. He didn't need to; he was unquestionably one of the most successful people in Hollywood. He had pretty much done it all. In his sixties, he signed up to work on yet another film, 20th Century Fox's *The Flight of the Phoenix*, in 1965. It starred James Stewart, Hardy Krüger and Peter Finch, and was about a large cargo plane that crashes in the Sahara Desert, and how the survivors then build another airplane out of the remaining parts and use it to fly back to civilization.[130]

The aircraft used was the Tallmantz Phoenix P-1, which was an FAA-certified one-off aircraft designed by Otto Timm, and built solely for the film. It was made up of a North American T-6 Texan engine, cowling, propeller, undercarriage wheels, cockpit controls, Beechcraft C-45 Expeditor wings, a North American L-17 Navion wheel used as the P-1's tailwheel and Tallmantz-designed and constructed fuselage, wing roots and skids.[131] Filming took place in the Buttercup Valley in southern Arizona. The temperatures were in the 140s. Tallman was supposed to fly that day, 8 July 1965, but had suffered a shattered knee during a fall at his home, so Mantz took off from the airport in Blythe.

Mantz flew the P-1 several times, learning what it could and would not do. Bobby Rose, a longtime Hollywood stuntman, was in the seat behind Mantz. The plane wasn't capable of taking off from the sand, so they concentrated on filming the shot involved doing a touch-and-go to simulate a lift-off. The first pass went well, but the director wanted a second pass for 'insurance'. As the plane touched down, the wheels struck a small sandy hump of sunbaked dirt that started to drag heavily at the undercarriage. Mantz gave the engine full throttle, and the plane broke free of the sand. It travelled about a hundred yards with Mantz pulling back on the stick. However, the bump had broken the back of the aircraft, and it split in two, tumbling over at 90mph on the desert floor, breaking up in the process. Mantz died instantly when the engine crushed him. Rose, standing behind in the rear of the makeshift cockpit, had strapped himself to a stringer. He was able to release the belt and kick free of the plane. He broke his shoulder blade but eventually flew again.[132]

More than 400 people attended Mantz's funeral at Hollywood's Forest Lawn Memorial Park. His pallbearers included the actor James Stewart, American military general and aviation pioneer James Doolittle, film director John Ford and Charles 'Chuck' Yeager, the first man to exceed the speed of sound in level flight. He left a photo of Amelia Earhart on his desk. In 2006, the International Council of Air Shows inducted Paul Mantz into its Hall of Fame, naming him the 'King of Hollywood Pilots'. He died the way he lived: flying for the cameras.[133]

A few days after Mantz's death, Tallman faced his own tragedy when doctors amputated his leg because of a massive infection that had resulted from his broken kneecap. Despite the loss of his leg and his close friend, Tallman retrained himself to fly using only one leg and returned to stunt flying. Later, he worked on such films as *The Blue Max*, *Catch 22* and *The Great Waldo Pepper*. Tallman was killed in an air crash on 15 April 1978 after failing to clear a ridge near Palm Springs, California, due to poor visibility.[134]

Frank Clarke

Known mostly for his prominent role as Leutnant von Bruen (and double for von Richthofen in combat scenes) in Howard Hughes's 1930 production *Hell's Angels*, Clarke was both a Hollywood actor and stunt pilot. He was born in California on 29 December 1898. He came into prominence when he moved to Venice, California, and learned to fly, purchasing a war-surplus Curtiss JN-4. His first exploits were as a stunt pilot, with a risky midair transfer from one aircraft to another reported in local media on 4 October 1919. Clarke was positioned on the top wing of a Curtiss Jenny, and after two misses, was able to catch the landing gear of the aircraft flown by fellow aviator Al Wilson. Newspapers heralded the feat as a 'first' of its kind.[135]

A 'born' pilot, Clarke was hopping passengers at Venice Field in 1918 on the same day he soloed. His good looks won him the lead role in the flying film serial *Eagle of the Night* (1928) at Pathé Studios. Clarke soon realized that Hollywood was eager to employ a group of pilots, who each would create elaborate aerial stunts. In a lengthy career, he was able to not only fly and double for other actors such as James Cagney but also operate camera aircraft and act as a cinematographer. Clarke was a charter member, along with Pancho Barnes, of the Associated Motion Picture Pilots.

An off-and-on rivalry with Mantz often culminated in either pilot getting a coveted job. Clarke began to extend his involvement in films by taking on more demanding assignments. Don Dwiggins in his biography on Mantz wrote: 'Clarke also insisted on writing his own scripts, calling for such suicidal stunts as landing on top of a speeding passenger train. He came closer to disaster on this one when a wheel stuck between two cars; it came free when the train rounded a curve.'[136] Clarke was also involved with such productions as *The Lost Squadron* (1932), *Ace of Aces* (1933), the 1935 serial *Tailspin Tommy in the Great Air Mystery*, *Men with Wings* (1938) and *The Flying Deuces* (1939).

On 13 June 1948, Clarke was with a pilot friend, Mark Owens, flying his Vultee BT-13 Valiant to Kernville, California, en route to visit a retired fellow Hollywood flying buddy, Frank Tomick. Clarke decided it would be amusing to drop a bag of manure on Tomick's cabin. Clarke pushed the throttle forward in what was to have been a dive-bombing run. Tomick watched in horror as the plane plunged straight down into the ground and exploded. The sack of fertilizer had jammed behind the control stick, locking it. *The San Bernardino Sun* reported on 14 June 1948, that sheriff's deputies 'investigated the crash of a converted Army training plane in which two Hollywood movie studio workers were killed. The victims were identified as Frank Clark, [*sic*], stunt pilot, and Mark Owens, both of Los Angeles.'[137]

Chapter 8

Women in Aviation

They have been called ladybirds, angels, sweethearts of the air and aviatrixes, but rarely have they just been called pilots. Technological innovations of the twentieth century opened up new careers for many, but opportunities in these fields tended to be available to males only.

The relatively young technology of aviation was no different, but a new kind of 'modern woman' dared to fly. Few can name more than a handful of women pilots of the early twentieth century, but, by 1935, there were between 700 and 800 licensed female pilots and unrecorded numbers of unlicensed others in the United States.[138]

Women often had to work hard to prove themselves as capable as men in the field. The American author, politician and public conservative figure, Clare Booth Luce, wrote, 'Because I am a woman, I must make unusual efforts to succeed. If I fail, no one will say, "She doesn't have what it takes." They will say, "Women don't have what it takes."' Pioneer aviator, Claude Grahame-White felt that women were 'not temperamentally suited to handle the controls of an airplane'.

Female pilots were most numerous during the 'Golden Age of Aviation' which took place during the interwar period roughly from 1919 to 1942. It was a time of great economic fluctuation, but it was also the beginning of great social change, especially concerning the women's movement. With the ratification of the Nineteenth Amendment in 1920, opinions about what women should and could do started to shift. Women encountered a new set of paradoxical gender roles and were caught between the 'true woman' of the domestic sphere and the 'modern woman' of the machine age. Ironically, society idealized both the traditional conception of how women ought to be and the evolving concept of the modern woman, thus prohibiting women from truly attaining either ideal without facing social consequences from some group.[139]

America's first female pilots provide examples of this dilemma women faced by being caught between a man's world and the life of domesticity. Four women especially – Neta Snook, Pancho Barnes, Amelia Earhart and Jackie Cochran – embody the triumphs and struggles women faced in overcoming the paradox as America transitioned from first-wave feminism to second-wave feminism. Women became pilots so they could experience the exhilaration of taking to the skies for adventure, civic duty, profit and challenge, but, unknowingly, they also became feminist pioneers by courageously testing the cultural gender expectations and roles of their day. By navigating this dilemma that all women faced, America's first ladies of flight ultimately advanced the women's movement and became feminist pioneers.

The public in the early twentieth century was 'air-minded', fascinated by and with a ravenous appetite for stories about the pioneers who piloted the new technology of incredible flying machines. Aviation was written about in magazines and newspapers, talked about on the radio, seen in popular films, and was always the main attraction at fairs and other events. Sport aviation records were highly publicized and were as popular in some circles as horse racing or auto racing. The public could not get enough of their adventure tales and was captivated by the idea that women could take to the skies as naturally as men.[140]

Barnstorming gave rise to sport aviation as stunt pilots began challenging themselves to break records. Sport aviation is just what the name implies: flying for sport. Pilots who flew for sport often participated in air races (sometimes called derbies) and tried to break land, speed, altitude and other kinds of records. Many women who flew as barnstormers also became sport aviators and those who flew just for the sport were often also involved in commercial aviation as flight instructors.[141]

The era of female fliers also marked the beginnings of the 'machine age' with the new technologies of the automobile and airplane gaining popularity as the modern way of living. Women faced dual forces of oppression due to the rise of this technology. On the one hand, women were shut out of technology for the same stereotypical justifications that females have always faced whenever they made an effort to gain access to the public sphere. The major argument against women participating in technology, and therefore the workplace, was that it just was not in the 'nature' of females to possess the capacity to learn the skills and knowhow needed to operate machines. In an essay written in 1929 entitled, 'Milady Takes the Air', pilot Bruce Gould summarized the cultural climate of scepticism at the time. In it, he wrote, 'women by nature are impulsive and scatter-brained', that they 'don't like to mess around with machinery', and that women were 'all right in the rear cockpit, or the upholstered cabin; anywhere, in fact, except in the pilot's seat'. Women were ridiculed and stereotyped even further when they attempted to use technology 'belonging' to men. As Amelia Earhart wrote in her book, *The Fun of It*, women 'are considered guilty of incompetence until proven otherwise'.[142]

Anita 'Neta' Snook will probably almost always be remembered for being the woman who taught Amelia Earhart to fly, but her career and life were just as interesting as other female aviation pioneers. Snook was a representative of female commercial aviators because her career consisted of being a student at a flight school, testing aircraft and other aviation technology for the British government, barnstorming, transport, aerial advertising, managing an airfield and becoming a flight instructor. In all of her occupations, Snook's experience illustrates the difficulty for women trying to gain a foothold in the blossoming aviation industry in the early years from the late 1910s to the early 1920s.[143]

For women pilots, it was quite difficult to earn the respect as professionals because of the gender stereotype that females could not comprehend technical or complicated machinery. Women have often been portrayed as technological buffoons when it came to operating things like automobiles or airplanes. This was a common perception of Americans during this time – which still lingers today.[144]

The Fashion

Fashion in the 1920s represented modernism for women who were determined to free themselves from the extravagant and restrictive styles of the Victorian era. Cotton and wool were the abundant fabrics of the time, with Rayon being introduced as a substitute for silk in stockings and some undergarments. The old method of buttoning and lacing garments was also replaced with easier fasteners. Hooks and eyes, buttons, zippers or snaps were all utilized to fasten clothing.

With the constrictive corset – the essential undergarment to make the waist thinner, being replaced by the looser-fitting chemise or camisole, trends of shorter, low-waisted dresses and revealing styles became more accessible, masculine and practical, creating the emergence of 'The New Woman'. 'Flappers' was a popular name given to women of this time because of what they wore. Bobbed hairstyles, cloche hats and the casual, haphazard fashion of a mixture of brightly coloured clothes, scarves and stockings with bold, striking Art Deco geometric designs characterized the era.

The leading fashions and trends were rolled down stockings and galoshes, long strands of pearl beads, cigarette holders, headbands and feather boas. Fashion also attracted unprecedented publicity from the movie studios that publicized pictures and photographs of their famous movie stars, such as Norma Shearer, Joan Crawford, Clara Bow, Louise Brooks, Marie Provost and Marlene Dietrich, who were idolized by millions of women who wanted to emulate them. Another fashion trend was the flat-chested, boyish *garçonne* look, and the women who wore men's clothing. The avant-garde style of knickerbockers, loose-fitting breeches gathered at the knee, were adopted as a fashion statement by women, often accompanied by a shirt and tie. Amy Johnson borrowed the knickerbockers or jodhpurs trouser fashion from men as a comfortable and practical form of dress for female aviators of the era. Amelia Earhart wore knicker pants, men's shirts, a leather flight jacket, an aviator hat and goggles.[145]

Fred Hattom, of Standard Flying Schools, published an article in *Aero Digest* in 1930:

> When a girl enrolled for a flying course, all the instructors at the school went into a huddle and lots were drawn to see who would have the task of teaching her. She usually was aggressive, a daredevil type whose sole purpose in learning to fly was for the novelty and thrill she got out of it. Stunts delighted her, and she invariably went in for them after her first solo.
>
> Today, the schools are enrolling and training the fair sex to such an extent that the lady student is no longer a novelty. Many schools have found it necessary to give up the single standard idea and give special attention and consideration to the training of women fliers. Standard Flying Schools at Los Angeles has one of the heaviest feminine enrollments in the country. The soloing of a number of

these students who showed flying ability far exceeded expectations, a complete reorganization of teaching methods was put into effect. A complete line of women's flying clothing was stocked by the Accessories Department, and special attention was given to the type of flying equipment selected so that lady students would not have to be padded with cushions to enable them to reach the rudder pedals.

In the past, it has been customary for the average school to use a standard make open biplane with dual controls that were not designed for instruction purposes. The majority of these planes used for training were practically out of the question for women students. The older deficiencies have been corrected in the modern training planes and the new designs are built for both male and female training. When sitting on a parachute, the student of short stature can easily reach all the controls and still be in a natural position.

Since the Department of Commerce rating came into effect, schools have been more careful in the acceptance of students because of the requirements of the percentage who must finish and graduate. Before this requirement, it was found that approximately 50 percent of the girl students dropped out within the first six hours. Those who discontinued the course were faddists, whereas the remaining fifty percent were intensely serious and completed their training.

Not every instructor can teach women to fly. The 'hells' and 'damns' of an instructor's vocabulary must be eliminated entirely in the training of ladies. The instructor must make his corrections and explanations in a soft manner. There is no decided difference between the learning ability of the blonds or brunettes. It is found that the athletic type girl makes the better flier and learns faster than the domestic type. They require constant explanation and repetition of actual flight maneuvers and are a little slow to think quickly in a tight pinch. The 'moneyed' young ladies are inclined to slide through their course with the least effort possible, as their objective is learning solely for the pleasure and exhilaration of flying. Those who work for their money and take up flying are more serious to get all that the course offers.

Out of 1,500 students to complete training at Standard, one of the best was Ulela Francis Snook, wife of the Army round-the-world flier Henry Herbert Ogden. She had been in a plane only once before enrollment, and after six hours she was ready to solo, but because of the twelve-hour dual rule at Standard, she continued her training. Of the 1929 group of students, Elizabeth Kelly showed a remarkable sense of direction, and never at any time was she in doubt as to her whereabouts while in the upper realms. Vera Dawn Walker determined to equal the ability of good stunt pilots. The gyrations of her plane and the smoothness with which she handled the ship always received the plaudits of her instructors. It is believed that during the coming year, schools that consider women students more seriously will experience greater enrollment as well as a larger volume of ship sales. It is time to adopt the proved policy of the automobile dealer – Cater to the woman.[146]

Katherine Stinson

Katherine Stinson was born in Fort Payne, Alabama, on 14 February 1891, twelve years before the Wright brothers made their first successful flight. She was raised in Mississippi and became interested in flying in 1911 when she participated in a balloon ascension. She had planned to study music in Europe so that she could be a piano teacher, and to earn enough money for her trip, she decided to become a stunt pilot. After convincing her parents of her intentions, she asked Max Lilgenstrand (Max Lillie) of Chicago to instruct her. Lillie looked at the petite young woman and promptly rejected her because of her sex and diminutive size (5 feet 5 inches and weighing 101lb). Flying was a dangerous pursuit in 1912, and many would-be pilots were killed, but this didn't deter Stinson. She constantly had to prove herself and eventually persuaded Lillie to take her up in one of his planes, and after a mere four hours of instruction, she was flying alone. Lillie then agreed to teach her stunt flying, and Stinson's career in aviation was underway. On 12 July 1912, she obtained her licence (No. 148) from the Aero Club of America, becoming only the fourth American woman to do so.[147]

She qualified as a pilot in a Wright Model B pusher, and from the beginning, she earned a reputation for her fussiness about aircraft maintenance. She blamed the death of her Swedish-born instructor, Max Lillie, on inattention to maintenance. Lillie, who was the holder of the very first Expert Aviator's Certificate, was killed on 15 September 1913 in Galesburg, Illinois, when a wing collapsed on his aircraft as he was making a turn. Mrs Lillie fainted in the grandstand when she saw her husband fall. He was crushed by the engine, which landed on his head and chest, and died shortly after spectators reached him.[148]

As 'The Flying Schoolgirl', Stinson toured the country as an exhibition pilot, thrilling thousands of viewers with her stunts at county and state fairs, and being paid as much as $500 for an appearance. She quickly became a pioneer of the skies, racking up many 'firsts' – the first precision flyer, the first to do preflight inspections, the first to fly solo at night, and the first pilot to perform skywriting, broke her competitor Ruth Law's distance record, and tirelessly promoted aviation around the world. Before long she not only relinquished her plans to study music but also inspired her family to become involved in aviation. In 1913, Katherine and her mother, Emma, founded the Stinson Aviation Company in Hot Springs, Arkansas, the family's home at the time. She gained a reputation for meticulous attention to the care of her machines, and sought out and was approached by the best mechanics at aerodromes for overhaul and repair.

Stinson became the first woman pilot to fly airmail, but after an unsuccessful attempt to establish an airmail route in Texas, she and her family moved to San Antonio, where she and her sister Marjorie began giving flying instruction at her family's aviation school in Texas. Its first students were from Canada and the U.S. 1st Aero Squadron. Exhibition work kept Katherine on the road, while Marjorie, and later, Eddie, Katherine's younger brother, became instructors. Eddie doubled as a mechanic joining Richard Hand, Dan Kiser and later, Robert F. Shank. Jack helped his mother, Emma, who he once described as the 'mainspring' of the school business.

Stinson, in the meantime, continued to make several record endurance flights. She was also the first pilot ever to fly at night, undertaking night skywriting when she flew over Los Angeles in 1915, using flares to spell 'CAL'. She flew a Curtiss JN-4D Jenny for fundraising tours for the Red Cross during the First World War and was inducted into the U.S. Aviation Reserve Corps, as its only woman, in 1915.

When Lincoln Beachey, the famed exhibition pilot, was killed on 14 March 1915, Stinson bought the wreckage of his plane to get the engine – an 80hp Gnome rotary – for a specially commissioned Partridge & Keller airplane she was having built (and selling her Wright B to pay for). With her new airplane, she became the first woman to perform a loop. Stinson later added to that by inventing a manoeuvre of her own – the 'Dippy Twist Loop' (a loop with a snap roll at the top).[149]

In 1916, with the war in Europe raging, the Royal Canadian Flying Corps began sending their cadets to the Stinson School for training. Stinson became known as 'The Flying Schoolmarm' and her students as 'The Texas Escadrille'. The school closed at the end of the war in 1918, and Stinson became a draftsman with the Aeronautical Division of the U.S. Navy.

In 1917, Stinson broke Ruth Law's non-stop flight record by flying the 606 miles between San Diego and San Francisco. A major event in Stinson's aviation career was an exhibition tour of Japan and China in 1916/17 (becoming the first woman to do so). Mechanic Frank Champion (and Emma) travelled with her among crates of aircraft, parts, equipment, maintenance tools and gifts. She flew her Partridge-Keller and a spare Laird biplane. Tens of thousands of spectators admired her and fellow aviators' skills with the airplanes.

While at the Edmonton Fair at Calgary in 1918, Stinson was appointed an official mail carrier and handed a sack of first-class mail. The mail had been stamped 'Airplane Mail Service, 9 July 1918, Calgary, Alberta' for the occasion. A huge crowd gathered to see her take off aboard a Curtiss Stinson Special, heading from Calgary to Edmonton, complete with mail, but seven miles north of Calgary, her airplane developed mechanical problems, and she had to land for repairs. She returned to Calgary where she started again, following the old Calgary and Edmonton Railway line. Stinson flew over the Edmonton Exhibition grounds at about eight o'clock, landing in front of the grandstand on the infield. This was the first official airmail flight in Western Canada, second in Canada only to a Montreal–Toronto run completed two weeks earlier by Captain Brian Peck. The achievements of this young American pilot were considerable. At a time when women were not considered 'scientific' enough to understand how to drive a car, Katherine Stinson was flying an airplane solo. Her skill and determination proved that flying was not reserved for the male sex.[150]

Bessie Coleman

Long Island's black community turned out nearly 1,000-strong for the big air show at Curtiss Field in Mineola on 3 September 1922. The cause of all the excitement was Bessie Coleman, making her first flight in America since her return from France, where she had become the first African-American woman, and also the first Native American, to hold a pilot licence in the world.[151] Very few American women of any race had pilot's licences by 1918, but those who did were often white and rich. Coleman, then 29 years old, was rejected by American aviation schools because she was black and a woman. Undeterred, she learned French and moved to Paris, and earned her licence from the Fédération Aéronautique Internationale on 15 June 1921.

Upon her return to the U.S., she still faced discrimination but found work barnstorming where, as a stunt pilot she dazzled crowds as she parachuted from planes and performed aerial tricks. She primarily flew Curtiss JN-4 Jenny biplanes and other aircraft which had been army surplus aircraft left over from the war. She made her first appearance in an American air show on 3 September 1922, at an event honouring veterans of the all-black 369th Infantry Regiment of the First World War. Held at Curtiss Field on Long Island near New York City and sponsored by her friend Abbott and the *Chicago Defender* newspaper, the show billed Coleman as 'the world's greatest woman flier'[152] and featured aerial displays by eight other American ace pilots, and a jump by black parachutist Hubert 'The Black Eagle' Julian.[153]

Coleman quickly became a media sensation and was popularly known as 'Queen Bess' and 'Brave Bessie',[154] soon becoming a high-profile pilot in notoriously dangerous air shows in the United States. Coleman quickly realized that to make a living as a civilian aviator she would have to become a barnstorming stunt flier, performing dangerous tricks for paying audiences. But, to succeed in this highly competitive arena, she would need advanced lessons and a more extensive repertoire. Returning to Chicago, Coleman could not find anyone willing to teach her, so in February 1922, she sailed again for Europe.[155] Six weeks later, she returned to Chicago to deliver a stunning demonstration of daredevil manoeuvres that included figure eights, loops and near-ground dips to a large and enthusiastic crowd at the Checkerboard Airdrome – now the grounds of Hines Veterans' Administration Medical Centre, Illinois, and near Cook County Forest Preserve.[156]

She quickly gained a reputation as a skilled and daring pilot who would stop at nothing to complete a difficult stunt. In Los Angeles, she broke a leg and three ribs when her plane stalled and crashed on 22 February 1923.[157] Despite the setback, Coleman became a highly popular draw for the next five years. Invited to important events and often interviewed by newspapers, she was admired by both blacks and whites. She had hoped to start a school for African-American fliers, but about ten minutes into a practice flight with another pilot, William Wills, in Jacksonville, Florida, in 1926, the plane unexpectedly went into a dive and then a spin at 3,000 feet above the ground. At 2,000 feet (610 metres), Coleman – she had not fastened her seat belt because she planned to make a parachute jump the next day, and wanted to be able to look over the cockpit sill to examine the Brendan – was thrown from the aircraft. She was killed instantly when she hit the ground. She was 34 years old. Wills was unable to regain control of the plane and died upon impact when it exploded and burst into flames. Although the wreckage of the plane was badly burned, it was later discovered that a wrench used to service the engine had jammed the controls. While there was little mention in most media, news of her death was widely carried in the African-American press, and 10,000 mourners attended her ceremonies in Chicago.[158]

Lillian Boyer

From late 1921 to late 1928, Lillian Boyer, American aerial stunt performer, dazzled huge crowds at fairs in twenty-two states as she took to the air in a Curtiss Jenny biplane piloted by the well-known flier William S. Brock, and risked her neck in ways marvelling spectators had never seen. She was the first woman to transfer from a speeding automobile to an airplane, and her stunts included hanging by one hand from the skid under a wingtip, balancing on her head, standing with her feet under a strap while Brock looped the flying machine, doing stunts on a ladder and making parachute drops. Her most dangerous stunt was called 'The Breakaway', although she always maintained that she was never afraid. She would leave the cockpit but take a thin cable with her and attach it to one of the struts. A mouthpiece was on the cable, and Brock could reel in the cable from his cockpit. But the spectators, watching from 3,000 feet below, did not know that.

The *Los Angeles Times* of 19 February 1989 – the month that Boyer passed away at the age of 89 – printed parts of her scrapbook:

> After I'd do a few things on the tip of the lower wing, I'd put the mouthpiece in and climb over the wing to the skid, do one thing and another and then hang there a minute and let go. The 'Ahs' and 'Ohs' would start. They thought I was falling. Then, the cable would go taut and I'd hang here under the plane, do a spread eagle and other tricks. As long as my weight was on the cable, there was no way I could open my mouth. Then, Mr Brock would lower the ladder and I'd grab it, let go of the mouthpiece, and do a few more tricks on the way up.
>
> Despite the show being called Lillian Boyer's Flying Circus, she had a contract with Mr Brock. They would get $1,000 to $1,200 a day, and always tried to insist on three days at a fair (sometimes they would get a week), but all Boyer wanted was $100 a day. Brock got the remainder and paid all my expenses, the mechanic, and took care of the plane. A hundred dollars a day clear was big money.

'Pancho' Barnes

Florence Lowe 'Pancho' Barnes was the granddaughter of Thaddeus Sobieski Constantine Lowe who had been a 'Civil War hero, pioneering balloonist, renowned inventor, promoter, and showman'. A privileged child with an odd lifestyle, Barnes once performed ballet with Anna Pavlova and often rode horses with her neighbour George Patton. Few outside aviation circles of the day knew about this woman who was one of the most vibrant and outrageous personalities of the early twentieth century.[159]

Barnes, who had spent four months abroad in Mexico, got caught up with revolutionaries, but managed to escape the attention of authorities by disguising herself as a man and began to use the nickname 'Pancho'. She returned to San Marino, California, with an inheritance bequeathed to her on her parents' death. In 1928, while driving her cousin Dean Banks to flying lessons, she decided to learn to fly and convinced her cousin's flight instructor, Ben Caitlin, a First World War veteran, of her desire that same day. She soloed after six hours of formal instruction.[160] Barnes brushed aside any thoughts of being manipulated – she was always looking for the next adventure, and just wanted to fly and be paid for it.

Barnes had her own barnstorming show called the 'Pancho Barnes Flying Mystery Circus of the Air' and became so skilled in flying acrobatics that Lockheed, one of the most celebrated aircraft manufacturing companies of the day, asked her to test fly its newest aircraft. They specifically wanted a good female pilot to test their planes, reasoning that their aircraft would be more marketable if potential buyers could see how 'easy' a woman could fly the planes without difficulty or danger.[161]

In 1925, Pancho traded in an apartment building in Los Angeles for an eighty-acre alfalfa ranch – the Rancho Oro Verde in the dry lake desert not far from Muroc Army Air Base, and by 1938, it was open to Pancho's friends, movie stars and fellow pilots. Two years later, it had been expanded to 380 acres and had a thriving dairy, cattle and hog business. There was also a bar and café, which she named the 'Happy Bottom Riding Club' (also known as 'Rancho Oro Verde Fly-Inn Dude Ranch'). As the proprietor, Barnes would later offer a free steak dinner to pilots when they personally broke the sound barrier for the first time.[162] (It started when Chuck Yeager broke the sound barrier in the Bell X-1 on 14 October 1947.) Eventually, the ranch also included a hospitality business with an all-female staff and it became a destination of choice for test pilot relaxation.[163]

A hangar was also being built at her 'airport' to complement the start of her civilian pilot's training course. Civilian visitors and military men alike flew into the strip to stay; during the height of the club's success, there were over 9,000 members worldwide. It was not unusual to find heads of state, high-ranking military men, actors, famous writers and artists at her bar and restaurant. Relations grew sour in 1952 after a change of command at Muroc when it became Edwards Air Force Base, the main reason being the increase in flights out of Edwards, along with an increase in flights at the Pancho's club landing strip.[164]

Barnes began her flying career in the spring of 1928 at the Puff Derby and won the eighty-mile contest by completing the race twenty-four minutes ahead of the other well-known entrants. Despite a crash in the 1929 Women's Air Derby, she returned in 1930 and won the Tom Thumb race from Los Angeles to Santa Paula on 9 August 1930, and later that month, competed in the Women's Air Derby. She set a Los Angeles–Sacramento round trip speed record on 1 March 1931, for which the Governor of California presented her with a trophy that noted that she was considered 'America's fastest woman flyer'.

In 1929, Barnes made her Hollywood debut by stunt flying in Howard Hughes film *Hell's Angels*, (which was Jean Harlow's breakout role, and cost more than $4,000,000 to produce, making it the most expensive film of its time) and through the connections Barnes made during the making of that movie, gained more jobs at Hollywood, working on other films such as *The Aviator*, *Young Eagles*, *Air Mail Pilot*, *The Lost Squadron*, *The Flying Fleet*, *The Dawn Patrol* and *The Flying Fool*. Despite a crash in the 1929 Women's Air Derby, she returned in 1930 under the sponsorship of the Union Oil Company to win the race – and broke Amelia Earhart's women's world speed record on 4 August, with a speed of 196.19mph, flying a Travel Air 'Type R' Mystery Ship.[165]

The 'Type R' Mystery Ships were a series of wire-braced, low-wing racing planes built by the Travel Air Company. Five 'Type R's were built in complete secrecy (the builders even going so far as painting the windows on the factory to keep the curious press from getting a look at it), from which they got their name, and made their appearance at the 1929 Cleveland Air Races.

Besides being an admirer and friend of Barnes, the new base commander, General Albert Boyd, would berate her if her clientele came too close to military airspace and flight paths. Subsequently, the air force prohibited servicemen from visiting the club, destroying the vast majority of her business, leaving Barnes feeling particularly betrayed because she and the government were in the middle of negotiations regarding establishing a fair price for her business and property at the time. When the government added a suit (when allegations surfaced that the club was being used as a brothel) to appropriate the ranch, Barnes countersued for slander, harassment, unlawful acquisition of land and conspiracy. But on 13 November 1953, shortly before the lawsuit concluded, the ranch was destroyed by fire.[166]

Barnes died on 30 March 1975, and personnel from Edwards Air Force Base hold an annual barbecue on the site of 'The Happy Bottom Riding Club' in remembrance of Barnes and the ranch.[167] Visitors may still see the remains of the pool, the restaurant's foundation (including the chimney) and the barn. From the air, an outline of the airstrip is visible.[168] Barnes herself had a biography and a documentary made about her life in aviation: *Pancho Barnes* was a 1988 American made-for-television biographical film starring Valerie Bertinelli, Ted Wass, James Stephens and Cynthia Harris. The film was directed by Richard T. Heffron and premiered on CBS on 25 October 1988. *The Legend of Pancho Barnes and the Happy Bottom Riding Club* was a 2009 documentary film that chronicles the life of aviation pioneer Florence Lowe 'Pancho' Barnes. It was produced and written by Nick Spark and directed by Amanda Pope. Featuring interviews with test pilots Bob Cardenas, Bob Hoover and Chuck Yeager, astronaut Buzz Aldrin and biographers Barbara Schultz and Lauren Kessler. Narrated by Tom Skerritt, Kathy Bates is the voice of 'Pancho' Barnes.

Phoebe Jane Omlie (Fairgrave)

Phoebe Jane Fairgrave was born on 12 November 1902, in Des Moines, Iowa, and as a young girl fell in love with aviation after seeing an air show. Unhappy with secretarial work following her schooling in St Paul, Minnesota, she headed for a Minneapolis airfield, which was operated by Curtiss Northwest Flying Company, and started pestering pilots to take her aloft. Growing tired of her persistent questions, pilot Ray Miller, at the instigation of the airfield manager, took her up for a ride, intending to scare the petite teenager away. He made a few loops and a nosedive or two, hoping to make her feel sick and get her to finally leave them all alone. The plan backfired because the ride only succeeded in making the 17-year-old more determined to learn to fly.

Fairgrave used a $3,500 inheritance left to her by her grandfather to purchase a plane, a Curtiss JN-4D, and to justify the venture to her parents, she found work as a stunt performer for the Fox Moving Picture Company's popular Saturday Matinee serial *The Perils of Pauline*, which starred Pearl White, and propelled her into fame in the process. The job required her to wing-walk; her pilot during filming was Vernon Omlie, a First World War veteran and flying instructor at Curtiss Field. Omlie taught her how to fly, despite his fellow instructors thinking she was too young and diminutive (and possibly just too female) to become a pilot. It was while learning to fly her plane that Fairgrave began to consider the possibility of performing acrobatics on the wing with a seasoned pilot at the controls high in the sky, a dangerous-looking stunt then coming into vogue.

After some months spent honing her skills, she announced that she would set a world's record for women's parachute jumping. She proposed to leap from the dizzying height of 15,000 feet almost three miles above the astounded citizens of Minneapolis, a bold move in 1921 – particularly for a teenage girl.

During the time she spent practising on her record-breaking parachute jump, she also learned how to impress the press. After she informed her buddies at the flying field of her new objective, she stopped by the St Paul's *Pioneer Press*, and let them in on her plans. Their subsequent coverage of the jump and later stunts enhanced her reputation as a 'daring angel of the skies'.

Fairgrave was dressed in her riding breeches, her goggled leather helmet and her oversized basketball shoes with the extra-suction soles, and arrived shortly after 3 pm for the well-planned publicity stunt on a field outside St Paul, Minnesota, on 10 July 1921. 'Thousands lined the fence around the Curtiss Flying Field,' stated to the *Pioneer Press*. Omlie eased the large Curtiss Oriole down the gravel runway, lifted the plane's nose and eased it over the treetops. They climbed steadily, to an altitude of 15,200 feet. When they reached that height, almost three miles above the thousands of onlookers scattered over the pastures far below, Fairgrave began her show. She crawled out to the end of the right wing and strapped on the big parachute she had so carefully folded a few hours before. Then she stood up uneasily – and jumped. The 'chute opened properly, and Phoebe floated lazily downward. When she reached the ground a few minutes later, she was a world record-holder. No woman had ever before made a parachute jump from such an amazing height. The *Minneapolis Sunday Tribune* blared Fairgrave's accomplishment from its front page.

Following the jump, Fairgrave teamed up with her pilot, Omlie, for a barnstorming tour of the Midwest. They married the next year and then spent another gruelling and dangerous summer crisscrossing the country. Phoebe developed and performed the 'double parachute jump', which involved jumping from a plane, deploying a 'chute, cutting it loose, and then, after free-falling, deploying a second 'chute. They were sometimes paid as much as $2,000 to make an appearance, but never less than $500.

There was no way that the Omlies could charge admission to watch Phoebe perform her high jinks in the sky, but by the time most people had watched that slip of a girl dancing the Charleston, hanging by her teeth or changing planes in midair, hundreds of feet above the ground, the public was hooked. Most were also eager to pay handsomely for the thrill of an airplane ride, during which they could see their own homes from high in the sky.

As the barnstorming tour expanded, Omlie and Phoebe took on another pilot as a partner: Glenn Messer, an established barnstormer from Des Moines. Vernon insisted on planning and practising every stunt over and over on the ground before they performed it in the air. Theirs was one of the first teams to transfer a 'beautiful young girl' from one plane to another while both were flying a mile above the ground. Vernon found a barn in Iowa with a long runway from front to back where they could practise the stunt. They rigged a trapeze from the roof, in the middle of the runway, so that when Messer hung by his knees from it, his hands would be at the same height as Phoebe's when she stood on the seat of a buggy on the ground.

After Phoebe and Messer became comfortable with the necessary handclasps and movements required for her to transfer safely from the buggy seat to the trapeze, Vernon attached horses to the buggy and slowly approached Messer, who was hanging from the trapeze. He gradually increased the speed of the buggy until Phoebe and Messer could make the change smoothly even when the horses were at a gallop.

The first time they tried it in the air, Messer hung from the axle of the upper plane. But that brought the plane's propeller much too close to Phoebe. They solved the problem by hanging a rope ladder from the axle, which allowed Phoebe and Messer to climb into the receiving plane after the transfer.

In 1923, the Omlies were invited to open the first airport in Memphis, Tennessee, but for the daring performers, the barnstorming mystique was beginning to pale by the end of that year. What had started as glamorous fun began to look and feel very much like work, and it certainly wasn't an instant ticket to wealth, fame and adulation; it caused them some serious financial woes. On one occasion, a hotel owner in a small Illinois town impounded Phoebe's luggage during a tour while they scrounged for money to pay the bill. As they tried to figure out how to turn their act into a serious vocation, Vernon and Phoebe focused more and more on Memphis, which they believed might make a good base of operations. In 1925, the flying circus finally arrived for a brief stay in the city and then moved along to the next location – without the Omlies.

In 1927, Phoebe became the first woman in America to be granted a transport pilot's license (#199) by the Department of Commerce, and later, in 1933, became the first woman to receive an airplane mechanic's licence (#422). In 1929, the Mono Aircraft Company hired her to provide publicity by flying their planes. In the summer of 1928, she flew her 65hp Monocoupe to 25,400 feet, setting a new altitude record. That same year, she was the only woman competitor in the National Reliability Air Tour. During the race, she became the first female pilot to cross the Rockies in a light aircraft.

She entered the first Women's Air Derby which took place on 18 August 1929, flying a Monocoupe 90. She completed the 2,350-mile course, travelling from Santa Monica, California, to Cleveland, Ohio, in twenty-four hours and twelve minutes. She also set an altitude record of 24,500 feet and went on to set more records at the 1929 and 1930 National Air Races in Cleveland.[169] She went on to win the 1930 Dixie Derby and the 1931 Transcontinental Handicap Air Derby.

Phoebe was asked by Eleanor Roosevelt to help campaign for her husband in the presidential race and took to the air in support of Franklin D. Roosevelt. In 1933, the new president appointed Phoebe special advisor for air intelligence to the National Advisory Committee for Aeronautics (NASA's predecessor) where she served as a liaison between NACA and the Bureau of Air Commerce (FAA's predecessor).

When a commercial flight that Vernon had passage on crashed and killed all passengers, Phoebe quit her job at NACA and returned home to Memphis. In 1937, she co-authored Tennessee's aviation act and helped establish a system of state-supported schools for training civilian pilots. Her training programme subsequently became the model for the CAA's civilian training programme. In 1941, Phoebe returned to Washington, as a senior flying specialist for the CAA, to coordinate their aviation activities, Works Progress Administration, the National Defense Commission and the Department of Education.

She resigned from the CAA in 1952 believing that increasing government regulations were inhibiting aviation's growth. After leaving,

Omlie tried her hand a cattle ranching and running a café and hotel. She failed at both enterprises. She did some public speaking, making her last appearance in 1970. She moved to Indianapolis, where she remained until she died in 1975. She suffered from alcoholism and lung cancer.[170]

The Women's Air Derby

It was Charles Lindbergh's heroic thirty-four-hour transatlantic solo flight in May 1927 that legitimized flying as a skill, stoked public interest and attracted millions in investment in flying as a means of travel, with the fliers finding themselves elevated to a new category of 'star'. By 1929, 9,098 men and 117 women held flying licences in the United States. Very few among the latter who were trying to make a living at flying had any permanent career options open to them, despite women having made news of their feats in the air, pushing back against a patriarchal aviation culture. Harriet Quimby flew the English Channel in 1912 three years after Louis Blériot, and in 1921, former wing-walker Phoebe Jane Fairgrave Omlie broke the world parachute jump record by jumping from 15,200 feet (4,600 metres). In the same year, Iris Louise McPhetridge Thaden (Louise Thaden) flew to 20,260 feet (6,175 metres), a record for a female aviator. Many female fliers resorted to air circuses – travelling carnival-style troupes of aviators who set up for business for a few days in the remote hinterland towns to entertain crowds with wing-walking and trick flying and then moving on.

Air races became a popular spectator sport in the 1920s when civilian aviation was becoming organized and aviators were setting records and benchmarks. An All Women's Air Derby took place during the 1929 National Air Races, despite the jibes put out by the American film star and humourist Will Rogers about the event being a 'Powder Puff Derby', the name by which the race is most commonly known. The women pilots were often called 'ladybirds', 'angels' or 'sweethearts of the air'. Amelia Earhart wrote, 'We are still trying to get ourselves called just "pilots".'[171] To qualify for the race, pilots had to have had at least 100 hours of solo flight, including a minimum of twenty-five hours of cross-country flying (these were the same rules that applied to men competing in the National Air Races). The twenty competitors, eighteen of whom were from the United States were:

- Florence 'Pancho' Lowe Barnes, a pioneering aviator and a founder of the first movie stunt pilots' union, and who famously declared that 'Flying makes me feel like a sex maniac in a whorehouse with a stack of $20 bills'
- Marvel Crosson, the first female pilot to earn a commercial licence in the Territory of Alaska
- Amelia Earhart, the first female aviator to fly solo across the Atlantic Ocean, and a founder member of the Ninety-Nines organization of women pilots
- Blanche Noyes, who flew for the air mail service
- Ruth Elder, actress and known as the 'Miss America of Aviation', and a charter member of the Ninety-Nines
- Clare Mae Fahy, the wife of aeronautical record holder Herbert J. Fahy
- Edith Folz, the first female transport pilot in the state of Oregon
- Mary Haizlip, the second woman in the U.S. to qualify for a commercial pilot's licence
- Jessie Miller, an Australian aviator
- Opal Kunz, the chief organizer of the Betsy Ross Air Corps, and a charter member of the Ninety-Nines
- Mary von Mach
- Ruth Nichols, a founder member of the Ninety-Nines
- Blanche W. Noyes, who was among the first ten women to receive a transport pilot's licence
- Gladys O'Donnell
- Phoebe Jane Fairgrave Omlie, the first woman to receive an airplane mechanic's licence
- Neva Paris
- Margaret Perry
- Thea Rasche, a German aviator
- Louise Thaden, aviation record holder
- Evelyn 'Bobbi' Trout, the endurance flier who was known for night-flying
- Vera Dawn Walker.

Walter Beech's Travel Air was the airplane of choice with seven in the race. Two racers were flying enclosed cockpit jobs, Amelia Earhart in a Lockheed Vega with a Wright J5 engine and Edith Foltz in an Eaglerock with a Kinner. Amelia flew in a dress and Edith in her famous Foltzup outfit, which converted from jodhpurs to a skirt. 'Pancho' Barnes was attired in flying jodhpurs and a sporty beret, and smoking her standard black cigar.

Nineteen pilots took off on 18 August 1929 on the cross-country course that dealt with immense deserts and high mountain peaks from Santa Monica, California, with stops en route to the destination of Cleveland, Ohio, that included San Bernardino, California; Yuma, Arizona; Phoenix, Arizona; Douglas, Arizona; El Paso, Texas; Pecos, Texas; Midland, Texas; Abilene, Texas; Fort Worth, Texas; St Louis, Missouri; and Cincinnati, Ohio. At each stop, the pilots often overnighted for refuelling, repairs, and to be treated to media attention and celebrity banquets. Their navigation tools were limited to looking for landmarks, following roadmaps and flying along rail lines.

That nine-day journey made the survivors famous, signalling American women's full-fledged entry into aviation, but it did not come without tragedy. Twenty-nine-year-old Marvel Crosson died in a crash in the Gila River Valley in Arizona, apparently caused by carbon monoxide poisoning.[172] Crosson was flying a new Travel Air Speedwing Chaparral, provided by Earle Brewster, Arizona's Union Oil district manager.[173] There was a public outcry demanding the race be cancelled, but the pilots got together and decided the most fitting tribute would be to finish the derby.[174] Blanche Noyes noticed smoke seeping in from the baggage compartment, rapidly filling her plane. From little more than 3,000 feet above the wide plains of West Texas, and with no time to search for a good landing place, she brought the plane down quickly, crashing through bushes. Noyes leaped out and threw sand on the plane, scorching her fingers. After putting out the fire and repairing the damage, Noyes finished fourth, just behind Amelia Earhart in third. Louise Thaden was the winner in the heavy Class D (engines with 510–810 cubic inches or 8,400–13,300cm^3), while Phoebe Omlie won the light Class C (engines with 275–510 cubic inches or 4,510–8,360cm^3).[175]

The Ninety-Nines

The International Organization of Women Pilots, known as the 'Ninety-Nines', was formed when twenty-six licensed women pilots met at Curtiss airport in Valley Stream, Long Island, on 2 November 1929. The meeting had been called by Amelia Earhart (who would become its first president in 1931) following the Women's Air Derby. All 117 women pilots who were licensed at the time were invited, and the group is named for the ninety-nine of them who attended the meeting or expressed an interest in forming a group that would offer mutual support and advancement of women pilots.[176]

Charter members included Amelia Mary Earhart, Ruth Elder, Viola Gentry, Fay Gillis Wells, Mary Goodrich Jenson, Florence Gunderson Klingensmith, Opal Kunz, Ila Fox Loetcscher, Ruth Rowland Nichols, Phoebe Jane Fairgrave Omlie, Theodora 'Thea' Rasche, Marjorie Claire Stinson, Iris Louise McPhetridge Thaden (the first vice-president and treasurer of the Ninety-Nines) and Eleanor 'Nellie' Zabel Willhite. Other notable early members included Florence Lowe 'Pancho' Barnes, Margaret Adams, Ruth Blaney Alexander, Suzie Azar, Janet Zaph Briggs, Katherine Sui Fun Cheung, Jacqueline 'Jackie' Cochran, Betty Gillies, Nancy Hopkins Tier, Alviine-Johanna 'Elvy' Kalep, Peggy Kelman, Dorothy 'Dot' Lemon, Anésia Pinheiro Machado, Katherine Stinson, Manila Davis Talley, Evelyn 'Bobbi' Trout, Hermelinda Urvina Mayorga, Nancy-Bird Walton, Jessie E. Woods and Edna Gardner Whyte.[177]

Ninety-Nines members supported the goals of the organization by being active in numerous aviation activities, including aviation education seminars in the community; air racing, from the Powder Puff Derby, which took place during the 1929 National Air Races, to the Palms to Pines Air Races (which ran consecutively for forty years until 2009) and the Air Race Classic; and air marking by volunteering their time to paint airport names, compass rose symbols and other identifications on airports and the National Intercollegiate Flying Association (NIFA). Most regional and national NIFA competitions have '99s' on their panels of judges.[178]

In 2014, the Ninety-Nines was inducted into the International Air & Space Hall of Fame at the San Diego Air & Space Museum. As of 2018, there were 155 'Ninety-Nines' across the globe, which includes a 'virtual' chapter – the 'Ambassador Ninety-Nines' – which meets online for those too busy or mobile to be in one region for long.[179]

Timeline of Notable Women in Aviation

1784 One 4 June, Élisabeth Thible became the first woman to fly – in a hot air balloon.

1798 On 10 November, Jeanne Geneviève Garnerin (née Labrosse) was the first woman to solo in a balloon. She also became the first woman to parachute, from an altitude of 900 metres, on 10 October 1799.

1819 On 6 July, in the Tivoli Gardens, Paris, Marie Madeleine Sophie Blanchard became the first woman to lose her life while flying, when her hydrogen-filled balloon caught fire and she fell to her death.

1880 On 4 July, Mary Myers, better known as 'Carlotta, the Lady Aeronaut' was the first American woman to solo in her own lighter-than-air passenger balloon.

1896 On 14 February, Mary Anita 'Neta' Snook was born. Neta was the first woman aviator in the state of Iowa, the first woman to run her own aviation business and the first woman to run a commercial airfield.

1897 On 24 July, Amelia Mary Earhart was born. On 17 June 1928, she became the first female aviator to fly across the Atlantic. She and her navigator, Fred Noonan, disappeared over the central Pacific, near Howland Island on 2 July 1937, during an attempt to make a circumnavigational flight of the globe.

1901 On 22 July, Frances Lowe 'Pancho' Barnes was born. She was a pioneer aviator and a founder of the first movie stunt pilots' union. She raced in the Women's Air Derby in 1929, and in the following year broke Amelia Earhart's world women's speed record with a speed of 196.19mph (315.74kph).

1906 On 11 May, Jacqueline 'Jackie' Cochran was born. A prominent racing pilot, she set numerous records and was the first woman to break the sound barrier on 18 May 1953. Emma Lillian Todd was identified by *The New York Times* of 28 November 1909 as being the first woman in the world to design airplanes, which she began doing in 1906.

1908 In September, Madame Therese Peltier became the first woman to fly solo in a powered, heavy-than-air airplane (a Voisin-Delagrange I) – the flight being made at Turin, Italy.

1910	Baroness Raymonde de Laroche obtained a licence from the Aero Club of France, on 8 March, making her the first licensed female in the world. She was killed on 18 July 1919 when an experimental aircraft she co-piloted, crashed after going into a dive. On 16 September, Bessica Faith Raiche made the first accredited solo flight by a woman in the United States, when, at Hempstead Plains, New York, she took off and skimmed over the airfield a few feet off the ground.
1911	On 1 August, at the age of 36, Harriet Quimby took her pilot's test and became the first American woman to earn an Aero Club of America aviator's certificate. On 16 April 1912, she became the first woman to fly across the English Channel.
1916	Ruth Bancroft Law was the first woman to loop the loop in an airplane and was the first person to fly a plane at night. She also set a Chicago–New York air speed record.
1915	In May, Marjorie Claire Stinson became the first female airmail pilot in the United States, flying 30 miles from Seguin to San Antonio, Texas.
1921	Bessie Coleman became the first African-American woman, and also the first Native American, to hold a pilot's licence.
1922	On 5 October, Lillian Gatlin became the first woman to fly across America as a passenger, making the journey by travelling in post office airmail planes following their regular transcontinental routes.
1929	The first Women's Air Derby (Powder Puff Derby) was held in August. Louise Thaden won, Gladys O'Donnell took second place and Amelia Earhart took third place. Florence Lowe 'Pancho' Barnes became the first woman stunt pilot in the motion picture industry (in Howard Hughes' *Hell's Angels*).
1929	Amelia Earhart became the first president of the Ninety-Nines, an organization of women pilots named for its ninety-nine charter members.
1930	Anne Spencer Lindbergh (née Morrow), wife of pioneer aviator Charles Lindbergh, became the first woman to earn a first-class glider pilot's licence.
1934	Helen Richey, after winning the premier air race at the first National Air Meet for women in Dayton, Ohio, became the

first woman pilot hired by the Greensburg, Pennsylvania-based commercial airline, Central Airlines, making her first regular civil flight on 31 December.

1936 Beryl Markham (née Clutterbuck) took off from Abingdon, Oxfordshire, England, on 4 September, and became the first woman to fly across the Atlantic from east to west, and crash-landed (due to icing of the fuel tank vents) at Baleine Cove on Cape Breton Island, Nova Scotia, Canada, twenty hours later. Louise Thaden and her co-pilot Blanche Noyes won the Bendix Trophy Race, which took place on 4 September, and was the first victory of women over men in a race in which both men and women could enter. Laura Ingalls finished in second place.

1938 Hanna Reitsch was a German aviator and test pilot who became the first woman to fly a helicopter (a Focke-Achgelis Fa 61) and was the first woman to be licensed as a helicopter pilot.

1939 Willa Beatrice Brown was the first African American woman to earn a pilot's licence in the United States, and the first African American woman officer in the Civil Air Patrol. In 1940, she was appointed coordinator of the Chicago units of the Civilian Pilot Training Programme; the Coffey School of Aeronautics was selected by the U.S. Army Air Corps as a feeder school to provide black students to its pilot training programme, from which 200 students went on to join the Tuskegee Airmen.

1942 Nancy Harkness Love and Jacqueline Wilson made separate efforts to organize women flying units and training detachment, resulting in the formation of the Women Airforce Service Pilots (WASPS) in **1943**. Starting August, WASPs flew more than 60 million miles before the programme ended in December 1944, with only 38 lives lost from 1,830 volunteers and 1,074 graduates.

1964 Geraldine 'Jerrie' Mock was the first woman to pilot a plane around the world. The journey from Columbus, Ohio, in a single-engine Cessna 180 (registered N1538C) christened the *Spirit of Columbus*, began on 19 March, and ended at Columbus, Ohio, twenty-nine days later, on 17 April.

1973 Emily Howell Warner was an American airline pilot and was hired by Frontier Airlines on 29 January, when no other women were working as pilots for any of the major commercial airlines.

She became the first woman airline captain in 1976. U.S. Navy announces pilot training for women, with 24-year-old Judith Ann Neuffer being the first female candidate in the programme at Pensacola, Florida, ahead of seven other women, four of them civilians.

1974 Sally Dale Murphy was the first female to qualify as a United States aviator, graduating as the first female U.S. Army helicopter pilot on 4 June.

1977 The United States Congress passed a bill in November recognizing WASP pilots of the Second World War as military personnel, not civilians, as an acknowledgment of their service and accomplishments during the war. President Jimmy Carter signed the bill into law.

1978 The International Society of Women Airline Pilots (ISWAP) formed this year with twenty-one pioneering female airline pilots and has grown to represent women in over 90 airlines and 35 countries.

1984 Beverly Lynn Burns became the first woman to captain a Boeing 747 when, on 18 July, she commanded People Express transcontinental aircraft 604 from Newark International Airport to Los Angeles International Airport.

1994 In June, Victoria Louise 'Vicki' Van Meter was the youngest pilot (at 12 years old) to fly across the Atlantic from Augusta, Maine, to Glasgow, Scotland, in a Cessna 210 Centurion. On 21 April, Jacquelyn Susan 'Jackie' Parker became the first woman qualified to fly an F-16 combat plane, and was assigned to a Viper Squadron.

2001 Polly Vacher made a lateral solo circumnavigation of the world between January and May in her single-engine Piper PA-28 Cherokee Dakota (G-FRGN) for the charity Flying Scholarships for the Disabled, making her the first woman to fly around the world in the smallest aircraft to be flown solo around the world by a woman, via Australia and across the Pacific.[180]

Countless other daring female pilots who broke the stereotype remain anonymous and lived feminism through their actions, if not their words as well. Their triumphs and struggles as females in a male-dominated industry showcased their fearless determination in the early twentieth century. They may not all be remembered like Amelia Earhart, but without their efforts to change gender norms, many women today would not be flying and would not be living their dreams.

Chapter 9

Movies and Television

The first known wing-walking instance was back in 1911. This was before it became more 'common'. Colonel Samuel Franklin Cody built a biplane in England and took his two stepsons for a flight from Laffan's Plain. The two boys stood on the lower wing of the plane. Stunt pilots sought to impress people with their skills and tricks, either alone or in groups called 'flying circuses'. With no safety measures in place at all, the phenomenon grew rapidly, and despite a high number of performers being killed, they just kept going against the odds, creating new ideas for their stunts to beat the opposition and attract the larger paying audiences. Some did handstands while others hung from the wings by their teeth; many learned to transfer from one plane to another. It was not long before wing-walkers started to transfer not only from plane to plane in the sky but also from ground vehicles such as cars, trains and even boats, onto planes.

Wing-walking had also been used by the U.S Air Corps for midair refuelling, which allowed for more long-distance flights, and was a practical use of the wing-walk phenomenon. In August 1913, Commandant Felix locked the controls of his 80hp D.8 Nieuport-Dunne biplane over France and climbed out along the lower wing, leaving the plane to fly itself.[181]

The movie industry was never far behind and quickly turned their cameras to the skies, making full use of the air thrills that excited the audiences. The Wright brothers' first flight in the Dominguez 1909 Air Rally (as well as several others) were shot as moving pictures and shown to the public. Soon, the stars themselves took to the air, with actress Mabel Normand possibly the first celebrity aloft in the Keystone short, *A Dash Through the Clouds*, in 1914.

Stunt pilot and film actor Ormer Locklear, who had given his first public performance involving wing-walking stunts in November 1918, quickly realized the necessity of understanding planes and aerodynamics, studying angles, mathematics, engineering and mechanics to strengthen safety concerns. He would weaken areas of the plane to be involved in crashes, to ensure easier crack-ups and hopefully fewer injuries. To provide added protection, he padded and protected cockpits with iron or steel, created rescue crews to immediately pull pilots from the wreckage, and ensured that a doctor and nurse were always on standby. However, Locklear was killed alongside co-pilot Milton Elliot on set, when his plane crashed into the ground due to a lighting issue while filming *The Skywayman* in 1920. The tragic accident was kept in the film upon its release.

Richard Grace

Early films captured flying stunts by building large stands atop high hills and shooting angles that made it appear stars were aloft in the area. By the early 1920s, studios hired veteran aerialists to devise spectacular air stunts to energize moviegoers, stunts which also goosed the adrenaline of the thrill-seeking pilots. Richard 'Dick' Grace stands out as perhaps Hollywood's top daredevil sky pilot of the times, who performed flying stunts for Tom Mix's film, *Sky High*, in 1922, and other films, sometimes flying planes into buildings, diving and spinning as if in trouble. The pilot didn't focus on hitting marks but judged his distance and spots from landmarks like buildings and trees.

The *Los Angeles Times* of 22 March 1925, reported that Sunset Productions had signed Grace, 'famous stunt aviator to a long-term contract and started production on a series of sensational serial feature thrillers to be released on the independent market'. The first film in the series, *Wide Open*, featured Grace performing a change from one plane to another without a ladder, jumping upside down so that he could grasp the plane with both his hands, which he felt was less risky. Grace would hang under the wings with his legs wrapped around the landing gear before jumping into the lower plane. He performed the stunt twice, once in close-up and once for long distance. The cameraman required a second take for this shot, because of the high wind, which held up the third take. Hanging upside down for so long caused blood to rush to Grace's head, and the cutting wind shredded his clothes. He missed dropping into the plane and risked falling one and a half feet in front of the propeller, but luckily caught the carbine wire on top of the wing, which caused him to complete a full forward somersault onto the strut before the pilot helped drag him into the cockpit.

Grace inspected and reworked the 200 Spads and Fokkers, former British and German warplanes, to ensure pilots' safety for William Wellman's 1927 silent war film *Wings*, for Paramount Pictures, which starred Clara Bow. Wellman hired in actors Richard Arlen and Buddy Rogers (who had aerial combat flying experience) to enhance the authentic feel of the film by having them actually fly in the air and performing some of their own stunts or to film shots of dogfights. Second Lieutenant Clarence S. 'Bill' Irving acted as an adviser to Wellman and developed an airborne camera system that could capture close-up scenes of the actors and pilots in moments of combat. When Arlen, Rogers and other characters are shown in close-up while flying, they are indeed working the planes themselves and flying so that the German fighter planes can be seen behind them.[182]

Acclaimed for its technical prowess and realism upon release, the film became the yardstick against which future aviation films were measured, mainly because of its realistic air-combat sequences; it went on to win the first Academy Award for Best Picture at the first annual Academy of Motion Picture Arts and Sciences award ceremony in 1929,[183] the only silent film to do so. Grace successfully performed his difficult stunts swooping, diving and crashing for the film, but severely injured himself in what should have been a simple crash after turning over a plane. Grace exited the plane and posed for photos with director Wellman, before later collapsing. Doctors discovered he had broken his fifth vertebra and fractured the sixth, encasing his neck in a cast and putting him into the hospital. Doctors informed him that if he ever stunted again, crashed planes or took a blow to the head, he would die.[184]

Grace worked as the aerial coordinator for the 1928 American silent romantic war film *Lilac Time*, which starred Colleen Moore and Gary Cooper. An article in *The New York Times* on 1 July 1928, entitled, 'Metier of Plane Crashing', the film's director George Fitzmaurice described three air crashes, 'All of them were made by a young man who specializes in that sort of thing – a member, one gathers, of a particularly unusual club of queer trades.' The article reported that Grace would fly anytime and anywhere, guaranteeing to 'crash-up anywhere at all, and does so without injury to himself'.

The article went on to describe how Grace and his crew built extra padding around the cockpit, reinforced the edges with iron and steel, and then tied old mattresses and canvas over to cover the work. After Grace crashed, if the recovery team saw smoke and Fitzmaurice blew the whistle, the team would run and pull the pilot from the plane, otherwise, they would wait fifteen seconds before pulling Grace from the wreckage. After one crash, a wheel hit a rut and forced the plane on its nose; the speed before crashing shoved the motor back to about three inches from Grace's chest. Newspapers reported that this spectacular nose-dive for *Lilac Time* was filmed near El Toro, spinning the motor into the ground and back into the plane, destroying the engine and breaking one wing.

Grace worked again with Wellman for the filming of *Young Eagles*, starring Buddy Rogers and Paul Lukas, private pilots. Grace once again planned aerial stunts and performed crashes himself, including flying a biplane into the edge of Lake Sherwood on one wing, bouncing end over end, and landing upside down in the lake. Afterwards, he told *The New York Times* for a story on 1 January 1930, 'Crashing and writing are my lines and I like both too much to cut either. And it isn't so dangerous after all – that is, if you know what to do and the time to do it.'

Grace had survived over forty film crashes by the early 1930s, but gradually saw most of his wonderful work replaced by trick photography with models, the Dunning Process and other special effects.

The Dunning Process was a matte creation technique patented by the American cinematographer Frank D. Williams in 1918. Unlike previous matte techniques, the Williams process relied on the properties of film. Firstly, the actors were filmed in front of a black background – although white or blue backgrounds were used later – and that was printed on high-contrast film several times until a copy known as the holdout matte was achieved, which showed the black silhouette of the actors over a completely white background. That copy was inverted to make the cover matte, with the background black and the foreground white. Upon integrating the holdout matte and the desired background, the image was printed upon the white parts of the film while keeping the black silhouette untouched. Then, the original film was united with the new material and, using the cover matte, it was printed upon the white parts, the white silhouette, to achieve the final copy.[185]

The Famous Players-Lasky Company produced the 1919 silent film *The Grim Game*, which was directed by Irvin Willat, and starred Harry Houdini and Ann Forest. Filming took place at DeMille's Airfield No. 2, over which the aerial sequences were to feature a new stunt, where Houdini would hang by a rope from an aircraft and drop into the cockpit of an aircraft flying below. The film company advertised for a stunt double to take Houdini's place, and despite Houdini scorning the idea of using stand-in, Robert E. Kennedy, a former army air force flight instructor, applied for and received a contract for the dangerous stunt.

The midair collision in the movie was not scripted and was a real accident caught on film over the skies of Santa Monica, California. David E. Thompson was flying with Kennedy, who was doubling for Houdini, hanging from the landing gear. As the two Curtiss JN-4 Jennys lined up at 4,400 feet, a sudden gust of wind pushed Thompson's aircraft into the lower aircraft, which was flown by Christopher Pickup, and his landing gear got jammed into the top wing of the lower aircraft. As the two aircraft spun down, Thompson's aircraft flipped upside down while Al Wilson, flying the camera aircraft, followed the tangle of aircraft down.[186] Both aircraft managed to free themselves at about 200 feet and were able to land, although Thompson's aircraft was still upside down. No one was killed, and the story was rewritten to incorporate the accident. Publicity supporting its release on 25 August 1919 was geared heavily toward promoting this dramatic 'caught on film' moment, claiming it was Houdini himself dangling from the aircraft.[187]

In the wake of *The Grim Game*, and hiring Ormer Leslie 'Lock' Locklear, the foremost stunt pilot of the time, Carl Laemmle, head of Universal Pictures, planned a series of aviation features that would highlight the aerial stunts performed by Locklear, who would also be the star of the films. The film director, Jacques Jaccard, was contracted to produce *The Great Air Robbery*, a 1919 six-reel silent American drama, which starred Ormer Locklear, Allan Forrest and Ray Ripley.[188]

Locklear starred as Larry Cassidy, a flyer in the United States Postal Service, who faced a deadly foe, Chester Van Arland (Ray Ripley), the leader of the 'Death's Head Squadron', which was intent on stealing a $20,000 shipment of gold that would be on a midnight flight to Washington. Van Arland possesses the medal that airmail pilot Wallie Mason (Allan Forrest) was awarded for his war service in France, and has also kidnapped Mason's girlfriend, Beryl Caruthers (Francelia Billington). He offers to return the medal in return for inside information about the gold shipment. Cassidy is able to stymie the gang's plans, using his aircraft to chase down Van Arland and rescue Mason's girlfriend.[189]

The film was released on 30 December, and showcased the talents of stunt pilot Locklear, considered at the time as the foremost aviation stunt man in the world, and depicted pilots flying air mail, the first film to deal with the subject. Principal filming started in July at DeMille Airfield No. 1, which had been leased by Universal Studios, which also leased Locklear's own Curtiss JN-4 Jenny, mounted on a raised wooden platform at the airfield to facilitate the filming of close-ups. Stagehands moved the wings up and down to simulate the aircraft in flight. The portrayed air mail aircraft were prominently displayed with the 'CB' logo on their fuselages and rudders, while the 'Death's Head Squadron' had skull and crossbones markings.[190]

Jack Frye and many other Black Cats performed aerial scenes for the now-famous 1929 Howard Hughes movie *Hell's Angels*. However, at the time, Howard demanded many stunts that were at the limit of safety, and many of the most daring stuntmen of the day refused to do the scenes, even at generous fees. The movie segment described below is the crowning example of this end and was thought to be much too dangerous by the aviators who performed for the movie, many of whom thought it would only end in death to the actors. In the end only two men were found to perform the dramatic feat for the overzealous Hughes.

During a shoot for *Hell's Angels*, noted movie stunt man Al Wilson was piloting a 16-passenger Sikorsky S-29A. The plane was disguised for the filming to give it the appearance of a forbidding looking German Gotha-Giant bomber which (in real life) was powered by powerful twin Mercedes motors. At the plane's maximum ceiling of 7,500 feet, the script directed Wilson to deliberately force the massive plane into a steep dive over San Fernando after it was (staged) to be shot down. Al was supposed to pull out of the dive at the last minute and land the behemoth safely. The final cut would show only the dive and supposed crash. Black Cat in training Philip Jones hid in the plane and released sacks of 'lamp black' over fans which spewed the soot out to simulate smoke.

As the primitive machine careened toward the fast-approaching ground a wing started to separate and Al realized he was not able to pull the ship out of its death dive so he bailed with a parachute. In the screaming dive and enveloping soot, the 29-year-old stuntman Phil Jones didn't realize that the pilot had ejected, and found himself trapped upside down in the forward cabin where he was forced to ride the ship to its destruction and his death. Phil's mangled body was later extracted from the wreck after the ship exploded on impact in an orange grove. This scene was scheduled to be performed by Black Cat 'Fronty' Nichols, but Jones had offered to do it for less money. Nichols was replaced. Poignantly it was to be the last stunt Jones did for the film on a ship he had worked on for the last 18 months (in many shoots). The death shot was left in the movie – filmed by three different camera ships.

After the tragedy, a coroner's jury investigation found pilot Wilson negligent and determined he had 'violated the rules of the air'. An indignant public shared the jury's consensus that Wilson had safely floated 'merrily' to the earth while his passenger was trapped in a fatal dive. According to official findings, Wilson failed to warn his aircraft mechanic stuntman Phil Jones, before he deserted his ship too hastily at an elevation of 6,500 feet, which would have only been allowed if he had made sure Jones was safely out of the ship first. (Johnson maintained that he bailed at about 5,500 feet and yelled for Jones to bail.) The guidelines for abandoning a ship in peril at the time was 1,000 feet. In the panic, Johnson was thought to have not been aware the pilot had ejected at all. The investigation resulted in Wilson's membership being revoked by the Professional Pilots' Association while the United States Department of Commerce suspended his licence for three months and fined him $500. The accident haunted Wilson from then on.

During the oft-terrifying filming of *Hell's Angels*, Howard Hughes decided he wanted to fly a particular scene himself. He was never satisfied with the stunts of the pilots working for him. Members of the Black Cats had recently taught Hughes to fly at $50 a lesson (per Fronty Nichols interview). Once Hughes was sufficiently trained (but certainly not skilled for movie stunts), he took off and tried to do a stunt in the film. Unfortunately for him, this required more experience than he could muster and the flight ended in a death dive and ugly crash near Inglewood. Hughes was hospitalized with severe injuries. This was the first of several bad crashes in the life of the brash Hughes which were all the result of his carelessness (or at least his not following safety guidelines of the day). In the company of the Black Cats though, perhaps safety was just a moot point.

The last of their many memorable events was a stunt at the annual Stanford University versus University of Southern California football game at the Los Angeles Coliseum. Pilot Bon MacDougall, with Spider Matlock and Fronty, were hired to fly over the stadium and drop parachutes with footballs which were in the colours of both colleges. While Spider and Fronty climbed on to the wings and waved to the crowd releasing footballs at half-time, Bon found himself struggling with a weak engine – almost on the verge of a stall. The radiator was leaking and spraying water on the spark plugs which was making the plane misfire enough so Bon could not maintain the altitude needed to clear the bleachers. He frantically signalled Spider and Fronty to get in the plane and off the wings where their weight was hastening the plane's descent. After they dived for the fuselage, Bon was able to gain enough lift to clear the top stadium seats and 75,000 spectators by mere inches. Bon spotted an empty lot where he was able to side-swipe in and land. The public was not impressed. After the three deplaned, they left the ship marooned, and on shaky legs took a taxi back to the stadium and stayed for the rest of the game. The near-disaster was the death knell for the group. Bon, Fronty and Spider, decided their luck had run out many times over and it was time to disband with what was left of their fleeting nine lives.

Those Magnificent Men in Their Flying Machines; Or How I Flew from London to Paris in 25 Hours 11 Minutes (1965) was a period comedy. In 1910, newspaper mogul Lord Rawnsley (Robert Morley) decides to offer a large cash sum to the first pilot to successfully cross the English Channel. Aviation experts from near and far enter the race, including the underhanded Sir Percy Ware-Armitage (Terry Thomas), wild American flyer Orvil Newton (Stuart Whitman) and British ace Richard Mays (James Fox). Orvil and Richard come out as the front-runners, but both men are distracted by Rawnsley's daughter, Patricia (Sarah Miles).[191]

The Tarnished Angels (1957) was a melodrama by Douglas Sirk based on the 1935 novel *Pylon* by William Faulkner. Disillusioned First World War flying ace Roger Shumann (Robert Stack) spends his days during the Great Depression making appearances as a barnstorming pilot at rural air shows with his parachutist wife LaVerne (Dorothy Malone), worshipful son Jack (Chris Olsen), and mechanic Jiggs (Jack Carson) in tow.[192]

Ace Eli and Rodger of the Skies (1973) was a movie by Steven Spielberg, and centres on a barnstorming pilot (Cliff Robertson) and his son (Eric Shea) as they fly around the United States in the 1920s, having adventures along the way.[193]

The Great Waldo Pepper (1975) starred Robert Redford in a movie about a disaffected First World War veteran pilot who missed the opportunity to fly in combat and examines his sense of postwar dislocation in 1920s America.[194]

Nothing by Chance (1975) was an American documentary film based on a book by Richard Bach that centres on modern barnstorming around the United States in the 1970s. One of the driving forces behind the production, star Richard Bach, was a pilot in real life and recruited a group of his friends who were also pilots to recreate the era of the barnstormer, and the accidents that led to aviation regulations by the Air Commerce Act.[195]

Days of Heaven (1978) was a romantic period drama directed by Terrence Mallick, starring Richard Gere and Brooke Adams, in which a barnstorming troupe visits a farm and performs.[196]

The Gypsy Moths (1969) was an American drama directed by John Frankenheimer, starring Burt Lancaster, Deborah Kerr and Gene Hackman, based on the 1955 novel of the same name by James William Drough.[197]

The MTV show *Nitro Circus* features Travis Pastrana, Jolene Van Vugt and Erik Roner wing-walking on a biplane without 'chutes or harnesses.[198]

The Fall Guy (1981–6) was an action-adventure television series originally airing on ABC about a Hollywood stuntman (Lee Majors) who moonlights as a bounty hunter (Colt Seavers) using his skills as a stuntman to catch the bad guys. A scene in the intro shows a biplane running through a farmer's field and crashing ('barnstorming') into the side of a barn.[199]

Gladys Smith Roy

Gladys Smith (Roy) was born in Minneapolis in 1904, and attended the public schools of the city, graduating from South High School in 1921. Shortly after her graduation, she had her first airplane ride with her brother, Lieutenant Chadwick Smith, at Robbinsdale airport. On her second trip in the air, she crawled out on the wing of the plane and made a parachute jump which decided her career. From that time, she became a professional stunt performer. She was married to Arthur J. Roy and used the name of Gladys Roy in her stunt work.

The Western Vaudeville Managers' Association was Roy's booking agent, who booked her into fairs across the West. Roy also did stunt work for Lord Motor Car Company, as well as exhibition work for John P. Mills Real Estate, and various other real estate exhibitions and auctions.

She later became a wing-walker and became famous for dancing the Charleston, walking blindfolded across the wings, and playing tennis with Ivan Unger on the upper wing of an airplane in flight.[200]

Roy established an enviable record as a parachute jumper and held records for women for short-distance parachute jumping (at just 100 feet) to 16,100 feet. She was known, too, as a flying movie stunt actress. She appeared in *The Fighting Ranger* in 1925, but was thrown from a horse during the production and seriously injured. During the state fair, in 1926, Roy leaped from a speeding plane, and in the descent her parachute plunged swiftly through an air pocket 100 feet from the ground, causing her to fall heavily on her back and to dislocate her hip.

On 15 August 1927, Roy was at Watson Field, Youngstown, Mahoning County, with Miss Evelyn Wilgus, from Russells Point, who had just won Miss Ohio title, and was to participate in the Atlantic City bathing beauty contest. Roy and Miss Ohio were at the flying field for the filming of the picture *The Queen of Ohio Meets the Queen of the Air*. The movie was nearly completed when the young aviatrix started the engine of her plane, stepped down from the fuselage and unconsciously walked into the propeller. The plane was motionless on the ground at the time of the accident. Struck twice, the blade tore away her skull, Roy died in hospital shortly afterwards.[201]

Tiny Broadwick

Georgia Ann 'Tiny' Broadwick, later known as Georgia Brown, was an American pioneering parachutist and the inventor of the ripcord, and became the first woman to perform a parachute jump above 2,000 feet (610 metres). During her career, she made more than 1,100 jumps. Born Georgia Ann Thompson in 1893 on a farm in Granville County,

North Carolina, 'Tiny' – so nicknamed due to her small size [202] as she weighed only 85lb (39kg) and was a mere 5 feet tall – became an instant headliner, dressing in a ruffled dress, bloomers and bonnet, and earning the description of 'the Doll Girl'.

Tiny married at the age of 12, and a year later had a daughter. She found herself an abandoned mother two years later, in 1907, and working in a cotton mill. A farmers' strike provided a hiatus from her gruelling job, and during this time, went along with some of her friends to attended the state fair at Raleigh, where she saw the act 'The Broadwicks and their Famous French Aeronauts', which was part of the Jones Carnival. The act was used to draw the crowds and involved the ascent of a hot-air balloon. The performers went up in the balloon's basket, then climbed over the side and floated back down to earth with parachutes. After the show she talked to Charles Broadwick, the owner, and asked if she could become a part of the act and travel with the group. Broadwick could see that Tiny, with her beauty and diminutive stature, would be a great draw card and agreed to hire her. So, she joined the travelling troupe, leaving her daughter in the care of her parents.

To ease travel arrangements, she later became Broadwick's adopted daughter, although she has also been referenced as his wife (with her own family later unclear on the relationship).[203] Most states have a minimum marriage age for minors with parental consent, ranging from 12 to 17 years old.[204]

Maude Broadwick, the wife of Charles Broadwick, was an aeronaut with Riddle's Southern Carnival Company. On 8 November 1905, she was witnessed by around 1,000 spectators to cut the tether ropes of the balloon so her husband could make an ascension and subsequent parachute drop, but as the balloon quickly rose, she was seen and hanging on the ropes between the balloon and the parachute after getting caught up in the balloon's tethers. After she had reached a distance of 200–300 feet, she dropped to earth and was killed instantly as she hit the ground.

In 1906, Broadwick demonstrated an ingenious solution he had devised to protect the parachutist from such dangers. He simply folded the canopy and its suspension lines into a pack, which he then strapped to his back. What deployed the parachute was a lightweight cord called a static line. One end of this line was attached to the balloon and the other to the peak of the parachute canopy. As the jumper left the balloon, his weight would pull the static line taut and yank the parachute from the pack. The line would then snap while the canopy deployed.[205]

Tiny Broadwick began performing aerial skydives and stunts while wearing a 'life preserver', or parachute, designed by her adoptive father, making her first jump out of a hot air balloon on 28 December 1908. The skydiving family travelled around and performed at fairs, carnivals and parks.[206] While Tiny made at least two jumps at an exhibition at Chicago's Grant Park during the week of 16 September 1912,[207] she is mostly credited as being the first woman to parachute from an airplane, over Los Angeles on 21 June 1913, with aviator Glenn L. Martin as the pilot.[208] While demonstrating parachutes to the U.S. Army in 1914, the static line became entangled on the tail assembly of the aircraft on her fourth jump, so for her next jump, she cut the static line short and did not attach it to the plane. Instead, she deployed her chute manually by pulling the shortened, unattached line while in free-fall in what may have been the first planned free-fall jump from an airplane. This demonstrated that pilots could safely escape aircraft by using what was later called a ripcord.

In 1912, Tiny Broadwick married Andrew Olsen, divorced, then, in 1916, married Harry Brown, and stopped parachuting for four years. That marriage also ended in divorce and she retained the name Georgia Brown thereafter. She returned to jumping again in 1920 for two more years, finally retiring in 1922 due to problems with her ankles.[209]

Jersey Ringel

Dubbed 'The Ace of Air Acrobats', Philip Harry 'Jersey' Ringel was born in Newark, New Jersey, in 1894, and in 1917, at the age of 23, was performing all sorts of stunts on the wing of an airplane flying about a 1,000 or more feet from the ground. He was the star performer of Jersey Ringel's Air Circus, and his greatest crowd-thrilling stunt was to stand up on the upper wing of his plane without holding on while it was looping the loop. He was the only man who performed the stunt, and it is doubtful whether anyone else has ever attempted to even try it.

He appeared with the well-known British champion racing car driver Larry D. Stone many times around the country, with Stone behind the wheel of his race car, a Preston Motors' Premocar Magic Special Six Duesenberg (No. 7), circling a huge track with Ringel just 10 feet above him as they executed a passenger (most often Louis 'Bugs' McGowan) exchange via a hanging rope ladder.

Ringel was piloting a Waco biplane on 24 February 1930, carrying George Tarbell Patten, president of Southern Fliers, Inc., and Dr Lyle B. West, Patten's family physician, to the bedside of Patten's partner's wife, who had been injured in an automobile accident in Clearwater. Poor visibility caused Ringel to misjudge the landing field at Marietta, Georgia. The engine stalled, and the plane fell into a spin, going into a nose dive approximately 100 feet in the air. Dr West and Mr Patten were killed in the crash and Ringel was seriously injured, dying later on 3 March.[210]

Chapter 10

Wing-Walkers

Outlawed

In 1936, the U.S. government outlawed wing-walking below 1,500 feet (457 metres), which essentially doomed aerial stunting; audiences could no longer easily see stunts performed above that altitude. Federal regulations also required stunt people to wear parachutes, whether it was part of the act or not. And as if those changes were not enough, increased insurance premiums soon followed. Essentially, wing-walkers and stunt pilots could no longer afford to perform because of significantly greater expenses and their inability to excite audiences with stunts that appeared to have them walking the line between life and death. Although a handful of performers would continue to wing-walk into the 1950s and 1960s, it was difficult for them to capture their audience's attention the same way their predecessors had during the glory days of stunting, an era when audiences could truly suspend their certainty about whether a wing-walker was going to live or die.[211]

Flying had changed after the war, as had people's attitude towards it. Aviation was dominated by the arrival of the jet age. In civil aviation, the jet engine allowed a huge expansion of commercial air travel, while in military aviation it led to the widespread introduction of supersonic aircraft. Much of the interwar magic was lost along the way as new goals were being set, such as breaking the sound barrier, the development of quieter, faster and more comfortable airliners in which passengers could enjoy a comfortable ride at 20,000 feet or more, and the first steps being taken towards travelling into space.

There were still air shows with amazing displays of flying skills, and despite the wing-walkers being safely tethered to their Boeing Stearman biplanes, the glamour, spectacle, sounds and atmosphere were just the same as it was when young, brave Ormer Locklear came up with a stunt that was guaranteed to wow the crowds and went for dramatic 10-feet strolls along the wing of his warplane in 1918.

Revival

A few wing-walking teams operated in America in the 1970s, with stuntmen and women having restrictions that included being attached to the upper wing centre section. In 1987, barnstormer Vic Norman, who had founded AeroSuperBatics Limited in 1982,[212] brought an American-style barnstorming solo Stearman wing-walking act to the European air show public, sponsored by Yugo Cars. Soon after, he received sponsorship from Cadbury and became the Crunchie Flying Circus. This lasted for almost a decade, during which time a home base was set up at RAF Rendcomb, Gloucestershire. In 1999, the team got fresh sponsorship from St Ivel and became the Utterly Butterly Barnstormers, followed by the French skincare company Guinot from 2007–9, and then Breitling from 2010–17. In recent years, their four Stearman PT-17s have been flying as the unbranded AeroSuperBatics Wingwalkers.

World Airshow News announced on 11 June 2018, that Greg Shelton was the 2018 recipient of one of the most prestigious awards in the air show industry: the Bill Barber Award for Showmanship. Shelton had started flying lessons in 1982 using a Piper J-3 Cub and then a Starduster to fly aerobatics. Less than a year later, he bought a T-6 Texan project, and spent the next four and a half years restoring it to flying condition, and then started flying it at air shows in 1990. As the years passed, Shelton also performed his shows in a Yak-52 and then a Yak-55M. In 2003, he sold the Yak and bought a 1943 ex-military training aircraft – a 450hp Boeing 'Super' Stearman (N4442N) (painted in patriotic red, white and blue) with the view to starting a wing-walking act.

Ashley Battles, from Augusta, Georgia, started flying at the age of 16, and wing-walking from the age of 20. She has been a pilot since 2000 and has so far obtained her commercial certificate, multi-engine, instrument and several type ratings.[213] She decided to get out of the cockpit and into the sky when she heard that Greg Shelton was looking for a wing-walker at that time. Battles had never wing-walked and Shelton had never flown a wing-walker, but they made it through their 'baptism by air'. Battles performed her routine while (uniquely) wearing a Wonder Woman costume. She retired in 2013 after ten years on Greg's wing, and currently holds the world record for remaining on the wings of a plane for a staggering four hours and two minutes. Shelton provided the wing-walking entertainment at the 52nd MCAS Yuma Airshow & Open House, on 15 March 2014, with Samantha Albrecht on the wing for the first time. After Albrecht's deployment – she is currently one of three performers with Third Strike Wingwalking, home of the highly sought 'Double Barrel' dual wing-walking act – Greg enlisted his wife, Ashley, as a wing-walker from the beginning of 2015. Equal part mentor and hero, he has been Ashley's flying partner ever since. From 2016, they offered a unique night wing-walking performance in addition to their traditional daytime show, during which Ashley wears a special lighted costume that allows her to be seen atop Greg's wing as she waves to the crowd during their fully aerobatic night air show.

Safety First

Formed in 1957 at Croydon before moving to Redhill, Surrey, the Tiger Club brought the prewar sense of fun back into civilian flying. Lewis 'Benjy' Benjamin came up with the idea of introducing a wing-walking act. Tiger Moth (G-ARAZ) was then modified, although the CAA was not keen, and tests with a mannequin followed. Benjy himself went aloft as the first live wing-walker on 4 March 1962. He stood against a frame fitted to the centre of the top wing and secured with two harnesses while the Tiger Moth aircraft which, with its 130hp engine, cruised at 70mph. Too slow to loop the loop with a man on top, the man in the rig stayed upright and quite motionless throughout the flight apart from arm semaphores.

In more recent times, the improved rig designed and manufactured for wing-walkers had to undergo complete stress analysis, as well as requiring full approval from the CAA in the UK of the materials, construction and interface with a Boeing Stearman aircraft. The wing-walker or wing-rider is held securely in place by a five-point safety harness with locking pins to prevent accidental release. It has now been accepted as a major modification for a Boeing Stearman aircraft.

Emiliano Del Buono, CEO of 46 Aviation SA, which he established in 2009, displays and operates Warbirds in the Swiss town of Sion. He also owns and pilots a 1943 Boeing-Stearman PT-13D Kaydet (N450D), and with his English-born wife, Danielle, who has over 1,000 wing-walks to her credit, recreates the nostalgia and romantic spirit of the 1920s barnstorming days.

The aircraft, which is fitted with a Pratt & Whitney R-985 engine to replace its original 220hp Lycoming R-680, has been specifically modified for wing-walking duties to gain its legal certification. The modifications include two additional ailerons, which allow for a better rolling rate and more agility; with Danielle's weight and air resistance on one side or the other of the aircraft, the extra control surface is very useful to counteract the efforts. A cable is also fitted, and runs from the front cockpit and up the mast as a safety line for when Danielle climbs up to the top wing. There, she is attached to the safety lines by a system similar to the Swiss via ferrata, which consists of an attachment loop, energy-absorption system, lanyard and two carabiners. It works by connecting her harness to the steel cable running through iron rods along the via ferrata trail, which allow her to detach one to move to the next safety point while still being attached to the previous one. Anti-slip tape also covers the areas that Danielle uses to provide a secure-foot feeling as she manoeuvres for her performance. The javelin on the left wing has also been padded for additional comfort for Danielle during the rolls and loops.

Deaths

Professional gymnast and wing-walker Gordon McCollom (25), of Costa Mesa, California, the wing-walker for Joe Hughes (who had one of the most spectacular wing acts of the decade), was killed at the Reno Air Circus on 12 September 1975. McCollom was standing on the wing of the modified 'Super' Stearman PT-17 (N121R), which was flying in an inverted position, ready to grab a ribbon that was stretched across the runway, but during the very low pass, a 'freakish' downdraft pushed the Stearman down. McCollom was killed instantly when his head scraped the runway. The Stearman's rudder was ripped off before Hughes could climb again, roll upright and land the airplane.

A father and daughter, Ronald G. Shelly (61) and Karen Shelly Duggan (31), from Fauquier County, Virginia, who performed as a stunt-flying and wing-walking team, were killed during a show in Concord, New Hampshire, on 26 June 1993, when their modified Boeing Stearman PT-17 (N58212) suddenly lost altitude from around 200 feet while pulling out of a slow roll down the runway and crashed into the ground, catching fire immediately.[214]

Pilot Robert Copas and wing-walker Lisa 'Lace' Maxwell died on Sunday 1 May 1994, when their Tiger Moth biplane (VH-UNA) crashed as they entertained children terminally ill with cancer near Sydney. The airplane burst into flames on impact, killing Maxwell, who was strapped to the upper wing. The pilot sustained 100 per cent burns and later died in hospital. According to the investigation report, the engine failed soon after take-off because of a problem with the carburettor needle. The problem had already been identified on similar airplanes in other countries but had not resulted in an airworthiness directive in Australia. The pilot tried to perform a flat turn to get back to the runway by kicking the rudder. This resulted in a stall and spin which killed both occupants.[215]

In 2011, 48-year-old Todd Green fell 200 feet to his death at an air show at Selfridge Air National Guard Base, in Harrison Township, Michigan, while performing a stunt in which he was transferring from the top wing of a Boeing A75N1 Stearman (N49739) to the metal skid of a Hughes 269C helicopter (N7505B) which hovered just above him. He had made two unsuccessful attempts, but the third was fatal.[216]

That same year, Amanda Michelle Younkin-Franklin received 70 per cent burns in a plane crash during a performance in southern Texas when the engine lost power. Amanda and husband Kyle Franklin were performing a wing-walking routine on 12 March at the Air Fiesta 2011 at Brownsville-South Padre International Airport, Cameron County, Texas, when the engine of their Waco UPF-7 biplane (N30136) lost power. Amanda was able to climb off the wing and into the forward cockpit seat before the forced landing, according to the National Transportation Safety Board's preliminary report, but she died two months later, on 27 May. The pilot, her husband, Kyle, was also seriously injured, sustaining facial injuries in the incident – shoulder harnesses were not available in the rear seat, and the pilot was not wearing a helmet – but was discharged from the hospital on 28 March, and continued outpatient physical therapy.[217]

Wing-walker Jane Wicker, 44, and pilot Charlie Schwenker, 64, were killed instantly on 22 June 2013, when their 450hp Boeing IB75A Stearman (N450JW) crashed in front of thousands of horrified spectators at the Vectren Air Show, near Dayton, Ohio. No one else was hurt. The biplane was flying upside down close to the ground with Wicker strapped to the lower wing. The aircraft suddenly twisted and nose-dived, crashing to the ground. It bounced, broke apart, and was immediately engulfed by a fireball. The show was cancelled for the rest of the day, but resumed the next day, while the National Transportation Safety Board investigated the crash.[218]

On 20 October 2018, 34-year-old Canadian rapper Jonathan James 'Jon James' McMurray, from Los Angeles, California, died attempting to wing-walk while filming a music video. McMurray fell off the wing too close to the ground to deploy his backup parachute.[219]

Notes

1. James Spaight, *Aircraft in War*, London, Macmillan & Co., 1914, p. 3.
2. James Spaight, *Aircraft in War*, London, Macmillan & Co., 1914, p. 14.
3. John Terraine, *White Heat: The New Warfare 1914–18*, London, Guild Publishing, 1982
4. 'Air Aces of the First World War', www.iwm.org.uk.
5. James Spaight, *Aircraft in War*, London, Macmillan & Co., 1914, p. 3.
6. Mats Deland, Mark Klamberg & Pål Wrange, *International Humanitarian Law and Justice: Historical and Sociological Perspectives*, Routledge, 18 September 2018.
7. John Terraine, *White Heat: The New Warfare 1914–18*, London, Guild Publishing, 1982.
8. U.S. Centennial of Flight Commission, 'Aerial Reconnaissance in World War I', retrieved 6 March 2014.
9. John Terraine, *White Heat: The New Warfare 1914–18*, London, Guild Publishing, 1982, p. 31.
10. John Terraine, *White Heat: The New Warfare 1914–18*, London, Guild Publishing, 1982, p. 32.
11. John Terraine, *White Heat: The New Warfare 1914–18*, London, Guild Publishing, 1982, p. 31.
12. Terry C. Treadwell, *America's First Air War*, London, Airlife Publishing, 2000.
13. E. F. Cheesman (ed.), *Reconnaissance & Bomber Aircraft of the 1914–1918 War*, Letchworth, UK, Harleyford, 1962, p. 9.
14. www.wright.nasa.gov.
15. James E. Tobin, *To Conquer the Air: The Wright Brothers and the Great Race for Flight*, Simon and Schuster, 27 April 2004
16. The Wright Story, www.wright-brothers.org.
17. www.photojournal.jpl.nasa.gov/catalog/PIA24438
18. The Wright Story, www.wright-brothers.org.
19. 'Big Men of Finance Back the Wrights', *The New York Times*, 23 November 1909.
20. Tom D. Crouch, *Aero Club of Washington: Aviation in the Nation's Capital, 1909–1914*, p. 44.
21. Frank Wicks, *Trial by Flyer*, archived from the original on 29 June, 2011
22. The Wright Story, www.wright-brothers.org.
23. *The New York Times*, 18 September 1908, retrieved 17 October 2010.

24. The Wright Story, www.wright-brothers.org.
25. 'Aviators Blame "Mountain Sickness" for Death of Daring young Hoxsey', *The Tacoma Times*, 2 January 1902; via *Chronicling America*.
26. James Collins, *Test Pilot*, Sun Dial Press, 1 January 1935.
27. Carroll F. Gray, 'Cicero Flying Field: an article on the historic Chicago airfield', retrieved 29 December 2020.
28. 'Aviator Parmelee Plunges to Death. Caught by Treacherous Gust of Wind While Giving Exhibition Flight in Washington State', *The New York Times*, 2 June 1912, retrieved 21 July 2007. 'Philip Parmelee, the aviator, was killed here today while giving an exhibition flight from the fair grounds. Parmalee was the flying partner of Clifford Turpin, whose airship flew into the grandstand at Seattle Thursday, killing two persons and injuring fifteen.'
29. www.thosemagnificentmen.co.uk.
30. Rheims Aviation Meeting, *Flight* magazine, No. 519, 28 August 1909.
31. www.thosemagnificentmen.co.uk.
32. John Harding, *Flying's Strangest Moments: Extraordinary but True Stories from Over 1100 Years of Aviation*, Pavilion Books, 25 May 2006.
33. Peter Reesse, *The Men Who Gave Us Wings: Britain and the Aeroplane*, Pen & Sword, 2 April 2014.
34. British Civil Aviation in 1913, Royal Air Force Museum, archived 12 December 2008.
35. Iain MacFarlaine, 25 July 2005, www.findagrave.com.
36. www.thosemagnificentmen.co.uk.
37. www.theaerodrome.com.
38. *The New Daily Mail Prizes*, *Flight*, Volume 5, Issue 223, 5 April 1913, p. 393.
39. Department of Civil Aviation, 20 August 1941.
40. 'The Postal History of ICAO: The Conquest of the Channel, 1909'. www.applications.icao.int.
41. www.thosemagnificentmen.co.uk/manchester/.
42. John Harding, *Flying's Strangest Moments: Extraordinary but True Stories from Over 1,100 Years of Aviation*, Pavilion Books, 25 May 2006.
43. 'Conversion by Sight', *Flight* magazine, 28 August 1909, p. 516.
44. Henry Serrano Villard, *Contact! – The Story of the Early Aviators*, Dover Publications, 2002.
45. www.fly.historicwings.com, August 2013.
46. Thomas Van Hare, *The Circuit de l'Est*, www.historicwings.com, 8 August 2013.
47. *Rheims: The First Aviation Meeting*, www.thosemagnificentmen.co.uk.
48. www.aviation-safety.net.
49. Second Dole Plane Crashes; Pilot Dies, *San Pedro News*, 12 August 1927, retrieved 29 February 2020, *The New York Times*, 12 August 1927.
50. Freak Construction Fatal to Rogers, *Healdsburg Tribune*, United Press, 13 August 1927, retrieved 29 February 2020.

51. www.thisdayinaviation.com.
52. www.aviation-safety.net/wikibase/60096.
53. www.thisdayinaviation.com.
54. Three Planes 150 Miles Out at 2pm, *Healdsburg Tribune*, 16 August 1927, retrieved 3 March 2020.
55. *San Pedro Daily Pilot*, Vol. 14, No. 273, 18 August 1927.
56. 'Above & Beyond: Aunt Mildred', Airspacemag.com, retrieved 2 December 2016.
57. *Benton Harbor News Palladium*, 19 August 1927.
58. Howard Gutner, *Cedric Gibbons and the Art of the Golden Age of Hollywood*, Rowman & Littlefield, 17 September 2019.
59. J. R. Vernon, 'The 1920–21 Deflation: The Role of Aggregate Supply', *Economic Inquiry*, July 1991, p. 572–80.
60. Anthony Patrick O'Brien, *Depression of 1920–1921*, Garland Publishing, New York, 1997, p. 151–3.
61. Surviving the Dust Bowl, www.pbs.org.
62. Carl M. Cleveland, *'Upside-Down' Pangborn: King of the Barnstormers*, Aviation Book Company, 1978.
63. Martin Caidin, *Barnstorming: The Great Years of Stunt Flying*, Duell, Sloan and Pearce, 1965.
64. David H. Onkst, U.S. Centennial of Flight Commission, www.centennialofflight.net.
65. Carl M. Cleveland, *'Upside-Down' Pangborn: King of the Barnstormers*, Aviation Book Company, 1978.
66. *Popular Aviation*, December 1934, pp. 368, 400.
67. *Los Angeles Times*, 7 December 1931.
68. Phil Scott, The Blackbirds, www.aopa.org, 1 July 2009.
69. 'The Coloured Air Circus in 'Perry Mason was Real', *Last Daily*, 13 August 2020.
70. *Black Wings: The Life of African American Aviation Pioneer William Powell*, www.airandspace.si.edu, 2 February 2016.
71. Elizabeth Winter, *William J. Powell (1897-1942)*, 1 December 2007, www.blackpast.org.
72. The Coloured Air Circus in 'Perry Mason was Real', *Last Daily*, 13 August 2020.
73. Phil Scott, *Air Facts*, June 2012.
74. Barbara Crane, 'Pilot to Relive Historic Mail Flight', *Birmingham Post-Herald*, 24 March 1975.
75. www.bhamwiki.com/w/Glenn_Messer.
76. *Sedalia Weekly Democrat*, 15 February 1935, p. 4.
77. www.vintageairphotos.blogspot.com.
78. Airplane Rides Poster (anon) Moberly Airport, 28, 29, 30 September, and 1 October, 1935.
79. www.thehenryford.org/collections-and-research.
80. *The Southeast Missourian*, 11 February 1935, p. 3.

81. 'Tales from the Flying Circus, Part Deux', www.vintageairphotos.blogspot.com, 12 March 2013.
82. *The Grantham Journal*, 29 July 2911.
83. *Flight*, 20 March 1931, via wwwflightglobal.com.
84. 'Airisms from the Four Winds', *Flight*, 6 March 1931, via wwwflightglobal.com, retrieved 18 November 2012.
85. www.pbs.org.
86. www.charleslindbergh.com.
87. *The Atlantic Challenge: Alcock and Brown Take the Atlantic*, centuryofflight.net, retrieved 16 June 2012.
88. 'Arthur Goebel, Jr: Forgotten Golden Age Daredevil', Paige W. Christianse, *Aviation History*, March 2006, via www.historynet.com.
89. www.coloradoaviationhistoricalsociety.org.
90. Jared Ingersoll Dowell, *Lincoln Beachey and the Stunt Flying Epoch*, p. 15, 14 April 2003.
91. www.nationalaviation.org.
92. Jared Ingersoll Dowell, *Lincoln Beachey and the Stunt Flying Epoch*, p. 20, 14 April 2003.
93. Jared Ingersoll Dowell, *Lincoln Beachey and the Stunt Flying Epoch*, p. 26, 14 April 2003.
94. E. D. Weeks, *Lincoln Beachey's Last Ride*, American Aviation History Journal, p. 105, 1961.
95. Frank Marrero, *Lincoln Beachey: The Man Who Owned the Sky*, Scottwall Associates, p. 52, 28 March 1997; E. D. Weeks, *Lincoln Beachey's Last Ride*, American Aviation History Journal p. 106, 1961.
96. Arthur Mix, *My 82,000 Miles with Lincoln Beachey*, U.S. Air Services, p. 62, January 1962.
97. Alan Durkota, Thomas Darcey, Viktor Kulikov, *The Imperial Russian Air Service: Famous Pilots and Aircraft of World War I*. Flying Machines Press. pp. 201–204, 1995.
98. www.nationalaviation.org/our-enshrinees/beachey-lincoln.
99. 'Aerobatics & Spinning', www.thosemagnificentmen.co.uk.
100. Priscilla Long, 'Clyde Edward Pangborn, 1894–1958', www.historylink.org/File/7495, 12 October 2005.
101. Edward T. Heikell & Robert L. Heikell. *One Chance for Glory: First Non-stop Flight Across the Pacific*, Kindle ed., 2012.
102. 'Herndon v. Liberty', *Time*, New York City, 22 May 1933, retrieved 28 April 2008.
103. Edward T. Heikell & Robert L. Heikell. *One Chance for Glory: First Non-stop Flight Across the Pacific*, Kindle ed., 2012.
104. 'Clyde Pangborn, Wife to Kiss and Make Up', *The Milwaukee Journal*, 11 August 1940.
105. Cory Franklin, *America's State Fair Impresario: The Life and Times of Mike Barnes*, Lyons Press, 24 December 2019.

106. Rebecca Maksel, www.airspacemag.com, 7 April 2014.
107. 'Columbia's Crack-Up', www.historicmaurycounty.com.
108. David H. Onkst, www.centennialofflight.net.
109. Richard Branson, *Reach for the Skies: Ballooning, Birdmen and Blasting into Space*, Ransom House, 2011.
110. 'Barnstormers and Racers', Century of Flight, www.century-of-flight.freeola.com, retrieved 23 October 2014.
111. David H. Onkst, www.centennialofflight.net.
112. 'Barnstormers and Racers', Century of Flight, www.century-of-flight.freeola.com, retrieved 23 October 2014.
113. James H. Farmer, *Celluloid Wings: The Impact of Movies on Aviation*, Blue Ridge Summit, Pennsylvania, Tab Books Inc., 1984.
114. Stephen Pendo, *Aviation in the Cinema*, Lanham, Maryland, Scarecrow Press, p. 59, 1985.
115. 'Movie Review: The Screen', *The New York Times*, 16 February 1920, retrieved 22 October 2014.
116. Stephen Pendo, *Aviation in the Cinema*, Lanham, Maryland, Scarecrow Press, p. 6, 1985.
117. Viola Dana, 'Hazard of the Game', Hollywood interview by Kevin Brownlow, ITV, 1980.
118. Art Ronnie, *Locklear: The Man Who Walked on Wings*, Cranbury, New Jersey, A. S. Barnes & Company, 1973.
119. H. Hugh Wynne, *The Motion Picture Stunt Pilots and Hollywood's Classic Aviation Movies*. Missoula, Montana, Pictorial Histories Publishing Co., 1987.
120. Michael Paris, *From the Wright Brothers to Top Gun: Aviation, Nationalism, and Popular Cinema*, Manchester, UK, Manchester University Press, 1995.
121. Stephen Pendo, *Aviation in the Cinema*, Lanham, Maryland, Scarecrow Press, p. 6-7, 1985.
122. James H. Farmer, *Celluloid Wings: The Impact of Movies on Aviation*, Blue Ridge Summit, Pennsylvania: Tab Books Inc., 1984.
123. Gerald A. Schiller, 'Hollywood's Daredevil Pilot.' *Aviation History*, Vol. 13, no. 6, July 2003.
124. 'Paul Mantz', www.icasfoundation.org.
125. Henry M. Holden, 'Paul Mantz and the Last Flight of the Phoenix', www.airportjournals.com, 1 September 2004.
126. 'Paul Mantz', www.icasfoundation.org.
127. Henry M. Holden, 'Paul Mantz and the Last Flight of the Phoenix', www.airportjournals.com, 1 September 2004.
128. 'Paul Mantz', www.icasfoundation.org.
129. Stephen Joiner, 'Hollywood's Favorite Pilot', *Air & Space*, Volume 22, No. 5, October/November 2007.
130. 'Paul Mantz', www.icasfoundation.org.

131. Don Dwiggins, *Hollywood Pilot: The Biography of Paul Mantz*, Doubleday & Company, Inc., Garden City, New York, 1967; www.uswarplanes.net/phoenix5.html.
132. 'Paul Mantz', www.icasfoundation.org.
133. Don Holloway, *Aviation History*, May 2020.
134. 'Hollywood Stunt Pilots', www.century-of-flight.freeola.com.
135. H. Hugh Wynne, *The Motion Picture Stunt Pilots and Hollywood's Classic Aviation Movies*. Missoula, Montana, Pictorial Histories Publishing Co., 1987, p. 17.
136. Don Dwiggins, *Hollywood Pilot: The Biography of Paul Mantz*, Doubleday & Company, Inc., Garden City, New York, 1967, p. 41-42.
137. 'Two Movie Workers Die in Plane Crash' *San Bernardino Daily Sun*, San Bernardino, California, June 14, 1948, Volume LIV, Number 247, p. 1.
138. Julie Wosk, *Women and the Machine: Representations from the Spinning Wheel to the Electronic Age*, The John Hopkins University Press, 2001, p. 149.
139. Tom D. Crouch, *Wings: A History of Aviation from Kites to the Space Age*. New York, W. W. Norton & Company, 2003.
140. U.S. Centennial of Flight Commission, *Born of Dreams – Inspired by Freedom*, December 2003, www.centennialofflight.gov/index2.cfm, accessed 3 March 2008.
141. Dr John W. W. Mann, *America's First Ladies of Flight: A History of Feminism in Flying*, McIntyre Library, University of Wisconsin–Eau Claire, www.minds.wisconsin.edu, spring 1998.
142. Amelia Earhart, *The Fun of It*, Chicago, Academy Chicago Publishers, 1932, p. 10.
143. Patti Marshall, 'Neta Snook', *Aviation History 17*, January 2007, p. 21.
144. Neta Snook Southern, *I Taught Amelia to Fly*, New York, Vantage Press, 1974, p. 11.
145. www.american-historama.org.
146. Julie Wosk, *Women and the Machine: Representations from the Spinning Wheel to the Electronic Age*, The John Hopkins University Press, 2001, p. 156.
147. Debra L. Winegarten, *Katherine Stinson: The Flying Schoolgirl*, Eakin Press, 1 August 2000.
148. 'Aviator Killed at Fair', *The Evening Star*, 16 September 1913, p. 3.
149. D. Cochrane, P. Ramirez, www.airandspace.si.edu/stories/editorial/katherine-stinson-stunt-flier-record-setter.
150. Tatjana Obrazcova, www.50skyshades.com, 27 September 2015.
151. Nikki Grimes, *Talkin' About Bess, The Story of Aviator Bessie Coleman*, Franklin Watts, 1998.
152. Maria Lynn Toth, 'Daredevil of the Sky: The Bessie Coleman Story', *Los Angeles Times*, archived from the original on 5 November 2012.
153. 'Negress Pilots Airplane: Bessie Coleman Makes Three Flights for Fifteenth Infantry', *The New York Times*, 4 September 1922. p. 9.

154. 'Bessie Coleman', National Women's History Museum, retrieved 12 September 2019.
155. Doris Rich, *Queen Bess: Daredevil Aviator*, Washington D.C., Smithsonian Institution Press, 1993, pp. 37, 47, 57, 109–11, 115.
156. Ann Durkin Keating, 'Betty Coleman: Pioneer Chicago Aviator', *Encyclopedia of Chicago*, 2005, retrieved 28 February 2017.
157. 'Bessie Coleman', National Women's History Museum, retrieved 12 September 2019.
158. Daniel E. Slotnik, 'Overlooked No More: Bessie Coleman, Pioneering African-American Aviatrix', *The New York Times*, retrieved 12 December 2019.
159. 'Who is Pancho?', The Pancho Barnes Trust Estate Archive, www.panchobarnes.com, accessed 18 April 2008.
160. Karen Bush Gibson, 'Women Aviators: 26 Stories of Pioneer Flights, Daring Missions and Record-Setting Journeys', *Chicago Review Press*, 2013.
161. 'Women's Speed Mark Set: Florence Barnes Flies 196.19 Miles an Hour on Coast', *New York Times*, 5 August 1930.
162. 'Pancho', www.chuckyeager.org. retrieved 2 August 2013.
163. Karen Bush Gibson, 'Women Aviators: 26 Stories of Pioneer Flights, Daring Missions and Record-Setting Journeys', *Chicago Review Press*, 2013.
164. Alain Pelletier, *High-Flying Women: A World History of Female Pilots*. Sparkford, UK, Haynes, 2012.
165. Harold A. Skaarup, *California Warplanes*, iUniverse, Inc., Bloomington, 2012.
166. Rebecca Amber, *Edwards to Preserve Rancho Oro Verde*, www.webarchive.org, 2 December 2014.
167. William A. O'Brien, *Team Edwards celebrates Pancho Barnes Day*, 23 April 2014.
168. Laura Mowry, 'Welcome back Pancho – early test pilots handprints discovered', Edwards Air Force Base, archived from the original on 2 January 2012.
169. Kirstin Olsen, *Remember the Ladies: A Woman's Book of Days*, Main Street Press, Pittstown, New Jersey, 1988.
170. 'To Dance on Aircraft Wings', www.faa.gov.
171. Gene Nora Jessen, *The Powder Puff Derby of 1929: The First All Women's Transcontinental Air Race*, Naperville, III, Sourcebooks, 2002.
172. Gene Nora Jessen, '1929 Air Race', *99 News* magazine, 1999.
173. Julie Simpson, 'Star of the Clouds: The Story of Marvel Crosson, a Pioneer Pilot', www.coloradocountrylife.coop 31 July 2020.
174. Gene Nora Jessen, '1929 Air Race', *99 News* magazine, 1999.
175. Don Berliner, *Airplane Racing*. McFarland & Company, Inc., 2010, pp. 57–58.

176. 'Our History', Wayback Machine, archived 11 July 2016, www.ninety-nines.org.
177. 'Charter members of the Ninety-Nines', www.ninety-nines.org.
178. Ellen Nobles-Harris, 'Marking the Way', *99 News* magazine, March/April 2002, www.ninety-nines.org.
179. Linda Sprekelmeyer (ed.), *These We Honor: The International Aerospace Hall of Fame*, Donning Co. Publishers, 2006.
180. Jone Johnson Lewis, 'Women in Aviation: Timeline', www.thoughtco.com, 22 April 2019.
181. 'The Dunne's Doings', *The Aeroplane*, 4 September 1914, p. 268.
182. Tim Lusier, *Daredevils in the Air: Three of the Greats, Wilson, Locklear and Grace*, SilentsAreGolden.com, 2004, retrieved 2 February 2013.
183. 'Dorothy Wellman dies at 95', *Variety* magazine, 17 September 2009, retrieved 2 February 2013.
184. *Los Angeles Times*, 10 October 1926.
185. Graham Edwards, '"C" is for Composite', www.cineflex.com, 7 January 2014.
186. H. Hugh Wynne, *The Motion Picture Stunt Pilots and Hollywood's Classic Aviation Movies*, Missoula, Montana, Pictorial Histories Publishing Company, 1987.
187. Kenneth Silverman, *Houdini!: The Career of Ehrich Weiss*, New York, HarperPerennial, 1997.
188. Michael Paris, *From the Wright Brothers to Top Gun: Aviation, Nationalism, and Popular Cinema*. Manchester, UK, Manchester University Press, 1995.
189. 'The Great Air Robbery', www.en.wikipedia.org.
190. James H. Farmer, *Celluloid Wings: The Impact of Movies on Aviation*, Blue Ridge Summit, Pennsylvania, Tab Books Inc., 1984.
191. *Those Magnificent Men in Their Flying Machines or How I Flew from London to Paris in 25 Hours 11 Minutes* was released in 1965. BFI Film Forever, retrieved 20 October 2018.
192. *Variety Film Review*, 20 November 1957, p. 6.
193. Stephen Pendo, *Aviation in the Cinema*, Lanham, Maryland, Scarecrow Press, 1985.
194. *The Great Waldo Pepper*, Box Office Information, Box Office Mojo, retrieved 31 August 2014.
195. Stephen Pendo, *Aviation in the Cinema*, Lanham, Maryland, Scarecrow Press, 1985, p. 58.
196. *Days of Heaven*, Box Office Information, Box Office Mojo, retrieved 31 August 2014.
197. Variety Film Review, 20 June 1962.
198. www.en.wikipedia.org/wiki/Nitro_Circus.
199. Marcel Pazzin, www.hollywoodsign.org, 22 June 2017.
200. Rebecca Maksel, 'Tennis, Anyone?', *Air & Space* magazine, 29 January 2013, retrieved 26 February 2020.

201. *Star Tribune*, Minneapolis, Minnesota, 16 August 1927, p. 1.
202. Elizabeth Whitley Roberson, *Tiny Broadwick: The First Lady of Parachuting*, Gretna, Pelican Publishing Co., Inc., 2001.
203. Lisa Ritter, 'Pack Man: Charles Broadwick invented a New Way of Falling', *Air & Space* magazine, April - May 2010, retrieved 1 March 2013.
204. 'Child marriage is rare in the U.S., though this varies by state'. Pew Research Center. 1 November, 2016. Retrieved 21 February, 2017.
205. Lisa Ritter, 'Pack Man', *Air & Space* magazine, May 2010.
206. Helen Call, 'Woman – A San Diegan – Was First To Test Parachute For Government', *North Island Demonstration*, 29 October 1971.
207. Carroll Gray, 'Cicero Flying Field', www.LincolnBeachey.com, retrieved 13 May 2017.
208. Elizabeth Whitley Roberson, *Tiny Broadwick: The First Lady of Parachuting*, Pelican Publishing, 2001, p. 48; Thomas C. Parramore, *First to Fly: North Carolina & the Beginnings of Aviation*, University of North Carolina Press, 2003, p. 181.
209. Georgia "Tiny" Broadwick's Parachute', National Air & Space Museum, 12 March 2015, retrieved 21 June 2017.
210. *Aircraft Accidents*, doc. 319, Stanford University Library, 24 February 1931.
211. David H. Onkst, 'Wing Walkers', www.centennialofflight.net.
212. 'History of Wingwalking', www.aerosuperbatics.com.
213. *Jet Observer*, 24 July 2014.
214. Martin Well, *The Washington Post*, 27 June 1993.
215. www. aviation-safety.net/wikibase/407
216. *The Daily Mail*, 23 August 2011.
217. Sarah Brown, 'Wing Walker Amanda Franklin Dies', www.aopa.org.
218. Tom Dart, 22 June 2013, www.theguardian.com.
219. *The Globe & Mail*, retrieved 23 October 2018.

Glossary

AAA Contest Board was the motorsports arm of the American Automobile Association. The board sanctioned automobile races from 1904 until 1955, establishing Championship Car racing; modern-day IndyCar racing traces its roots directly to these AAA events.

American Stock Market Crash was a major American stock market crash (the Wall Street Crash) that started in September and ended in late October 1929, when share prices on the New York Stock Exchange collapsed.

Antitrust is a collection of federal and state government laws that regulate the conduct and organization of business corporations and are generally intended to promote competition for the benefit of consumers. The main statutes are the Sherman Act of 1890, the Clayton Act of 1914 and the Federal Trade Commission Act of 1914. These Acts serve three major functions. First, Section 1 of the Sherman Act prohibits price-fixing and the operation of cartels, and prohibits other collusive practices that unreasonably restrain trade. Second, Section 7 of the Clayton Act restricts the mergers and acquisitions of organizations that would likely substantially lessen competition. Third, Section 2 of the Sherman Act prohibits the abuse of monopoly power.

Army Air Service, also known as the Air Service, U.S. Air Service and before its legislative establishment in 1920, the Air Service, United States Army, was the aerial warfare service component of the United States Army between 1918 and 1926 and a forerunner of the United States Air Force.

Cradle of Aviation Museum is an aerospace museum located in Garden City, New York, on Long Island to commemorate Long Island's part in the history of aviation.

Deadstick, also called a dead-stick landing, is a type of forced landing when an aircraft loses all its propulsive power and is forced to land. The 'stick' refers to the traditional wooden propeller.

Flying Tigers was Captain Claire Lee Chennault's 1st American Volunteer Group (AVG), who fought the Japanese for seven months after the attack on Pearl Harbor in 1941.

Gosport System was a three-week intensive programme for training new Royal Flying Corps pilots designed by Major Robert Smith-Barry. Students learned first-hand how to fly in dangerous conditions, such as being able to get out of a spin, and learn to take the right action with engine failures, stalls and hazards, etc, rather than having to rely on just watching and learning from an instructor. The programme took place at Gosfield Airfield, after which the programme was named.

Kelly Act 1925. Congressman Melville Clyde Kelly introduced a resolution to permit private contracting of airmail service. This resolution, the Air Mail Act of 1925, was signed into law on 2 February 1925, prompting many companies to venture into the aviation field.

Lamp Black was traditionally produced by collecting soot from oil lamps.

Leutnant is the lowest officer rank in the armed forces of Germany (Bundeswehr), Austrian Armed Forces, and the military of Switzerland.
NAA. The National Aviation Authority (NAA) or Civil Aviation Authority (CAA) is a government statutory body in each country that maintains an aircraft register and oversees the approval and regulation of civil aviation. These include aircraft and equipment, operation of aircraft and equipment, licensing of pilots, air traffic controllers, flight dispatchers and maintenance engineers.

Parachute is a device used to slow the motion of an object through an atmosphere by creating drag (or in the case of ram-air parachutes, aerodynamic lift). Parachutes are usually made out of light, strong fabric, originally silk, but are now most commonly nylon. They are typically dome-shaped, but vary, with rectangles, inverted domes and others.

A variety of loads are attached to parachutes, including people, food, equipment, space capsules and bombs.

Prohibition was a nationwide constitutional ban in the United States on the production, importation, transportation, and sale of alcoholic beverages from 1920 to 1933.

Sesquiplane was a design of biplane in which the lower wing is significantly smaller than the upper. The word literally means 'one and a half wings'.

Waco 9 was the first of the steel-tubed fuselage aircraft design built by the Advance Aircraft Company (which became the Waco Aircraft Company c. 1929). The Model 9 was a three-seat open cockpit biplane with the ailerons on the upper wings extending outboard of the main wing surfaces.

Zephyr cloth is a sheer, lightweight cotton fabric, usually plain woven, used for dresses, blouses and shirts. It may be striped or checked. It is named after Zephyr, the Greek god of the west wind.

Bibliography

Bacon, Rev J. M., *The Dominion of the Air: The Story of Aerial Navigation*, c. 1902.
Bramson, Alan & Birch, Neville, *The Tiger Moth Story*, Cassell, 1964.
Brett, R. Dallas, *History of British Aviation 1908–1914*, Air Research Publications in association with Kristall Productions, 1988.
Caitlin Stamm, University Archivist, Saint Louis University, 3650 Lindell Blvd. St. Louis, MO 63108.
Chapman, Ted, *Cornwall Aviation Company*, Glasney Press, 1979.
Claxton, William J., *The Mastery of the Air*, Blackie & Son Ltd, second edition, 1915.
Cruddas, Colin, *Those Fabulous Flying Years*, Air-Britain (Historians) Ltd, Tonbridge, 2003.
de Havilland, Sir Geoffrey, *Sky Fever; The Autobiography of Sir Geoffrey de Havilland*, The Crowood Press Ltd, new edition, 20 July 1999.
Dealy, Jack. 'He Walked Away From 99 Crashes', *Flying* magazine, July 1951.
Dowell, Jared Ingersoll, 'Lincoln Beachey and the Stunt Flying Epoch', 14 April 2003.
Gibbs-Smith, Charles Harvard, *Aviation: An Historical Survey from its Origins to the End of World War II*, HMSO (London), 1970.
Gibbs-Smith, Charles Harvard, *The Rebirth of European Aviation, 1902–1908*, HMSO (London), 1974.
Gould, Arthur Lee, *The Flying Cathedral*, Methuen (London), 1965.
Grahame-White, Claude, *Aviation*, Carruthers Press, 2008.
Hadley, Dunstan (ed.), 'Only Seconds to Live: Pilots' Tales of the Stall and the Spin', *Airlife*, 1 July 1997.
Itai Vardi, *Auto Thrill Shows and Destruction Derbies, 1922–1965: Establishing the Cultural Logic of the Deliberate Car Crash in America*, Oxford University Press, 2011.
Jackman, William James & Russell, Thomas Herbert (via Octave Chanute), 'Flying Machine: Construction and Operation'. c. 1912.
Jarrett, Philip (ed.), *Pioneer Aircraft: Early Aviation Before 1914*, Putnam (London), 2002.
Harnisch, Larry, *Los Angeles Daily Mirror*, www.ladailymirror.com.
Loeffelbein, Bob, *Orange Coast Magazine*, May 1985.
Longyard, William Henry, 'Who's Who in Aviation History', *Airlife*, 1 April 1994.

Mace, Terry, 'A Fleeting Peace: Golden-Age Aviation in the British Empire', www.afleetingpeace.org, 2021.
Munson, Kenneth, *Pioneer Aircraft 1903–14*, Blandford Press, 1969.
Rayburn, Taylor, 'Death Diver!' *The Tennessean*, Nashville, Tennessee, 5 June 1955.
Reynolds, Randall, D., www.sedonalegendhelenfrye.com.
Staff, 'Pictures of Captain Frakes Crashing Plan Thru House', *The Lincoln Star*, 11 September 1938.
Start, Clarissa, 'An All-Around Daredevil', *St. Louis Post-Dispatch*, 23 August 1954.
'The Flight of Fearless Mabel', *Florida Times-Union*, 1999.
The San Diego Union, Wednesday, 26 November 1913.
Wilson, George T., *Aviation History*, June 2002.
www.222.opencockpit.net.
www.faa.gov.
www.thoughtco.com.
www.wright-brothers.org.

Index

Aerial Derby Race 69
Aero Club of America 6, 28, 124
Aero Club of Great Britain 25, 28
Aero Corporation of California 33
Aero Digest magazine 42
AeroSuperBatics Limited 160
Ahearn, Roy 50
Airco DH.4R 72
Airco DH.9 72
Airco DH.14a 72
Aikens, William 54
Airspeed AS.4 Ferry 79, 82
All Women's Air Derby 136
Angel, Eddie 49, 52
Angel, Jimmy 49, 52
Angel of Los Angeles 30
Ashcraft, Jack 50
Astley, Henry Jacob Delaval 62, 69
Aubrun, Emile 23–4
Avro 504K 77
Avro 534 Baby 72–5
Avro 534C 73
Avro 539 73
Avro 552 74
Avro 553 75

Baby Ruth Flying Circus 50
Baldwin Troupe 92
Banning, James Herman 54–5
Bantam 71
Barker, Henry 76, 82, 84
Barnard, Charles Douglas 75, 79, 84
Barnes, 'Pancho' 110, 117, 120, 129–30, 132, 137–41
Battles, Ashley 160
Beachey, Lincoln 23, 92–9, 109, 125
Beam, Bert Ward 102
Beaumont, André 61, 65
Bellanca J-300 101

Benjamin, Lewis 'Benjy' 161
Bendix Race 49
Berkshire Aviation Company 77
Birdling Monoplane 62, 69
Black Cats 33– 41, 49, 91, 150–2
Blériot, Louis 9–10, 12, 15, 16, 22–9, 136
Blériot Monoplane 11, 23, 61–2, 65
Boeing 80-A Clipper 59
Boulton & Paul P.9 75
Breese-Wilde 5 Monoplane 30–1
Bréguet Biplane 62
Bristol Biplane 61–2
Bristol 29 73
Bristol Type 32B Bullet 74–5
Bristol Type 77 74
British Empire Air Display Tour 76, 84
British Hospitals Air Pageant Tour 82
Broad, Hubert Stanford 74
Brock, Walter Laurence 70
Brock, Sr., Walter Stewart 'Billy' 50, 128, 129
Brooklands 11, 61, 72–5
Brooks, Bill 49
Bugs McGowan's Flying Circus 51, 157
Buhl CA-5 Air Sedan 31
Burdette airfield 33
Burns, Arthur C. 42
Butler, Alan Samuel 73–4

Caidlin, Martin 94–6
Cammell, Reginald Archibald 62, 67–8
Carr, Reginald Hugh 71
Carter, Larry L. 74–5
Cavalié, Juan Bielovucic 23
Cecil, Eugene 50
Chase, 'Bobby' 34, 41
Chamberlayne, Paul Richard Tankerville 71
Chanteloup, Pierre 12, 100

Chicago International Aviation Meet 95–6
Circuit de l'Est 23
Circuit of Britain Airplane Race 61
Civil Aeronautics Act 85
Cleveland Air Races 131
Cliff Rose Death Angels 52
Clover Field 39
Cochran, Jackie 120, 139–40
Cockburn, George 25–6, 28
Cody Biplane 61
Coker, Marie Dickerson 54
Cornwall Aviation Company 77, 82
Cotton, Frederick Sidney 72
(The) Coloured Air Circus 53–4
Courtney, Frank Thomas 73, 75
Cowdery (Cody), Samuel Franklin 61
(The) Crunchie Flying Circus 160–5
Curtiss, Glenn 6–7, 22–3, 25, 28–9, 93–5
Curtiss Oriole 133
Curtiss JN-4 'Jenny' Biplane 37–41, 47, 50, 88–9, 100, 103–8, 116, 125, 127–8, 149–50
Curtiss-Wright CW-16K 102

Daily Express 78
Dallas Spirit 31–2, 91
Dare, Jackie 42
Daughtry, Marie 55
Davis, Douglas 49
Davis, Jr., William Virginius 31, 91
Daytona Beach 51
de Haga Haig, Rollo Amyatt Wolseley 75
de Havilland 79, 82
de Lambert, Charles 15, 27
de Montalent, Oliver 62, 68
Del Buono, Emiliano 161
Deperdousin Monoplane 61
Dirigible 7, 92
Dole Derby 30
Doran, Mildred Alice 31–2
Draper, Christopher 71
Dyott, George 13

Earhart, Amelia 50, 111–12, 116, 120–2, 131, 136–41, 144
Edwards, Corinne 60

Eichwaldt, Alvin Hanford 31, 32
Elliott, Milton 'Skeets' 106
English Channel 15, 23–4, 136, 141
Erwin, William Portwood 31, 32

Fairfield Tribune 57
Fall, Joseph 'John' Stewart Temple 73
Farman, Henri 16–19, 22, 25, 27–8
Ferber, Louis Ferdinand 22, 25
(The) Five Blackbirds 49, 53
Flight magazine 76
Flight of the Phoenix 115
Flying Aces Air Circus 47
Fokker 84, 147
Foot, Ernest Leslie 74
Ford Trimotor 59
Forestier-Walker, Dring Lester 73
French Aero Club 28
Frost, Jack 31
Frye, William John 'Jack' 33, 35, 39, 42, 150
Fuller, Burdette 33–5

Garden, Oscar 77
Gathergood, Gerald 72
Gibson, Edmund Richard 'Hoot' 30
Gill, Howard Warfield 8, 23
Gipsy II, III 79
Gloster Mars 74, 75
Gordon Bennett Trophy 9, 22
Gordon, Rosalie 49, 100
Grahame-White, Claude 15–21, 119
Grand Prix de la Champagne 27
(The) Great Air Race 83
Greenwald, Sanford 'Sam' 34
Guthrie, Giles 76, 83

Hamel, Gustav Wilhelm 11, 12, 61, 64–5, 67, 69–70, 76
Hamersley, Harold Alan 72, 75
Hamilton, Charles K. 23
Harmon, Clifford B. 23
Hawker, Harry George 73
Henderson, George L. P. 71
Herndon, Jr., Hugh 50, 100, 101
Hinkler, Herbert 'Bert' John Louis 72–5
Hoanes, Charles 60
Houdini, Harry 141, 149

Howard Wright Biplane 62
Hubbard, Thomas O'Brien 73
Hucks, Bentfield 'Charles' 11–12, 70
Hunter Brothers Flying Circus 52

Ingle, Gladys 34, 38–40, 90
International Aircraft Corporation 30

James, John Herbert 'Jimmie' 73–5
Jensen, Martin 31, 91
Jim Crow Laws 53
John Tranum's Flying Circus 77
Johnson, Al 33, 35, 38, 40–2, 151
Johnston, Alvin Melvin 'Tex' 59
Jones, Phil 150–1
Jordan, William Lancelot 72
Julian, Hugh 53, 127

Kempton Park 69, 71
King, John R. 75
King's Cup 76
Kittinger, Joseph 47
Kitty Hawk 3
Knabenshue, Roy 7, 23, 92
Knope, Vilas Raymond 31

Langley, Samuel Pierpont 4, 6
Latham, Hubert 9, 15, 23, 25–8
Le Grande Semaine d'Aviation de la Champagne 9, 22, 24
Lefebvre, Eugène 9, 25–6, 28
Leblanc, Alfred 23–4, 26
Legagneux, Georges 23
Leicestershire Aero Club 63
Lincoln Standard Circus 31
Lindpaintner, Otto 23
Lockheed Vega 31, 34, 112, 137
Locklear Flying Circus 106
Longton, Walter Hunt 72, 74–5
Los Angeles Air Meet 92
Los Angeles Examiner 23
Los Angeles Times 41, 53, 129, 146
Love, Maxwell 54–5
Lund, Freddie 50

MacDougall, Ronald G. 'Bon' 33, 35, 37–8, 41, 43, 152
Mace, Terry 84–5

Mamet, Julien 23
Manly, Charles 4
Manton, Marcus Dyce 72
Martinsyde 73–5
Matlock, William 'Spider' 33, 35, 37–8, 152
McClellan, Heard 'Herd' 33
McEwan, James 82
Menefee, William 50
Morane-Saulnier 12, 70
Motion Picture Pilots' Association 110
Municipal Aerodrome Campaign Tour 78

National Air Race 54–5, 111, 135–6, 139
Negro Formation Flying Group 54
Nesterov, Pyotr Nikolayevich 11, 96–7
Nieuport Goshawk 73
Nieuport Nieuhawk LC.1 73–4
Nichols, Kenneth 'Fronty' 33, 35, 37–8, 151
Nisbet, Robert 72–3
Noakes, Jack 74
Noël, Louis 70
Norman, Vic 160

Omlie, Vernon 132–4
Ortweiler, Frederick John 74
Osborne, Fred 41

Pacific Aircraft Company 30
Paulhan, Isidore Auguste Marie Louis 6, 18–21, 23, 26–7, 93
Pedlar, John 'Auggy' 31
Pégoud, Adolphe 1, 10–11, 96–7
Percival Vega Gull 76, 83
Perry, Herbert Howard 74–5
Pixton, Charles Howard 61, 65–6
Pizey, Collyns Price 62, 66–9
Powder Puff Derby 136, 139, 141
Powell, William J. 53–5
Pride of Los Angeles 30
Prix de Lagatinerie 21
Prodger, Clifford B. 71

Quimby, Harriet 136, 141

Raynham, Frederick Philips 74–5
Reid, Edward D. Whitehead 75

Reynolds, Herbert Ramsay Playford 62, 69
Rhodes-Moorhouse 70
Richter, Jr., Paul E. 33, 42
Royal Aero Club 16–17, 20, 76, 85
Royal Flying Corps 56, 176

Saint, Howard John Thomas 72
Salmet, Henri 76
Saulnier, Raymond 15
Schlee, Edward 50
Schlesinger Air Race 76, 83
Schlüter, Paul Henry 31, 91
S.E.5a 74–5
Shell Trophy 70
Short, Shirley J. 106
Shultz, Wilmer Lower 50
Scott, Charles William Anderson 76, 82–3
Scott, Gordon 31
Shelton, Greg 160
Sky Devils Air Circus Tour 82
Smith, Charles H. C. 72
Smith, Merle 'Mudhole' 59
Snook, Neta 120–1, 140
Société Ariel 25
Sopwith 7F1 Snipe 72–3
Sopwith Camel 74
Sopwith Gnu 75
Sopwith Pup 73
Sopwith Schneider Cup 73, 75
Sopwith, Thomas 69
Standard Airlines 33
Standard Flying Schools 122
Stapp, William 'Bill' 34

Stinson, Jr., Edward Anderson 56, 58
Stocken, Reginald Herbert 74
Stuebenville Air Show 49

Tabnac, Jerry 33, 34
Tait-Cox, Leslie Robert 72–5
Tallman, Frank 114–16
Temple, George Lee 11
Teterboro Airport 49–50, 52
Thaden, Louise 136–9, 141–2
Tiger Moth 161, 163
Tissandier, Paul Albert Gaston 25, 26
Tomac, Frank 34, 40
Transcontinental Western Air 33
Trans-World Airlines 33
Travel Air 'Type R' Mystery Ship 131
Tremaine Hummingbird 30
Tully, Terence Bernard 73

Unger, Ivan 'Bugs' 33, 38, 40, 90, 154
Uwins, Cyril Frank 'Papa' 73–4

Valentine, James 61, 65, 70
Védrine, Jules Charles Toussaint 61
Victory Aerial Derby 70

Wells, Irvin 54–5
Westgarth-Heslam, Denis George 73
Willard, Charles 23
Wisconsin Special 51
Woodhouse, John Whitaker 75
Woods, Jessie 47, 49, 139
Woods, Jimmy 49
Wright, Orville 3–8, 110
Wright, Wilbur 3–8